Bernard Waters

Modern Training and Handling

Bernard Waters

Modern Training and Handling

ISBN/EAN: 9783743465046

Manufactured in Europe, USA, Canada, Australia, Japa

Cover: Foto ©Lupo / pixelio.de

Manufactured and distributed by brebook publishing software (www.brebook.com)

Bernard Waters

Modern Training and Handling

MARCHIONESS PEG.

Modern

Training and Handling

BY

B. WATERS
(KINGRAIL)

BOSTON
J. LORING THAYER PUBLISHING CO.
1894

Copyright, 1894
By J. LORING THAYER PUBLISHING CO.

PRESS OF
Rockwell and Churchill
BOSTON

CONTENTS.

MODERN TRAINING AND HANDLING.

CHAPTER I.

The setter and pointer—General appreciation—False sentiments relating to field sports—The dog commonly misunderstood—The Gordon setter—Degeneracy—Undesirable type—Few specimens—No public performances—Unimportance of the breed—The Irish setter—Uniformity of type—Symmetry—Field merit—Champion Elcho, Jr.—The English setter—Public estimation of superiority—Irregular breeding—Beauty of form—Marchioness Peg—Champion Paul Gladstone—Pegjim—Roderigo—Color — The pointer — Improvement—Champion Robert le Diable—The origin of the setter—Matter of speculation—"Setting spaniel"—Popular errors—No evidence of spaniel origin—Arguments against it—Characteristics of setter and pointer—The pointing instinct—Popular fallacies—Relative qualities—Prejudices—Staleness—Retrieving—"Inherited training"—Constitution and breeding—Will power—Weight and size—Strength and endurance—Objections to heavy dogs—Objections to light dogs—Conformation—Habits—The timid dog—The obstinate—The rattle-headed—The vicious—The sulky—The cunning—The enthusiastic—Modes of treating each—Knowledge of character.... 21

CHAPTER II.

Nomenclature—The paucity of field nomenclature—Its inconvenience—Absence of terms—Feathering—Breaking—Training—Handling. 55

CHAPTER III.

The amateur trainer—Faults of amateurs—Irregular temper; its ill effects—Necessity of studying dispositions—Irregular effort and

CONTENTS.

Inefficiency—Observing details—Advantages of habits of observation—Faultiness of over-training—Regular shooting and training incompatible—A knowledge of training results in skillful handling—The dog should be considered a reasoning animal—Loud commands unnecessary and offensive—Benefits of self-control—A good trainer must be fond of dogs—Manual dexterity required—No unnecessary force should be used—Bad effects of punishment on a dog's constitution... 60

CHAPTER IV.

General remarks on training—Faultiness of common methods—Pointing and ranging—The foundation of field work—No secret in training—Kind treatment conducive to success—The primary education the most difficult—No arbitrary system—Industry and enthusiasm—Compulsion and suasion combined—Dogs trained when too young—Perfection from skillful training—Erroneous theories—Inferior capabilities cannot be corrected—No short systems in training—Length of time required—Different stages of training—Training permanently fixed by habit—General irregularities of progress—General excellence desirable—Whimsicalities—Some dogs incapable of receiving a training—One thing at a time—Forgetfulness excusable—Lessons should not be too long—Advantages of companionship—Individuality of dogs................................. 67

CHAPTER V.

Instruments used in training—The spike-collar—The whip—The whistle—The checkcord—Their use........... 82

CHAPTER VI.

Commands—Analogy of methods in teaching all commands—Commands known by sight, sound and feeling—Association of ideas—Commands and signals commonly used—Come in—Go on—Heel—Drop—Hold up—Dead bird—Find—Fetch—Steady—Whoa—Commands in ordinary tones—Loud tones become habitual—Obedience to signals—Exclamations inartistic—Deceptive orders to be avoided.. 96

CHAPTER VII.

Preparatory training—Yard training—House training—Dog learns correct deportment from association—Ignorance of inexperienced dogs—Disagreeable traits in domestication—Placing feet on the person

—How corrected—Habitual **barking**—Dislike of handler is obstructive—Serious **demeanor in teaching**—Moderate lessons—Abrupt changes **confusing**—Age of puppy for yard training—The different commands—How each is taught...................... 101

CHAPTER VIII.

Retrieving—General **remarks**—Pointers easier to teach—Fidelity in teaching details—Poor retrieving—Disadvantages of retrieving—How corrected—A first-class retriever's **qualities**—Difficult branch of training—Calm exterior—Dog learns **trainer's expression**—Retrieving from water; its harmfulness—The Chesapeake Bay dog—The Irish water spaniel—**Two methods of** teaching retrieving—The "natural" method—Applied in puppyhood—No spectators at lessons—**Taking** advantage of playfulness—Manner of teaching the natural method—Tact required—Correcting bad habits—Effects of associated surroundings—No mouthing allowable—Common faults—"Give"—Importance of details—Long lessons objectionable—Variety of practice—Repugnance to grasping feathers—Regularity in teaching—Uncertain time required to teach retrieving—Rewards—Taking advantage of jealousy—Failure—Uncertainty of the method—Its faultiness—Ill effects of **punishment**—Retrieving not inherited—The force system—Accessory to the natural method—Its advantages—Erroneous beliefs—Dexterity required—Brutality unnecessary—Terror is obstructive—Faults in training—Preparatory use of collar—Overheated—First stage in training—Punishment—How to make a dog open his mouth—Willing dogs—Obstructive traits enumerated—How corrected—Second stage—Third stage—Rewards—Holding the dog's confidence—Hard mouth; how prevented—High head—Delivering the bird to hand—Picking up lost birds—Field retrieving—Faults necessary to correct—Marking the fall of birds; its value—When to begin—"Find"—Taught during puppyhood—How to teach the puppy to seek dead—Winged birds—"Steady;" how taught—Persistent effort necessary.................................. 118

CHAPTER IX.

Preparatory field training—Proper age to begin field work—Quails the best bird—Self-hunting experience necessary—Dog's capabilities injured by excessive restraint—Time required to give experience—How to avoid gun shyness—Dog's confidence must not be impaired—How to accustom the dog to the gun—Evils of working puppies together—Method taught after experience—Erroneous methods—Highest degree of working development—Value of ranging—Health essential to good work—Punishment for mistakes, erroneous—Good grounds, an advantage—Dog becomes careless when birds are scarce—The importance of a water supply—Birds are natural prey—" Off days "—Deafness and obstinacy—Deafness from exposure or careless shooting—Faults from jealousy—Errors in treatment of a puppy 160

CHAPTER X.

Pointing—The exquisite delicacy of the dog's nose—Variability of pointing—Wide nostrils no criterion of scenting powers—The olfactory nerves—Their distribution—The origin of the pointing instinct—Common fallacies—The use of instincts—Analogous traits in other animals—The origin of pointing unknown—The real use of pointing—The point not cataleptic—Pointing from compulsion—Pointing intelligently to the gun—Intelligent acts—Age at which the instinct appears—Instinct dormant till maturity—Disuse does not impair it—Hunting rabbits, a natural instinct—Early pointing no indication of superiority—Late development of the instinct—Speculative opinions—Pointing by sight; its faults—Pointing, how established—Steadying the dog on point—Caution necessary—The correct distance to point—Different dispositions—Punishment—One dog at a time—Dog should not be restrained too much—Dog should point on his own judgment—Abnormal development of the instinct—Dropping to point—Often caused by dropping to wing—Flushing to order—Its faults—Pointing larks, how corrected—False pointing—Flushes—Flushes unavoidable—How to treat flushing—Effects of wind on scent—The dog's love of approbation—Flushing caused by the voice—Shooting flushed birds............................ 171

CHAPTER XI.

Ranging—Advantages of unrestrained preliminary experience—Learning the habits and haunts of birds—The dog's memory of places—Marking the flight of birds—Hunting without training—The dog's intelligent methods of pursuit—Experience and inexperience—Education and experience combined—The principle alike for all sections—Length of time required—Faults of amateurs—Imperfect ranging; different forms, how corrected—Ranging should be regardless of wind—Speed necessary—Superiority of the fast dog—Dogs worked too slowly—The correct range—Its variability—Dog's range should be controllable—The cunning of the dog in methods of pursuit—The foxhound's intelligence—The greyhound—Running cunning—The setter and pointer learn by experience—Their imitative faculties—The method of the expert handler.................. 193

CHAPTER XII.

Drawing and roading, how performed—Good and bad performers—Scarcity of brilliant performers—High nose and quick execution—Drawing by body scent and foot scent—Slow roading by foot scent—Imperfect drawing and roading—Over-cautiousness a fault—Proper method to teach roading—When to assist the dog—Pottering—Uselessness of the whip—The puzzle peg; its worthlessness—When to work a puppy with a companion—Evils of working with an unsteady dog—Perfect liberty necessary—Disadvantages of constant restraint. 204

CHAPTER XIII.

Backing—Variability of backing—Backing is not instinctive—It develops with experience—Reasons against its being an inherent trait—Instinct—Instincts are strictly individual—The real uses of backing—Reasons for its being an intelligent act—Analogous acts of hounds—Backing the shooter—Backing the gun—Pointing and backing learned by dogs of different breeds—Peculiarities of individuals—False pointing detrimental—Uniformity of instincts—Variability of intelligence—Backing, how taught—Stealing points—Jealousy—Backing from compulsion—Advantages of a steady dog—Excessive backing—"Backing each other"—Correcting trained dogs.... 210

CHAPTER XIV.

Quartering—A mechanical manner of ranging—Preliminary experience required—How taught—Course must be up wind—Dog takes casts across wind—How conducted—Can only be practiced up wind—The difficulty of teaching it—Brace work—Many dogs are unfit for brace work—Theoretical brace work—Approximate correctness—Disadvantages of quartering—Memory and intelligence not exercised—Time wasted in quartering............ 222

CHAPTER XV.

Dropping to wing and shot—Similarity of commands—Dropping to wing or shot unnecessary—Its benefits overrated—Its disadvantages—Proper juncture to teach—How taught—Advantages of thorough preliminary training—Dropping to point taught unintentionally—Care necessary to avoid teaching it—Sulky and obstinate dogs—Dropping to points from fatigue—Judgment in selecting opportunities.. 227

CHAPTER XVI.

Turning to whistle—The dog's powers of observation—Different notes for different turns—Self-willed dogs—Force sometimes necessary—How applied—Long-continued lessons necessary............ 231

CHAPTER XVII.

Brace work—Formal brace work unpopular—Good dogs not always good brace workers—Equal speed and range desirable—Importance of independent work—Supplementary work—Thorough training, a necessity—Imperfect perception of sounds—Each dog should obey independently—The correct discipline in brace work—Discipline in retrieving—Using the dog's name as a command—Refinement in training—Observing formalities....... 233

CHAPTER XVIII.

Shyness—Different kinds—Hereditary shyness a fallacy—Often due to carelessness or punishment—Nervousness—Bad methods—Incurable gun shyness—Changed surroundings sometimes beneficial—Different methods with different dogs—Traits caused by gun shyness—Ill effects of punishment—Care necessary to avoid blinking—Degrees of gun shyness—Methods of cure—Running away—Trainers prefer untrained dogs—Blinking combined with gun shyness—Blinking from nervousness—Abandonment of points—Difficulty of curing blinking—Difficulty of detecting it—How cured—Benefits of chasing—Changing handlers—Prevention—Peculiarities of bolting—Slight causes often produce it—Uselessness of chasing a runaway—Different devices to capture—Breaking of the habit—Whipping erroneous—Running down with a horse—One lesson generally sufficient—Precautionary measures............................,... 236

CHAPTER XIX.

Unsteadiness—Natural effort of the dog to capture—Unsteadiness easily cured—Not always expedient in training—Gradual correction—Breaking from chasing rabbits—Similarity of methods—Caution necessary—Confirmed shot breakers—Ordinary treatment—The final method for bad cases—Any dog can be cured. 250

CHAPTER XX.

Trained and over-trained—Self-confidence and training combined—Different manner of handling for different sections—The properly trained dog—Over-training caused by ceaseless dicipline—Its evils—How cured—Its glaring inferiority in competition............ 254

CHAPTER XXI.

Conditioning dogs for field trials—Handling—Poor running condition leads to defeat—The value of thorough preparatory work—Sharp practice a poor resource—Skillful handling and poor dogs—False beliefs—Effects of change of diet, climate, etc.--Advantages of independent work—Preparatory work—Preserving speed by short work—Speed and nose—Three days' race—A steady, all day gait—Endurance—Regular work—Irregular effort in competition ; its weakness—Working with strange dogs—Age of Derby entries—Reasons for a liberal age limit—Uselessness of running "one season" puppies—Disadvantages in training them—Hints on handling—Conditioning for private field work—Hints on conditioning 257

CHAPTER XXII.

The intelligence of the dog—The dog is a rational animal—Common reasons against the dog's intelligence—Their fallacy—The intelligence proven by common phenomena—Instinct—Various definitions—Darwin's views—Instincts are for the preservation of the individual—Elementary principles of mind—Physiological dependence—The senses the only medium of knowledge—Analogies in brain structure—Reason—Sensation—Perception—Knowledge—The dog's knowledge only from experience—Memory—Association of ideas—Complexities of training—Improvement comes with experience..... 266

CHAPTER XXIII.

Field etiquette—The wholesomeness of field sports—The need of etiquette—Peculiarities of sportsmen—" Talking dog "—First principles—Rules of behavior—Selfishness—Conduct as a guest—Use your friend's cartridges—Shoot your friend's birds—Giving the wrong " tip "—Your dog is the best—Arrange the route to suit you—

'Wiping his eye"—Affected modesty—Gun pointed at a companion—Call a point loudly—Explain your misses always—Loaded gun whe riding—Keep your gun pointed at a pointing dog—Walk over a pointing dog—Shoot on your friend's side of the bevy—Always make the hunt a competition—Take all single shots—Invite yourself to go hunting—How to test your friend's gun.................. 282

CHAPTER XXIV.

Quails, snipe, ruffed grouse and woodcock—The best bird for training purposes—Quail shooting in the South—The best months for shooting—Habits of quails—Advantage of training in the South—Training from horseback—Hunting horses—Woodcock shooting—Its inferiority—Snipe shooting—Its variable character—Habits of snipe—Training dogs on snipe—Their abundance near the Gulf—Chicken shooting—Habitat—Extermination—Shooting out of season—The multitude of chicken shooters—No late shooting—Habits of chickens—Tameness of the sport—Method of hunting—" Marking " chickens—The need of water for dogs—Feeding and caring for dogs—Disadvantages of chicken shooting. 293

CHAPTER XXV.

The training of spaniels—Spaniel cannot equal the setter—His sphere of usefulness, cover shooting—The work of setters and spaniels compared—The range of spaniels—Training spaniels a simple matter as compared to training setters—Their manner of work—A bell useful—Giving tongue not desirable—Retrieving—The checkcord used with advantage—Teach the same commands taught setters and pointers—Few sections favorable to the work of spaniels—Type. 306

CHAPTER XXVI.

Guard dogs—No formal training—The education by companionship—St. Bernards, Mastiffs and Great Danes—Intelligence and good temper necessary—Vicious dogs—Education should begin from puppyhood—Powers of discrimination—Ill effects of chaining—Maturity.. 310

CHAPTER XXVII.

The training of foxhounds—Purity of blood essential—Careful training, as applied to pointers and setters, not required—Dogs for bears, deer and gray foxes—The criterion of excellence—Desirable qualities—Length of time a hound should be capable of running—Giving tongue—Manner in which a pack should run—Manner of regaining a lost trail—Qualities which render a dog worthless for running in a pack—" Running over"—Its disadvantages—Number of dogs in a pack—Shooting foxes unsportsmanlike—Training—Starting puppies —Age for training—Length and kind of lessons—Care necessary in first experiences— Rabbits, wild cats, gray foxes and red foxes— How to manage puppies—Advantages of broken dogs—Obedience to the horn—Ill effects of whipping—Plenty of time should be given in training—Bad effects of hunting a drag—Ill effects of harking off from trails—Dogs should not be left to themselves—Manner of training for deer and bears.............................. 313

CHAPTER XXVIII.

Guns—The vast trade in worthless grades—Gun for general shooting— For upland shooting—Cylinder bores—Their superiority for quail shooting—Disadvantages of a choked gun—Powder and shot charges —The 16 gauge—Length and drop of stock—Fit of a gun—Good cheap guns—Their price—" Balance " of guns—Guns bored for special loads—Sizes of shot—Carriage of dogs by rail—Their status in railroad management—Ill effects of long journeys—Neglect and its consequences—How to feed on journeys—Advantages of crating —Dangers when on chain—Gratuities to baggagemen—Their trials with dogs—Railroad traffic and regulations—Dimensions of a dog crate—Different styles of crates—Faults of dogs—Killing chickens and sheep—How cured....... 320

ILLUSTRATIONS.

	PAGE.
MARCHIONESS PEG (*Frontispiece*),	
CHAMPION ELCHO, JR.,	24
PEGJIM,	37
RODERIGO,	45
CHAMPION PAUL GLADSTONE,	50
FIRST LESSON IN RETRIEVING,	138
THE FIRST POINT,	176
AMERICAN FOXHOUND,	315
DOG CRATES,	329

INTRODUCTORY.

The general improvement in expert training, in this country, had its inception with the inauguration of field trials. There were a few, very few, expert trainers prior to that period, but they had a limited fame and their methods of training were known only to themselves. Each trainer affected to have some particular hobby in his particular system, which he claimed to be superior to all others, although as each maintained an air of secrecy in his methods it is difficult to imagine by what process one method could be compared with another. Considering training as an art, it had very little claim to it at that time. Even amongst those who professed to be experts, there were the widest differences of opinion in respect to the details of training, and the manner in which a dog should work after being trained. However, really expert trainers were so few that they were not a representative body of the average trainers. The typical trainer usually combined training with market shooting, and as the prices of training in such hands varied from ten to twenty-five dollars, the education of the dog was always subservient to the success of the gun, the latter being the most profitable. The dog was never required to do much more than to point and, with less certainty, to retrieve. The success of the typical old-time trainer as a hunter was usually erroneously accepted as conclusive proof of his ability as a trainer. Each section had one or more of such local celebrities; in many instances he was illiterate, a loafer in summer, a little dissipated periodically, and at all times had every indication of chronic, incurable seediness. As a class, they were no small factor in bringing the dog and gun into disrepute, the latter two being unjustly considered the cause of the evil instead of an available means to sustain it. But progress and a high grade of sportsmanship have sounded the death knell of the old order of things, and dissipated the false opinions and prejudices of society.

The first field trial in America was run near Memphis, Tenn., in 1874, under the auspices of the Tennessee Sportsman's Association, and had ten starters. For four or five years thereafter, the trials grew slowly; but gradually their advantages became known and served to awaken the interest of sportsmen. The inauguration of field trials brought the expert trainers to the front, and the competition and ample opportunities for comparison of methods caused general improvement. The importation of blue bloods from England was followed by the keenest of competitions, which resulted in the permanent supremacy of the imported dog over the native. The win of a dog in a public competition gave him an acknowledged meritorious reputation and greatly increased his monetary value and that of his related blood. To own dogs which were winners or had the superiority of a winning strain, was the strong desire of all progressive sportsmen. The spirit of rivalry or emulation which competition engendered created an active and widespread demand for better dogs. This in turn resulted in a large number of breeders to supply the demand. Many dogs were imported in addition to those native bred, and values constantly increased. The enlargement in the dog world served to permanently engage the entire time and attention of a class of expert trainers who adopted training as a profession, and as a higher grade of ability was required, the typical old-time trainer either became a market shooter pure and simple or was lost in the struggle for supremacy. It required several years, however, for the expert field trial trainers to outgrow the prejudices and antipathies, a legacy inherited from their predecessors.

The competition settled many controversial points in

INTRODUCTORY.   xix

training, made a general improvement in methods, corrected many erroneous details, and established more uniformity in systems, although, as in all systems brought to a high degree of refinement and which have variable intrinsic elements, there are yet a few unsettled points.

Dog training can never be reduced to a system of arbitrary rules. With many of the exact sciences, a theoretical knowledge may be exact so far as it goes, but in dog training there is always an unknown and variable quantity which governs the application of the training, namely, the disposition and intelligence of the dog. While a trainer may have an extensive theoretical knowledge, he must learn how to modify or extend his methods by actual experience. No science of training can supplant experience; they are mutually dependent. No two dogs have precisely the same degree of intelligence or the same habits, inclinations, disposition, etc., hence a certain course of education which might be eminently successful in one instance might be ruinous in another. While the system herein taught will serve to train any dog which is capable of being trained, the success depends on the manner of applying it. The amateur cannot expend too much pains in studying dog character, and thereto he must gain and hold the affections of his dog, otherwise he cannot succeed.

While field trials developed a higher grade of expert training, experts were not slow to learn that a dog too well broken, or rather one thoroughly broken for field work, was at a disadvantage in a field trial competition. One that was obedient to the whistle might mind all notes blown by either handler, and the same undesirable results with signals. The aim was to get a dog to be barely obedient; to be quick in locating and pointing his birds; to back so long as his competitor pointed, but not an instant longer; to whip in quickly and take the point from a competitor when possible, and to range at high speed. Although they are a very uncertain test of a dog's real merit, trials are not without educational benefits to sportsmen. However, from a training point of view, the obedience of field trial dogs is not the standard of a thorough education; nor is the training of such dogs a standard of the real abilities of the trainers.

This treatise is after the modern professional system of training. It combines the excellences of both the suasive and force systems of education, and contains an exhaustive description of the uses and abuses of the spike collar. The author, by way of showing his qualifications for preparing this work, would say that he was a professional trainer, field trial handler and reporter for a number of years, and several times acted in the capacity of judge. Taken thus in the aggregate, his experience and consequent opportunities to acquire knowledge from personal observation and practice have been second to none. Although written from a professional standpoint, therefore from what is considered the highest refinement of the art, it is intended for the use of the amateur trainer and sportsmen in general. While the principles are frequently repeated in their many different relations, it is none too clear for the use of the amateur; and even with the most elaborate explanation, he will find complications that will tax his judgment to overcome successfully.

Many of the principles and positions herein treated are more or less opposed to the recognized authorities of a decade ago, but the reader should bear in mind that field sports and their accessories have far outgrown the scope of the old authorities. Their beliefs and experiences are not our beliefs and experiences. Authorities, one after another, have to retire as the march of improvement leaves them in the rear, the perpetual struggle for supremacy making no exceptions.

MODERN TRAINING

AND

HANDLING.

MODERN TRAINING.

CHAPTER I.

THE SETTER AND POINTER.

The setter and pointer, so far as they have a history, have always held a high place in the appreciation of mankind; but the general elevation of the dog to the high grade and full appreciation to which his intelligence and worth entitle him may be said to have occurred in this country within the last two decades.

It is within the memory of comparatively young men, particularly in the East, when to take a dog and gun afield was considered as being an uncanny act for any one who had gentlemanly pretensions, and if the act was repeated a few times a lowering of social and financial standing ensued. Appreciation of the dog and gun was considered as being a depraved taste, which, in some vague manner, led to whole groups of depravities, and the man whose passion for sport afield with the dog and gun was great, and whose respect for social opinion was greater, hied covertly to the fields by early dawn, or unfrequented by-ways, much after the same manner as the wicked hunter does at present on sacred days. To neglect business was an unpardonable sin, life being an endless toil to store wealth, which was considered the object of life, not to make life nobler and more enjoyable. The renewed vigor of body and mind; the broader humanity; the training of eye and nerve; the beauties of nature, were all considered as vagaries; but these narrow beliefs have been swept away by general progress and enlightenment, and they only exist as shadows of the past.

It is strange that such companionable and valuable animals should have been neglected so long; stranger still that having such a wide and even distribution they should be so imperfectly understood by mankind. Every intelligent act was commonly ascribed to the impulses of instinct, and reason was not considered for a moment as being, first or last, a principle. Oftentimes men who could not solve the common material problems of life could, without the slightest hesitation, mental effort or previous study, decisively decide intricate psychological problems to their own infinite satisfaction; occasionally a bit more of the same kind of instinct would be beneficial if it had a wider existence in the scale of animal organisms.

Three distinct breeds of setters are recognized in this country, namely, the English setter, the Irish setter, and the Gordon setter.

The latter, as compared to his aboriginal parents, is a Gordon merely in name, he being so largely mixed with outcrosses on other breeds that the alien blood predominates. However, it may be mentioned that many years ago the Gordon was highly prized in England for his merit. The breed having long been owned by the Dukes of Gordon, it thus derived its name. Since the institution of field trials and the consequent more exacting demands of sportsmen in respect to working capabilities, the Gordon, so called, has constantly met with disfavor and progressively degenerated. Except by courtesy the miscellaneous scrub character of the breed hardly entitles it to the distinction of a true breed, if race type, numbers, pure blood and power of reproduction true to race characteristics are any criteria by which to determine it. So much is it degenerated in these properties that it is hardly worthy of consideration.

All bench show associations provide competitive classes for black and tan setters, which, nominally, are for Gordon setters, black and tan being their prevailing color; but such classification, being merely a distinction with respect to color, admits any other breeds of setters, or cross-bred setters, if they have the required color qualification; indeed, dogs of nearly pure English setter blood have won in black and tan classes at prominent shows within a not very remote period; thus the dog at first lost distinctive Gordon character, and at last ceased to have any fixed desirable character. At present, there are only isolated specimens owned here and there. The existing coarse, scrubby, inferior dogs, having mixed pedigrees, or pedigrees containing a few common, abstract proper names, or, as commonly occurs, having no known pedigrees, are not imputable to the existing bench show classification; on the contrary, the classification is consequential to the dog's unimportance. Bench show associations are not legislators as to the classification of breeds; they accept facts as they find them.

While there is a variable ideal type, there is the greatest irregularity and diversity of undesirable individual forms, the coarse, loose, unsymmetrical form being very common. The average winner in a black and tan setter class, classes by the way which are always numerically light, would not be considered worthy of notice in an Irish or English setter class. There are two or three dogs which have been shown, within the past few seasons, as superior specimens of the breed, presumably as it existed at some time in the past, but no new specimens are brought forward to succeed them.

The typical Gordon was heavily built, and, whatever symmetry of form may have been possessed by the parent stock, the inherent faultiness of a heavy type has resulted in coarseness and clumsiness. Some fanciers approve of the heavy type because it is a Gordon type, whereas the fact of such undesirable type is sufficient to condemn it, it being wholly inadequate for fast, prolonged work. It is strange that, considering its unfitness for working dogs, this type should be cultivated and perpetuated.

The public performances of the very few which have competed in the public trials, and the general reputation of the breed for inefficiency, are not such as to exalt it in the good opinion of sportsmen at large. There is a desultory attempt being made to establish a Gordon setter standard which will call for a lighter and more racily built dog, but this contemplated improvement is largely in the abstract, there being an undue proportion of good intention to imaginary performance; yet these spasmodic, vague, gentle attempts constitute the most tangible form of existence of the Gordon setter. A standard could not benefit the prevailing poverty of material naturally resulting from neglect, apathy of ownership, natural inferiority, smallness of numbers, formidable competition from more powerful breeds, and disfavor of sportsmen. In field sports the Gordon setter is a dim, fading landmark in the march of progress.

The Irish setter, as a breed, is not surpassed, if equaled by any other breed in uniformity of type and other race characteristics. The individuals of it have high average merit; and the more perfect specimens, of which there are many, possess a wonderful degree of elegance and symmetry of form. They are a deep, solid, blood-red in color, except a slight blaze of white on the chest or toes, which is usually present. There are occasional specimens of pure breeding which have more or less white markings; but the

CHAMPION ELCHO, JR.

white, if more than on the breast and toes, is considered undesirable, and is nearly all bred out, considering the breed as a whole. From time immemorial, it has been highly prized and guarded with care, hence it is a very pure breed. To preserve the purity of color and other characteristics, the best breeders judiciously avoid out-crosses on other breeds.

While the breed is not well represented at the field trials, and frequently not at all, it has many staunch admirers, and a powerful conservative support. The small representation in public field competitions naturally detracted from extensive records; nevertheless, it demonstrated its claim to recognition as possessing workers of a high order, and a percentage of those which ran were winners. It would, in any event, be impossible to compete on equal terms, the many owners of English setters, who are field trial supporters, being relatively overwhelming in numbers. No organized, vigorous effort has been made to bring them into regular public competition, although, as aforementioned, they have an extensive, powerful ownership, and a good record. Undoubtedly the breed would be greatly improved by representation in the general competitions, or if trials were inaugurated specially for it. The consequent general knowledge respecting the best individuals would result in greater precision in breeding a uniformly higher grade of field dogs, inasmuch as the best specimens could be selected. Subordinate causes, such as the indifference to public trials by the owners of one breed, may contribute largely to the ascendancy of other breeds in public estimation, failure to compete being unjustly considered as equivalent to real defeat. This assumption might be reasonable if dogs were kept strictly for racing purposes, but the larger part of sportsmen value them for private shooting.

That this setter has high working qualities is manifested

by the large number of practical sportsmen who keep them for field work.

At all the important bench shows the Irish setters compete in large numbers. Their evenness of type, rich coloring, fine symmetry and graceful, spirited carriage always evoke the highest admiration.

Champion Elcho, Jr. (Elcho—Noreen), whose portrait is elsewhere given, is universally recognized as a dog of exquisite symmetry of form, and refinement of race characteristics united with substantial physical development; qualities which must be possessed in a high degree to gain pre-eminence over his race. He was born June 1, 1881, is owned and was bred by Dr. William Jarvis of Claremont, N. H., a gentleman who has spared no effort to secure the choicest blood; and the results, as shown by his breeding large numbers of dogs of uniform excellence for several years past, distinguish him as an eminent and skillful breeder. Elcho, Jr. has won championship honors in nearly every city in this country in which bench shows have been held; and his work in the Eastern Field Trials received very complimentary notice by the sporting press. He has the reputation of being an excellent field dog. Taken all in all, he has a wonderful combination of beauty and merit.

The English setter, considered as a field dog, is the superior of all others as shown by the records of public competitions, extensive ownership, common reputation and the opinion of authorities. The enormous numbers of the breed and common distribution are prime factors in maintaining its ascendancy, aside from questions relating to competive superiority.

From its wide distribution, general popularity and financial value, an innumerable multitude of small breeders, frequently inexperienced, who breed wholly or partly for profit, which militates against uniform improvement in the breed, are common. These adverse conditions are more fully delineated in the chapter on Breeding.

However, the more eminent and skillful breeders produce dogs of rare excellence, dogs which have no superiors. By the reputation of a few breeders, the reputation of the breed, as a whole, is maintained at a high standard, the worthless strains, unfortunately, profiting by it; for if the owners of the worthless strains can trace any relationship, near or remote, to eminent individuals, they never fail to claim the merit of reflected luster.

Taking the better bred families now into consideration, they undoubtedly are marvels of combined beauty of form and working capability. Dashing, agile, fast and enduring, quick and accurate in execution, they are the racers of the hunting field.

By referring to the portraits, the exquisite symmetry and characteristics of the breed will be noted. The artist has caught the expression and individual peculiarities with admirable fidelity, and the portraiture is truthful.

Marchioness Peg, whose portrait is given in the frontispiece, was bred and is owned by Dr. N. Rowe of the *American Field*, Chicago. She is handsomely marked black, white, and tan, and is by Druid (Prince—Dora) out of Peg (Leicester—Dart). She is very symmetrical and handsome, rating with the high class bitches of America. In the trials of the National American Kennel Club, run at Patoka, 1879, she divided second and third with Countess May. Pegjim, whose portrait is also given, is a son of Marchioness Peg by Cambridge, he by Gladstone out of Clip. He is magnificently proportioned, having a clean cut, typical head, lean neck, well shaped body, nicely shaped legs and feet, and fine general symmetry. He is a high class dog in the field. This breeding has produced some remarkably superior dogs, notably Jean Val Jean, winner of the champion stakes at the Eastern Field Trials Club's Trials, 1888. He also was bred by Dr. Rowe, and is by Mingo out of Twin Maud, she by Gladstone out of Clip; Mingo by Druid out of Star, thus forming the celebrated half and half breeding of Pegjim, Pegbid, Pegfly, Peg III, and Pegmatite, the lines of blood being the same through Marchioness Peg and Mingo on the one side, and Twin Maud and Cambridge on the other.

Champion Paul Gladstone is owned by Mr. S. L. Boggs of Pittsburgh, Pa. The portrait of Paul Gladstone shows him to be a dog of great symmetry and beauty. He has an enviable reputation, and has taken several special prizes for the best combined field trial and bench show record. He has also a long list of champion bench show winnings, and is noted as an eminent sire, and a dog of brilliant field merit.

Roderigo, owned by the Memphis and Avent Kennels, is by Count Noble—Twin Maud, and is well known to the sportsmen of America as combining the perfections of proved working powers, beauty and power of physical structure, and a successful stock-getter. He is a field trial winner, and holds a high place in the opinion of sportsmen as a performer of the highest capabilities.

Enough illustrations are given to show the higher types of the English setter, of the most popular lines of blood.

The prevailing color of the English setter is black and white, or black, white and tan; if the black and white ticked is approximately even, with or without a few black splashes, it is called blue belton; orange and white ticked, orange belton; lemon and white ticked, lemon belton. There are several other colors—solid black, liver, liver and white, white, roan; and these colors may be in different shades.

The pointer has been greatly improved within the past few years, field competition, energetic ownership and better breeding with respect to field form, being the prime causes of his advancement. The quick, snappy work of setters when on game, was always an insurmountable obstacle to the average pointer in competition with them; but the pointers have greatly improved in their execution, and undoubtedly in time, if **bred by selecting the best** working dogs, they will **be able to compete on an equal** footing with the setters. Some field trial associations have special stakes for pointers, which is a wise measure until such times as the pointers are bred in sufficient numbers to place them on an approximate equality.

However, decided improvement seems to be confined to individuals here and there and not to the breed as a whole. Taking into consideration the pointer's faultiness in becoming "stale" if overworked, that is, to become indifferent to hunting, and slow and pottering in his manner, and the long rest required to renew his ardor, also the loss of dash, pace and range nearly always exhibited after the third or fourth year, it is an open question whether the nature of the dog can be changed by the most careful selection to even equal the setters in working powers.

Having thus briefly considered the dog in particular, we will next discursively consider a few collateral topics.

The origin of the setter has greatly exercised the speculative faculties of many writers, and, finally, in most instances, they have comfortably settled on the theory that the setter is a variation from spaniel stock. There is no very good reason for this theory except that it has the least absurdity of the conjectures advanced. As to the proof adduced, there is none of the origin of the setter in a spaniel ancestry other than the vaguest tradition and conjecture, the latter being the chief support. It would be quite as reasonable, and quite as difficult to prove, that the spaniel is a variety of the setter. They both have certain analogies in form and habits; but, since there are analogous habits, instincts and peculiarities of physical structure more or less common to all dogs, they prove nothing in the absence of all direct evidence. So far as there is any trace of the setter in the past, it was then as truly a distinct species as it is at present, reproducing itself with its peculiar race characteristics, and showing no more tendency to variation from race forms or instincts than that common in any of the fixed breeds; for, in the oldest of pure breeds, no two individuals are precisely alike. Much stress has been laid on the fact that in ancient writings they were called a "setting spaniel," which is no direct proof of accuracy, as the term has not been proven to be general or correct in its application. It is more than probable that the term was used to distinguish the setter as a breed from the spaniel as a breed, which he in some respects resembles, or *vice versa;* this being still more probable from the then scanty, inaccurate nomenclature, careless observation, isolated ownership, and consequent lack of knowledge respecting them. Even in our own enlightened age, when knowledge is supposed to have some precision, the setter, as defined by Webster, is as follows: "A sporting dog of the hound kind that indicates, by sitting or crouching, the place where game lies hid. It partakes of the character of the pointer and the spaniel, and is generally regarded as having descended from the crossing of these two varieties." When the present at some period in the far future shall be the ancient past, and many existing facts and fancies shall weigh alike as vague hearsay; when the present form of the dog will have undergone great improving changes, and when the learned *savant* then is speculating on the aboriginal stock of the setter, he will learnedly point to that definition as decisive proof, and will tell the lesser *savants* that the definition was in Webster's Unabridged, the recognized official authority of the ancients;

therefore the setter will then be a hound, the product of a cross between a pointer hound and spaniel hound, and the speculation would be as reasonable as any which are advanced, at present, as to the origin. -

If the setter had a spaniel origin, there would be some evidences of it in the well known tendency of all animals to revert, at times, to ancestral types; yet in all cases of reversion in pure blooded setters, it is to the pure setter form. It may be said that the breed has been kept pure so long that the characteristics have become permanently fixed; that the origin is so far in the past that the tendency to reversion is lost; however, such is taking too much for granted as a negative argument; if it is that far in the past, we can know nothing of the origin. A breed is not so easily and distinctly established. Some intermediate gradation of forms would be preserved, showing a regular series, either continuous or broken, from the parent stock to the setter. It is hardly reasonable to assume the total destruction of all the intermediate groups and gradations, leaving the two breeds distinct without any sub-breeds showing unmistakable relationship to both.

It is well known that by selection of the best specimens in breeding, the forms of animals can be improved and changed more and more from generation to generation in accordance with the purposes of the breeder, as seen in the forms of horses for speed and draft, and in the forms of other domestic breeds; yet this susceptibility to change under certain conditions is confined chiefly to the physical forms, the effects of change being imperceptible in the habits and instincts of improved and unimproved horses, or other domestic animals. To maintain an improved breed up to the required standard of excellence, continued selection of the superior animals is necessary to breed from, else they by promiscuous breeding revert to the common forms.

If the spaniel had thrown off a variety, as it must have done to originate the setter (otherwise no change could have been effected), whether it was done little by little or at once, there is every probability that it would have been lost in the first generation or two, (1) from intercrossing with the pure parent type, (2) from the natural tendency to revert to ancestral prototypes, and (3) from the probability that the variation would not be cultivated and preserved. This may very well be conjectured; for if a family of setters at the present day showed a constant tendency to vary their forms and instincts with each succeeding generation till they became a distinct breed, the owner would condemn the progeny as being mongrel, inasmuch as it could not reproduce itself purely. Moreover, if the setter is a variety of improved spaniel, therefore a variety of spaniel, it and the parent stock would still have an inherent tendency to vary or throw off numerous varieties, for there is no probability that a variety would uniformly improve and breed with all the characteristic modifications, habits and instincts up to a certain degree useful to man, neither reverting to ancestral forms when neglected, nor varying into other forms when reproducing itself under constantly varying conditions of climate, selection, food supply, etc., and then become permanently fixed; but admitting the change in form, it is hardly supposable that it would be associated with changed instincts correspondingly useful to man, it having already been noted that changes of form are not accompanied by any perceptible changes in instinct, much less changes uniformly and relatively useful to man.

Setters and pointers have a great many characteristics in common; their hunting instincts and modes of pursuing their prey are the same in the general features, and there is a close analogy in race type and habits, the chief distinctive characteristic being the coat. If a typical setter is clipped

PEG JIM.

evenly and closely, there is an astonishingly close resemblance to a pointer, and many supposed distinctive characteristics are then clearly attributable to the difference in coat; however, there are some minor differences of physical structure and instincts which, while common to both breeds, vary in intensity in them. We will consider these peculiarities in a general way, for no hard and fast rule can be laid down in respect to relative peculiarities but what will have many exceptions, neither breed possessing a uniform fixedness of type or characteristics that admits of positive class comparison, barring the difference in coat.

The instinct to point appears at an earlier age in the pointer than in the setter, is more intense, and more uniformly present in the same degree of intensity in each individual; hence, there is not the same labor in perfecting them to work to the gun as there is with the setter; however, a few pointers, and, in a lesser number of instances, some setters, have the pointing instinct more strongly present than is necessary or desirable, since they will point on scents other than that of game, particularly when fatigued, and are content to back in place of pointing when working with another dog. This abnormal development of the instinct is rarely present in dogs which are properly bred. Setters as a class exhibit the instinct in a more irregular manner both with respect to the age when it appears and the intensity of it, although it is, in the greater number of instances, sufficient for the purposes of the hunter.

Certain particular points of superiority are claimed respectively for each breed by its admirers; but many of them have but a slight foundation in fact, while others are wholly fanciful. It is claimed that the pointer, owing to the shortness of his coat, can endure extreme heat with less distress and requires less water, and less frequently than the setter. After an extensive experience with setters and pointers, several years in succession, on the prairies chicken shooting, and on the quail grounds of the South, the experience comprehending vast tracts of territory, large numbers of dogs and all kinds of weather, the fact was noted that in excessively hot weather neither dog can perform well nor do without water more noticeably than the other. When dogs of either breed work under a hot sun, they require water plentifully, the differences in this respect being individual, and quite as distinct between individuals of the same breed as between individuals of the two breeds There is a difference observable in the two breeds as they first start into work in the season. When they are not in working condition, they suffer great distress while being abruptly hardened to the work in hot weather; but the pointer under like condition of work will get into working condition sooner and will have a slight advantage for a few days; yet this is subject to many exceptions. After the setter gets thoroughly hardened, he requires water no oftener than the pointer; nevertheless, both require it. Individual dogs of the most wonderful powers of endurance will be met with in each breed; ones which can run under a scorching sun with no visible distress, and require but a few laps of water occasionally. Others require a great deal of water, and appear to be constitutionally incapable of becoming accustomed to the heat, although they may work commendably well in a lower temperature.

An experience during one season, with one lot of dogs consisting of pointers and setters, from the peculiarities of the individuals, might lead the sportsman to believe that either the setter or pointer was the more enduring, accordingly as he observed the superiority in one or the other; but a single experience or a few experiences with a few individuals of each breed are not sufficient data for a definite conclusion. Men of large experiences usually agree on the main points; men of brief experiences always differ. Large numbers must have been seen under variable conditions through long periods of time; then the most diligent observation and unprejudiced judgment are necessary to arrive at a just conclusion. If the sportsman is absorbed in looking for excellences in his favorite breed, and for faults in others, he will be certain to retain his opinion unaltered, be the work what it may. It is no uncommon occurrence for a sportsman to believe that his dog is the superior worker in a hot competition when it is palpably evident to disinterested spectators that he is not above ordinary. Simple as it may seem to learn field work, it requires several years of extensive experience to be able to estimate the relative merits of dogs without prejudice; and many sportsmen never outgrow their favorite fancies, be they right or wrong.

Considering the two breeds as a class, the setter is much more dashing, quicker and enduring in his work, and speedier and wider in his range; and on birds his execution is much more rapid. A few individual pointers, at the recent field trials, have shown great improvement in this respect, yet the improvement can hardly be claimed for the breed at large. The pointer, however, is more easily trained and retains his training of the first season better; but he has one specially inferior property, namely, if overworked, which may be done in a few days or weeks according to the constitution or condition of the dog, he loses interest in his work, shortens his gait, contracts his range to an area of a few yards, and subsides to mediocrity. If his work is then continued, the evils are serious. It requires weeks and sometimes months to rest him sufficiently so that he will work with keenness up to his best form. This vapid state may be produced by starting the dog abruptly into hard work instead of conditioning him gradually for it, or by excessive overwork when he is in condition. Except in rare instances, the pointer begins to lose his dash and range after the third or fourth year, and as a matter of course, loses correspondingly in hunting qualities. The breed, however, is undergoing rapid improvement, and without doubt these objectionable qualities will be bred out in the near future. The improvement embraces the form; and by the establishment of more correct racing lines in the physical structure, and more will-power in his mental qualities, an animal of more endurance and dashing capabilities will be produced.

Setters, when thoroughly fatigued and worked down, even if overworked for weeks, simply need resting a sufficient length of time to recuperate, and they will then resume work with unabated ardor. They rarely lose their speed or vim except from accident, old age, or excessive breeding, the latter cause having a positive reducing effect on the working capacities of either setter or pointer, even if the use exists within a short period.

In both breeds the adverse conditions of life to which they are often subjected may have an injurious effect on their working powers. The food, kenneling and general care given, good or ill, may affect the dog accordingly.

In thick cover, heavy grass or briers, the setter has a decided physical advantage over the pointer, his longer coat serving as a protection; he can also endure cold and wet better than the pointer. Individual pointers will frequently take the most punishing cover quite as well as the best setters, yet it is demanding too much of them even if they have the courage, for, from the scratching and tearing suffered, they receive much punishment; thus, while they may have the courage they have not the requisite capabilities; however, in cockle-burrs, Spanish needles, beggar lice, etc., the pointer, from his short coat, suffers no particular inconvenience, while they cause the setter constant annoyance and distress, the cockle-burrs particularly. They get under his armpits, inside of his thighs, his flanks and under his feet, the pain forcing him to stop and pick them out with his teeth. Plucky setters will run regardless of them, but they chafe and gouge the skin into sores in the afflicted parts. This may be corrected by clipping the hair off, then the setter is on the same equality in this respect with the pointer. Or the difficulty may be overcome by trimming the hair closely about the armpits and inside the thighs, thus keeping the action free.

Neither setter nor pointer is fitted for retrieving from water in cold weather. Both suffer seriously from the exposure if long continued.

Some dogs are very intelligent, precocious, and pleasingly submissive; such may train easily, but the special aptitude shown in the beginning is no indication whatever that *no* training is necessary, although they may require less of it and apply it more quickly. Those which are born with a full knowledge of retrieving, a knowledge of a gun and its uses, a comprehension of orders, signals and field work, are never discovered by experts. Limited knowledge always encounters the marvelous. There are no dogs or families of dogs which inherit their training.

As a matter of course, it is desirable to have a dog as well-bred, symmetrical and graceful as possible, such being a source of constant pleasure and an ornament to a home. His value is greatly enhanced if he is a good worker, not so much with respect to his increased monetary value as to the superiority of the sport afforded by his superior capabilities afield; successful days—days of pleasant reminiscences— are largely due to a good dog's efforts. A well bred dog does not necessarily imply a weakly one. The well bred one should not be confounded with the poorly bred. The constitution and intelligence of the setter and pointer are of paramount importance; without these the value of the breeding is purely fictitious, either for work or breeding. An energetic disposition is also an important factor. Many dogs have fine symmetry, strength of form and perfect constitution, but have not the will power to work, or are constitutionally lazy. On the other hand, badly constructed dogs, from courage and determination, will work well when lame, footsore and fatigued, stopping work only when the hunt ends, or when physically incapable. Sometimes the light, lathy dog, apparently too fragile to run an hour without distress, will run day after day with undiminished powers and unabated ardor. Even dogs carrying an excess of lumber, as unnecessary bony and muscular development is called, will show great endurance when they have the necessary will and pluck, thus apparently upsetting all theories of the superiority of symmetrical physical structure ; however, the theory is correct as, given the other qualities of intelligence, constitution, pluck and speed, the symmetrical, strongly built dog will excel all others in endurance, but, as in the race horse, his powers must be as much in his head as in his heels.

Besides certain other analogies, the pointer and setter are, as a class, alike in weights, running from thirty to thirty-five pounds up to seventy or eighty pounds, and sometimes, though rarely, more. These weights may be considered as being the extremes. The average weights are from forty to fifty-five pounds, and these are by far the best for dogs in all kinds of work. They are capable of more prolonged exertion with less distress than the larger or smaller dogs. Large dogs are coarsely made as a general rule ; if well made, a rare exception, they have not the activity, vigor and will power of the small or middle weights. It is commonly said that a good large dog is better than a good small or medium sized one. The writer in the field trials or in field work has not observed that such assumption is the fact.

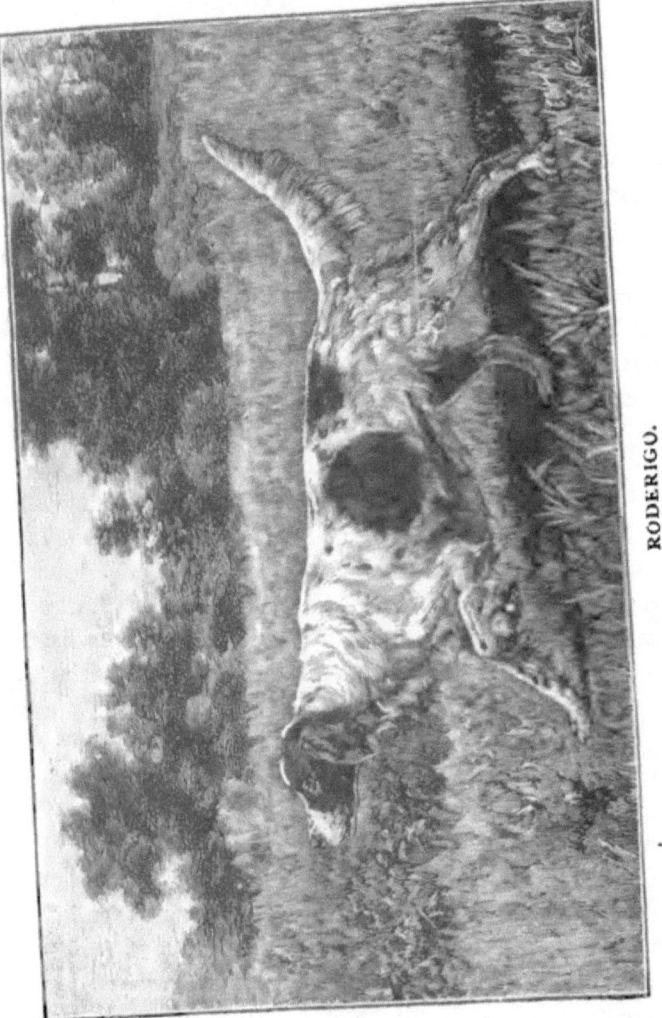

RODERIGO.

Analogous inefficiency in other animals tends to refute it, and these analogies are, strangely enough, usually cited to sustain it, by confounding strength on the one hand with endurance on the other. As a matter of strength alone, the large, well-made dog is the superior, but for fleetness and endurance combined, there is no comparison with the others. Thus a large, well-built man is superior to a small one in a personal encounter, but the statistics show that for great endurance they are inferior—particularly the army statistics show that in long marches, where the highest degree of endurance is required, the large men were decidedly placed in a lower grade. In horses the largest breeds have the greatest strength, but the racing horses are not the largest breeds. Taking the individuals of a racing strain as compared to each other, the fleetest animals are of medium size or smaller, the large animals being soon disabled if kept for speed even if they are speedy. Large dogs, from their great bulk and weight have the further disadvantage of being annoyingly inconvenient on hunting trips where it is necessary to carry them in a wagon, one large dog incommoding the occupants, and causing much discomfort. When traveling by rail they are difficult and laborious to handle if in a crate, and in such they certainly should be if the journey is at all long.

The small dog, while usually being very active and possessing great powers of endurance, also has certain disadvantages incident to his size and weight. Owing to the former they are extremely difficult to see when on point, if in cover which is at all close. Ordinary sedge grass will conceal them, the only visible sign of their presence being the line of motion observable in the top of the grass in the course the dog runs. It is difficult for them, owing to their light weight, to gallop through heavy sedge, weeds, briers, muddy ground, etc., and if the cover is mixed with briers, it is also exceedingly painful to them. These difficulties add greatly to the labor and fatigue of the work. However, good dogs like good horses come in all shapes—there are some forms of structure which, notwithstanding, are necessarily superior. A wide chest, with coarse, heavy shoulders is a decided disadvantage. The chest should be moderately narrow and deep, the ribs well sprung back of the shoulders to give lung room, and the shoulders so set as to play freely.

A short, thick neck is very undesirable. An excessively wide loin is more undesirable than a strong, narrow one; the latter is not necessarily an evidence of weakness as it may compensate by depth, by strong muscular development above and underneath. On the other hand a wide loin may be thin, and a broad square back and loin usually denote a slow gait, the correlated structure not being favorable to speed.

A dog which is awkward in his work from immaturity, being slow in developing, should not be confounded with the flighty, fidgety, nervously inferior kind which does not improve with maturity. A dog, slow in developing, may be discouragingly backward during his first season, but when mature he may be a fine worker. If the dog is rattleheaded or poor in judgment, very little should be attempted with him until he is aged sufficiently to steady him. It may improve his faculties, for though as a puppy he may be giddy, maturity may bring some intelligence. But also he may be naturally a fool, in which event it is a waste of time to attempt any training. It is much better to condemn him.

Dogs vary greatly in their habits, disposition, temper, intelligence, endurance, condition and general working capabilities. They exhibit all kinds and degrees of character and efficiency within the limits of their natural sphere; there are individuals which are too lazy to work, though able; ones which are willing to work but cannot learn formal methods; others which work till fatigued and then will quit; some have the energy without the ability, or *vice versa;* others will work diligently if permitted to have their own way; others will sulk if offended or restrained, or maliciously do the work badly; others are chilled if shown any unkindness. All the peculiarities of temperament have to be considered in training the dog and the methods adapted to them. So far as training is concerned, the characters commonly met with are the timid, the obstinate, the rattle-headed, the vicious, the sulky, the cunning, and the one which is difficult to handle from excessive enthusiasm.

The timid dog is the most difficult to train if handled improperly, harshness or continual restraint sometimes totally spoiling him, and always injuring his capabilities. He may have courage and energy when not in his handler's presence; this self-reliance must be preserved when the dog is in training, regardless of slow progress. If the dog's confidence is lost, there is then no training. One exhibition of temper, or inopportune punishment, may obliterate the effects of weeks. On the other hand, if handled gently, and developed by opportunity and experience, they frequently make excellent field dogs, and are handled with ease when trained. Punishment must be lightly and carefully applied; and none should be given, whatever fault is committed, when birds are being worked on, if there is any timidity with respect to them, or any gun shyness. All timid dogs should be thoroughly yard broken before any orders, except the most common and most easily obeyed, are enforced in the field; although the directions as given under the head of Preparatory Field Work should be observed at the same time. If the timid dog will chase birds and rabbits, and point, flush and run riot generally, so much the better; such faults are easily remedied in proper time; and the advantages are great. There are many intelligent dogs which are timid; also, there are some foolish ones. The latter class must not be trained by any arbitrary rules; the training must be applied as their powers and confidence develop; to teach and develop such dogs properly requires the highest skill of the trainer. They require punishment and correcting at times, but it must be applied with care; if properly applied, the dog can be educated to take ordinary punishment with comparative indifference. Herein trainers differ greatly; a good trainer can whip a dog, enforce obedience and retain the dog's confidence, while a poor one has a wonderfully positive talent for completely demoralizing and shattering a dog's ideas, affection, and hunting inclinations, at one punishment. Timidity is often combined with obstinacy or self will, which complicates the training a great deal and requires the exercise of the nicest judgment. The obstinacy must be overcome, yet the dog must not be cowed or his confidence lost, or any unpleasant associations established with field work. It is here apparent that to avoid possible complications the yard lessons should first be thoroughly inculcated. One mistake may retard the training for weeks; the dog may cease work, and no blandishments or commands thereafter will have any desirable effect on him; thus he may follow at heel during every hunt for an indefinite time. A dog of this disposition should never be taught to come to heel, or held there any important length of time before his training is well advanced in obedience, steadiness on birds, and general experience. There is no fault so difficult to overcome and none in which a trainer is so completely helpless as when a timid dog comes to heel and there remains. The trainer can only bide the dog's time. A sulky dog could be whipped from heel; but time must be allowed to efface the fears of the timid. However, a dog may begin his training with timidity, and acquire a great deal of boldness before it is completed.

The obstinate dog is usually very intent on having his own way, or on resisting the will of his trainer. Usually he is consistently obstinate and has very little respect for punishment; nevertheless, the obstinacy may be combined with timidity or cowardice. The thoroughly obstinate dog must be taken firmly in hand from the beginning, and a thorough yard breaking given. Cowing the dog slightly is often beneficial, providing that the trainer has skill enough to keep him within control; that is, can prevent him from running away. If he is taught to retrieve by force from the start, it usually has a beneficial, subjugating effect. It matters little when the training is begun, whether the trainer has any acquaintance with the obstinate dog, or *vice versa ;* the dog very soon learns to recognize his master, and if he is treated kindly between lessons, will soon learn to love him and recognize none other as his master. With a timid dog, it is necessary to gain his confidence before the training is begun. With the obstinate dog, it should be made an inviolable rule to enforce obedience to any orders, and every care should be taken to avoid giving any orders that cannot be enforced with a reasonable degree of certainty. For instance, if when afield, the dog is ordered to *Drop,* being some distance away at the time, there may be uncertainty about his obeying the command. If he refuses and an attempt is made to catch him, he may range safely out of reach. The attempt was an error on the part of his handler, for no command should be given under such circumstances, when there was a probability of a refusal to comply, with every advantage on the side of the dog. The trainer, knowing the peculiarities and reliability of his dog, might give him a command which he knew would be obeyed, such as *Come in ;* when caught, the desired obedience could be then enforced. However, if the yard discipline is thoroughly established with rigid adherence to prompt obedience in every detail, it is a positive advantage in all his after training; and the obedience, once thoroughly implanted, is permanent.

The rattle-headed dog, particularly if he has a hobby, is a trial and trouble to his handler. Devoid of intelligence, he performs his work as it may happen, and never comprehends the meaning or application of his education except the simplest parts which are related to the simplest work. He is forgetful because his memory is poor; he makes errors because he does not have a solitary plan in his work; his ranging is here and there, in likely or unlikely places, as it may happen; frequently he is a dog which means well, but as the friendship of some of the superior race is worse than their enmity, so the good intentions of the rattleheaded dog are generally materialized in glaring faults; he will point birds if he happens to go on them with favorable advantage of wind, position, etc., but he flushes them with equal *nonchalance* if he goes on them under unfavorable conditions. He profits very slowly by experience, making the same error a thousand times without any apparent concern. In his mature years, a dog of this kind may improve some; but having no understanding, he is always irregular and deficient in the exercise of his nose and legs. Unlimited opportunities afield are necessary to make anything desirable out of him.

The vicious dog is not common. Setters and pointers are very affectionate and mild in disposition. Once in a long while the vicious dog will be met with. After he has had a few lessons, he becomes cunning. He may attempt to fight when whipped, or while the spike-collar is used on him, or when the trainer attempts to put it on him; in the latter event he generally retires to a corner, growls, shows his teeth, and prepares for hostilities as his trainer advances with the collar. This should not deter the trainer in the

CHAMPION PAUL GLADSTONE.

least. The advance should be made slowly and steadily, catching his eye and holding it. The hands should be protected with heavy gloves. Reach out the left hand slowly toward him, and if he snaps at it, do not withdraw it. It is a thousand to one his snap falls short purposely, or, if he grasps the hand, it will be gently done. By no means attempt to take the hand forcibly away, and show no trepidation. Gently remove the hand and reach for his collar; after it is grasped, it is an easy matter to put the spike collar on him. There are some dogs so vicious that it is unsafe to trust to the influence of the eye or the fears of the dog. With such, when the left hand is advanced, the right should be held in readiness to give him a blow in the ear as he makes his attack, the left being withdrawn simultaneously; or make a feint of reaching quickly with the left, and quickly catch his collar with the right hand as he snaps at the left. If this cannot be done quickly and dexterously, it is better not to attempt it, as he might catch the right hand. Any trainer having the necessary nerve can put the collar on by one or other of these methods. But if the novice does not care to attempt it, he can whip the dog into submission. Give him a good, hearty whipping; if he growls when the hand is extended toward him, repeat it; continue the treatment till his collar can be grasped without any aggressive demonstration on his part.

A sulky dog is a very unpleasant subject to train. Whenever they are restrained in the exercise of their own will, they work sullenly and badly, if they work at all. This disposition has several different degrees. Some dogs will endure a certain limited quantity of restraint or correction before sulking, while others will sulk for hours at the first disagreeable occurrence. While a dog, having this nature, is in training, particularly after the yard breaking is completed, every care should be taken to keep him as cheerful as possible. If it is necessary to correct him when he is working in the field, it is better not to resume work until his good nature is restored. By aggravating this unpleasant trait, it can be greatly developed, much to the injury of the dog's value; hence the necessity of keeping it dormant.

The cunning dog displays admirable address in his schemes to have his own way. He flushes, affects an air of innocence and submission, and pretends it was an accident; he will pretend to misunderstand an order which is not pleasing to him, and will cheerfully proceed to work at something else, or go in some other direction which is more consonant with his inclination; he well knows when he is out of sight of his master, and can therefore flush and chase with impunity. At such times, if the whistle is blown, he is oblivious to it; but the moment his trainer comes in sight, he is all obedience and decorum. Like other animals endowed with reason, he may, in his peculiar way, be dishonest; when sent to retrieve a bird which fell out of sight he may eat it, although strictly honest when under the eye of his trainer. He learns a thousand little wiles and artifices, and by success in their exercise learns to play his master with the greatest *finesse*, if the master unhappily should attribute all his acts to pure instinct, and should therefore be unconscious of his inventive powers. A few wholesome corrections stimulate the dog's perceptions extensively. He knows when his tricks are discovered, and if once completely circumvented in all his wiles, he is cunning enough to know that working in his handler's interest is the more agreeable course to pursue.

The dog which is difficult to train from excess of enthusiasm usually comes gradually under control, if given work plentifully. Enthusiasm is one of the most excellent traits.

A general knowledge, at least, of the peculiarities of different dispositions is necessary, and must be duly observed in the methods of training.

CHAPTER II.

NOMENCLATURE.

Each art or science, possessing any general importance, has a comprehensive, supplementary, special language which serves to express, concisely and clearly, all the prominent peculiarities and relations of peculiarities belonging to it. Such abundance of technical terms is necessary, in treating of an art which has a variety of complex details, to afford the necessary forms of expression, and the consequent greater precision, fullness and conciseness.

Unfortunately, field sports, as related to the dog and gun, are an exception to the rule, the *technique* being loose, partly vague, inelegant, scanty and insufficient. This entails a great deal of unnecessary circumlocution and obscurity in all sporting literature, the finer thoughts and shades of color being lost in diffuse expressions or tiresome repetitions, or only the main ideas are given by reason of the trouble of constructing phrases to portray the collateral ideas.

It is strange that field sports should be the exception. Considering the general and uniform distribution of the setter and pointer, and the corresponding magnitude of field sports which exists at present, the care and importance attached to their breeding and training, and the many ages in the past during which they were highly valued, and the monetary value and facility afforded by an established sporting press for interchange of thought, it is astonishing that such poverty of nomenclature prevails. It would reasonably be expected that when field sports were in their beginning, the technical terms would be few and variable; it would also be expected that with their growth terms would multiply and have an established meaning. But field sports have been constantly progressing, while the nomenclature remains the same. The few terms in use are of the most primitive kind, generally being identically the same that were bequeathed by past ages, and were originally derived from the simplest words.

Pointing, backing, flushing, ranging, quartering, retrieving, pottering, roading, dropping to shot, wing or order, stealing a point, refusing to back, breaking a back, drawing, blinking, jealousy, gunshyness, footscent, body scent, running away or bolting, chasing, dropping to a point, are about all the terms which the nomenclature affords to express the *technique* of field work or training. All other incidental particulars, familiar to sportsmen, have no special nomenclature. This meagerness of terms is more apparent in the reports of field trials and descriptions of hunting experiences where common acts of the dogs are described at length in cumbersome terms again and again, and the few technical terms are repeated with tiresome frequency. Hence the narrations are lacking in the perspicuity, fidelity and vivacity which the scope and variety of the subject require. Even the common judgment and skill of the dog in finding birds, resulting from superior mental endowments combined with experience, is described by the very crude term "bird sense," plainly a misnomer.

Excepting the few literary productions which have superior merit from the talent of the writers, this paucity of terms undoubtedly contributes largely to the flatness and sameness of all the average sporting literature. Unless a writer has a fertile imagination and a copious vocabulary, this scantiness of technical material is sure to drag him down to the level of the commonplace, his writings taking rank with a multitude of spiritless, careless, insipid productions that might have passable merit if the authors had terms which would express their ideas.

The terms used to denote the education, and branches of education, to which the dog is subjected in preparing him for field work, and the details of field work, are also scanty and inexpressive. Even the terms *Training* and *Breaking*, used to denote the general education of the dog in respect to field work, have not the fixedness of meaning which they should have. Either term, if restricted to its common meaning, does not express the matter fully; and when used technically, there is no precise accuracy. While both are used as being synonymous by some experts in respect to the general education of the dog, by others they are used to designate different systems of training.

These terms, training and breaking, have different shades of meaning when applied to special branches of training; for instance, it may be said that a dog is trained to quarter his ground, or to range, and that he is broken from chasing, biting birds, etc., thus requiring both terms to express the several parts of education. However, these loose terms are much better than the multitude of acts which have no name, or which have an imperfect designation. In case a dog false points to such an extent that the hunter feels no certainty of birds being to his points, there is an unusual profusion of terms, for the act is called a false point when no birds are found, and the dog which habitually false points is called a false pointer. If two dogs back each other, the technical term is they "back each other." Here is a crude name for the act, but there is no technical term whatever to distinguish the dog which habitually causes the act; for it is commonly caused by a dog which will back while his companion is roading or puzzling over scent. Many common acts have neither terms to denote them nor the dog which performs them. For instance, the act of circling birds, heading them off and pointing them when they are running down wind; the habitual quartering or ranging entirely to the right or left of the shooter; the habitual turning in toward the handler at the end of each cast or irregularly ranging before or behind the handler; the habit of coming directly to the handler after each cast; the act of leaving the birds when found out of sight of the shooter, and returning to him to give notice of the find; the act of marking the flight of birds, bevies or single birds, and going directly to them or so near to them that by the dog's sense of smell he readily finds them; the act of flushing, whether done excusably, carelessly or willfully in an effort to capture the birds, or from jealousy, to prevent another dog from pointing; the dog which is proficient only in a special part or parts of field work as distinguished from the dog which is proficient in other or all parts; the dog which hunts intelligently, taking every advantage of cover, wind and ground, from the dog which ranges equally wide and fast, but without any intelligent plan,—all these have no technical distinction, although they are known to all sportsmen.

When a dog's actions denote that he has uncertainly caught a scent, or begins to road, it is commonly said that he "feathers," the term being derived from the display of feather a setter usually makes when he is conscious of game being near. This term is plainly inappropriate to express like acts of the pointer. The term "challenge" is used, by excellent authority, to denote this act, and it is much more expressive, accurate in meaning, and admits of comprehensive application.

It would seem that, there being so many large associations of sportsmen, some organized effort would be made to supplement and amend field nomenclature; but there appears to be no interest whatever with respect to it.

In this work the term training and breaking will be used interchangeably, the name being immaterial so far as the dog's education is concerned, the work, the methods and the dog's nature remaining the same, irrespective of such.

Handling is the manner of working and governing a trained dog, whether in private field work or a public competition, thus affording a term to distinguish between educational and working supervision.

CHAPTER III.

THE AMATEUR TRAINER.

The amateur trainer usually has the necessary enthusiasm and pertinacity, two qualities which are essential to the best success; but, in his first attempts, he invariably displays faults which are due to want of discipline in himself. The most common and serious fault is the irregular temper and the consequent much punishment and little teaching to which the dog is subjected. He does not consider that promiscuous, therefore misdirected, punishment, inflicted for not obeying commands which are not understood, is not training in any profitable sense of the term; on the contrary, it is decidedly injurious to the dog and obstructive to the training. The trainer should not set up his own knowledge as a standard for the dog, and by which to conduct the training, as many unconsciously do. He should intelligently study the dog's capabilities and peculiarities, modifying his methods and efforts in accordance with the dog's capacity. Ideas which appear simple and effective to the trainer may be comprehended with extreme difficulty by the pupil, particularly if the trainer has an imperfect system of teaching. The novice usually assumes that the dog has, at least, a fair knowledge of the English language, for he multiplies orders, and frequently has different orders for the same act. The ignorance of the dog is ascribed to obstinacy or stupidity, and punishment follows. If a strong man were to give a small boy commands which he did not comprehend, and immediately thereafter punish him for disobedience, such tutor would not be esteemed for his skill; yet such course would not be less absurd than the analogous one pursued by some amateurs. Other serious faults are irregularity of effort and inattention to details. The amateur may give the lessons properly for two or three days, then miss them for two or three weeks, and the dog is supposed to remember all, regardless of the fitful training. Proper care is not observed in correcting little imperfections of detail. Faults which could be corrected without trouble at their inception are permitted to grow and gain strength from habit, and are impatiently treated only when they injuriously affect the general training. Not infrequently a novice impulsively attempts to teach a whole system, or important branch of a system, or correct a grave fault, at one attempt, whereas he should have taken days or weeks. He, in his inexperience, is predisposed to believe that there is a fictitious valuation of the benefits accruing from a close observance of small details, hence he ignores them. Strict attention, systematically perfecting even the slightest details, is necessary to achieve success in training. Desultory efforts are but a short remove from no effort.

The amateur, besides being punctual and considerate, must acquire a habit of watchfulness and observation. To accomplish this requires constant effort of the will at first, but by cultivation it will become habitual. After a time, the trainer, if possessed of the proper qualifications, will be able to correctly interpret every action of the dog and anticipate his acts by his expression.

Some novices have the fault of training continually. The dog should not be made to feel that his life is one interminable lesson. While giving a lesson, the trainer should be painstaking and skillful, but when the lesson is ended, the training should be dropped for the time being, and the role of kind and indulgent master assumed. Ceaseless effort begets distrust or dislike; furthermore, the dog's mental faculties are not equal to long continued efforts without excessive fatigue, a trait which is also peculiar to the nobler animal.

It is also worthy of note that a trainer cannot train dogs successfully and at the same time indulge in regular shooting. It may be done after a certain loose fashion, but the education of the dog invariably suffers. The thousands of birds a man may have shot over a dog, or his expertness with a gun, is no criterion whatever in respect to his training capabilities. Training is a distinct art by itself of which shooting birds is merely a detail, hence experience in shooting is not necessarily experience in training. Experience, to be of value, must be correctly derived and associated. A fine shot, if an amateur, is rarely a good trainer, for the sufficient reason that he is so passionately fond of shooting he has no patience with obstructive delays to his pleasure, therefore he makes all else subservient to it. He does the shooting first and the training afterward, contrary to the correct method.

It requires just the same study, industry, natural capabilities and enthusiasm to make an expert trainer and handler as are required to become expert in any other art of equal complexity, hence it is apparent that the length of time required to learn the art is dependent on the amateur's aptitude and industry. If he cannot train a dog well even after studying and applying a proper system, his efforts are not without gain, for the knowledge will be serviceable in handling a trained dog. Good handling is a very desirable accomplishment, a thorough knowledge of it leading to a higher appreciation and better understanding of good work, the disposition of dogs, and a correct judgment of a dog's working qualities. From the experience gained, there is greater ability to control and handle dogs, every experience in any particular branch being beneficial in all branches.

No man can achieve success, or even passable success, as a trainer or handler, who looks upon a dog as a senseless piece of mechanism which works as the owner desires, and thus gaining its reward by the grace of servitude to the highest order of creation. To develop the highest capabilities, the dog must be treated kindly as a companion, as is his just merit.

The amateur should cultivate a calm, equable exterior. If he is excitable or easily irritated, showing it in voice and manner, it will directly or sympathetically affect the dog. If the amateur breaks shot himself when a bird is killed and deports himself unsteadily otherwise in shooting, he can rest assured that the dog will do likewise, whether broken or unbroken. Dogs are very imitative and sympathetic. They soon catch the excitement and unsteadiness of their handler, also the excitement and unsteadiness of unbroken dogs if hunted with such. Even when no game is present, the handler can excite and unsteady his dog by simulating a chase ; much easier is it then to excite him when game is present. The demeanor should be as placid and the manner as deliberate when shooting birds as if it were the most ordinary occurrence.

The ordinary tone of voice should be used, when possible, in giving orders, and it is possible whenever the dog is near enough to hear such tone. It is as equally effective as the loudest and is incomparably superior in refinement. Nothing is more disgusting than a bawling, bellowing delivery of orders. He who is loud, turbulent, devoid of field etiquette and offensively impulsive in his acts and utterances, will spoil the most capable dog in existence ; and if thereto he adds the weakness of finding fault with his dog, gun, cartridges and friends, and never finds a fault in himself, he cannot hope to be higher as a trainer than he is as a companion, unless he amends, which is hardly presumable, as there are very few precedents therefor. He who can be heard in the adjacent counties when a bird is flushed, or he who goes to the other extreme and praises his dog irrespective of the accuracy or inaccuracy of his work, can accept it it as an unalterable fact that as a skillful trainer he has mistaken his calling or diversion, as the case may be.

If the amateur fails in training a dog which possesses the proper natural qualities, the failure can only be ascribed to his own deficient skill or industry; for dog-training, as practiced at present, is an established art, and is followed as a profession year after year by a number of men. Given a dog having the required natural capabilities, there is not the least doubt as to successful training. Any part the dog will not perform willingly can be made compulsory.

It is absolutely necessary that the trainer either has a good temper, or self-control over such temper as he has, which practically is the same thing in dog training. All trainers are more or less impatient and irritable in their first efforts, but it is a weakness which should be suppressed as much as possible. The ideal trainer who is always patient and serene does not exist. By self-discipline a trainer can learn to control his temper; if he has not the will power to so control it, he is not the proper material for a trainer. Just so often as he loses his temper and inflicts unnecessary punishment, just so often does he do wrong and obstruct progress. No matter how refractory or stupid a dog may be, nothing is gained by gratifying ill temper. If the trainer's temper is impatient or fiery, yet controllable, it is no obstacle to successful training; indeed, the expert trainers, as a class, are not very mild tempered when crossed unnecessarily, but in the management of dogs they are patient, persistent, kind, and fond of dogs withal. A man's everyday disposition is no criterion by which to judge his temper as a trainer. He may be amiable, refined, and attentively kind in social and business life, yet, when training, may display terrible violence and unimagined fluency and resources of language; on the other hand, an ill-tempered man may conduct the training with the greatest patience and expedition; it can only be determined by actual trial.

Another prime requisite is that the trainer should be fond of a dog, otherwise he will not be sufficiently considerate in giving him time and opportunity to gradually and progressively learn the many things required of him. Men are intelligent beings of a high order, yet it would give the greater part of them, endowed as they are with reasoning powers, a severe task and many wearisome hours to learn to solve and intelligently explain, with the aid of the best masters, a simple problem in complex fractions, therefore he should be merciful to the dog which, he declares, solves problems by instinct with the disjointed instructions of all kinds of masters.

An exaggerated self-sufficiency, ignorance of methods, misconception of dog nature and impulsiveness, each and all detract from the novice's progress and efficiency. He should aim, by study and observation, to gain a thorough knowledge of methods. He should disabuse his mind of the idea, if it exists, that there is an arbitrary, inflexible method for training all dogs. To supplement the common methods, he must have natural fertility of resources to correct any unusual trait which may be undesirably exhibited. He should also recognize the fact that training is accomplished only by persistent, uniform effort; and without effort there is no training. After a perusal of the following chapters he will perceive that it is quite as serious a fault to be all method as to be without method. He can have so much educational method as to suppress the dog's hunting capabilities.

A fair degree of manual dexterity is very important, particularly in applying force to perfect a retriever. The awkward, forceless amateur who cannot put a checkcord on a dog without immediately entangling himself and every object within reach, or who gets the whip, checkcord and his hands mixed, every act going contrary-wise to his intentions, would do well to practice these acts by himself till he is proficient, thereby saving a dog much pain from his bungling. If he cannot attain the necessary dexterity, his special talent as a trainer lies in suasive methods, and he should cultivate it in that relation; for it is better to be an indifferent trainer than an inefficient infliction. On the other hand, the trainer who has great strength and dexterity should only apply such force as is necessary, and should proceed with due deliberation. Excessive punishment will injure a dog much more than is commonly supposed. A dog may start in full of fire and energy, and gradually become listless, the amateur frequently ascribing it to failing health, he not knowing that severe, long-continued punishment would produce it.

CHAPTER IV.

GENERAL REMARKS ON TRAINING.

The important subjects of ranging, pointing, backing, roading, etc., are dwelt upon at length, not so much with the intention alone of delineating the method of establishing a mere training in certain acts, as to describe the manner in which the dog should be developed and trained to the highest degree of his capabilities, with due regard to his natural powers and their subserviency to the purposes of the gun. It usually requires a long, ample experience to arrive at the highest degree of knowledge relating to field sports. If the sportsman is left to his own resources, it is generally acquired by slow, easy stages of evolution. No small part of this imperfection and dilatory progress is due to the common misconceptions respecting dog nature and instincts. By searching continually for complications where none exist; by assuming that the dog knows nothing but what he is taught; by enforcing artificial systems which are opposed to the dog's native capabilities, the true system, which is in harmony with the dog's nature and instincts, is, from its very simplicity, overlooked. Notwithstanding the general distribution of the dog and that every sportsman has more or less knowledge of the setter and pointer and the manner in which they work when trained, but comparatively few know anything of the real refinements in handling or training. This is thoroughly exemplified in the constrained manner in which the average dog works, or the perpetual whistling and commanding to which he is subjected when working.

There are some simple principles in dog training which should be understood and recognized at the start, namely, that the two principal elements in a dog's working capabilities are *pointing* and *ranging;* if these, as the foundation, are not well laid, the accessory natural qualities and whole educational superstructure. must be faulty. If a dog can point well, and cannot range, or *vice versa*, it is plain that his useful capabilities are of but little value. The importance of developing these properties to their full capabilities, together with the methods, is described in the chapters devoted to those subjects.

There is no secret in the art of training any more than what is embodied in diligence, skill, and fondness for the art. Some of the simplest parts and details are taught patiently at first, and the education is conducted step by step in easy gradations till the education is completed. In the latter stages; too great pains cannot be taken to have every command associated, as much as possible, with obedience, whether compulsory or voluntary; any deviation from this impairs progress and proper finish to the dog's training. Due care must be observed in the primary lessons respecting the control of the dog, for if he learns that he can evade certain orders by running away or keeping out of reach of his handler, he rapidly adds to his knowledge in respect to things which are not desired to be learned, and finally becomes unmanageable.

In conducting the education, the dog should be treated kindly and in good faith as a reasoning animal, which he is. If a trainer, firm in the belief that a dog cannot learn by experience, applies punishment promiscuously, he will soon learn that the dog, whether by reason or instinct, or without either, will, if opportunity offers, successfully avoid his trainer and his lessons. He will learn also that, after a very short experience, the dog will comprehend his aggressive purposes and can read his intentions so well that he can anticipate them by the expression of his trainer's countenance alone, even if the trainer's voice is sweetly modulated, and his manner seductive.

The primary education, as with all other animals, high or low, is the most difficult to teach; but, after the dog has learned his master's ways and comprehends some of the acts and orders, the remainder of the education is acquired with greater ease; indeed, if given judicious opportunity, he will learn a great deal himself by his observational powers alone. His character must be studied and understood, every dog, in this respect, differing from every other dog. By closely observing the habits, temper, disposition and intelligence of dogs, the trainer cannot fail to observe the diversity of character which exists. Also an astonishing number of intelligent acts and ideas will be noted, among which will be the one that the dog has a very correct estimate of his master's disposition and habits. If the latter does not believe that the dog is a rational animal, he would do wisely to study him still more closely, try to understand why he does certain intelligent acts, note his fixed habits of life, power of memory, will, etc., and then if he can not believe that the dog has reasoning powers, he can, without prejudice, conduct the training as if he did believe it, and he will progress with much more satisfaction to himself and comfort to the dog.

In the estimation of the average novice, a dog is a dog without any distinguishable differences of character or intelligence from those of every other individual dog, in about the same sense that one brick of a certain lot is similar to all other bricks of that lot, the natural inference then being that only one formal, arbitrary system is required in training. Nothing could be more erroneous. The temperament of each dog varies quite as much from that of all other dogs as one landscape differs from all others, and the trainer has quite as great a diversity of material to work upon as the artist has, although both have a few fixed, simple, elementary principles for the groundwork. Both artist and trainer must have a perfection and finish in the *tout ensemble* which is not reducible to formal rules. This ability is commonly called talent, but such does not comprehend it; it is really the ability resulting from love of the art, years of close study and hard work, and a few natural qualifications. Without the industry and enthusiasm, the talent is very little to the purpose.

A system of training is neither one of constant appeal to the whip or other punishment, nor a ceaseless attempt at suasion. The two must be combined in due proportion to the requirements of the pupil. However, as being of special importance, it should be noted that all punishment is purely corrective when properly used in training.

In the greater number of instances, the dog's training is hurried too much. The all-important point is to rush it through to a finish at the earliest possible moment. The true principle is to train the dog by easy gradations from the simple to the complex. As he progresses, he will learn to coadapt his methods to those of his handler from observing the success of methods, adjusting his work nicely and intelligently to subserve the purposes of the gun. By experience thus given, he acquires a full knowledge of all the varied and complicated details of field work and their purposes.

Also, as a rule, the education of dogs begins while they are too young. When the puppy is a year old he is young enough to start in training, and even then he should be worked with care and judgment. A year and a half is none too old, or two years if the dog has not been ruined by bad handling, although an earlier age is desirable. The dog's mental, muscular and nervous organizations are not sufficiently matured till he is a year old, at least. Occasionally a puppy is well developed at ten months; but very little is gained by working puppies at an early age, and there is always possible injury. With respect to the human subject, no intelligent man would advocate placing a ten year old boy in severe training in general athletics and a severe course of study at the same time. In such early training, neither the boy nor the puppy would have any comprehension of the application of what they were taught, besides which their organization would not be sufficiently matured to endure the severe mental and physical strain. In youth, the puppy's mind is immature and only adapted to such thoughtless improvement as is incidental to playfulness. His physique also has all the tenderness of immaturity, therefore his own free will should determine how much or how little exercise he will take. The same physiological laws which are universally recognized as applicable to the best development of children apply with like force and precision to the development of puppies.

The dog undoubtedly is capable of receiving a higher education than any other species of the lower animals, his natural fitness for his place in the economy of man's servitude demanding that he should have a peculiarly high education. All other domestic animals are controlled largely by mechanical appliances; the dog, if a long or short distance away, can be controlled, when trained, by a motion of the hand. He voluntarily co-aids his master in the pursuit of game, in a methodical manner; and from love of him, and comprehension of his purposes, he is faithfully reliable, and an intelligent assistant.

There is an important element in successfully developing

the dog's highest capabilities that is above methods and cannot be expressed in words any more than all the different colors of the rainbow, in their finest blendings, shape, relations, concentricity, and degrees of intensity, could be so portrayed. This refinement is in training the dog not only so that he will do the work, but so that he will have a full comprehension of its purposes and the interdependencies of all the different parts. He has then a full understanding of the acts of his master and loves to work for him alone, whereas, when he began, he worked solely for his own pleasure. To reach this refinement, the dog must be treated kindly as a rational animal. When he performs an intelligent act, he should be encouraged to know that he has done well. Do not make the mistake of thinking that he will not understand it. He will soon be on the watch to learn what acts are correct and pleasing, and worthy of approbation. He will learn by observation his master's moods and habits, and will take keen pleasure in working when he works and resting when he rests. There is a mutual bond of sympathy and understanding, a subtle comprehension, by which the dog works to the will of his master, when perfectly trained, without any commands; and the master comprehends every action and idea of the dog. This higher training borders on the realms of the psychological; yet that there is a time in the life of a properly trained dog when he will intelligently and accurately work without any supervision; when he comprehends his master's will or purpose by his actions or expression of manner; when he is happy only in his master's presence; when his knowledge comprehends every detail of the work, and when there is a mutual *esprit*, no expert, I believe, will dispute; still it must not be expected that the dog will reach all the higher capabilities of his nature before he is matured mentally, and has had skillful training and ample experience.

Many erroneous ideas prevail among novices in respect to the theory of training. It is commonly supposed that the setter and pointer are taught all branches of field work, even to pointing birds; hence, that stringent restraints and continual efforts are necessary to subjugate them. No more vicious theory could be imagined. They hunt naturally for themselves and learn methods much more accurately and effectively when left to their own experience and judgment. These natural capabilities are simply controlled sufficiently to subserve the purposes of the gun, and the process of reducing them to this state constitutes training. If the dog is inferior in any functional powers, the trainer can only make the best of such material as there is. Any natural deficiency is just so much gone from the dog's capabilities. For instance, if the dog is devoid of the pointing instinct, by giving a great deal of experience and training, he may be taught to stop on birds; but the act is then artificial and could be taught to a hound or cur in the same way. It is hardly necessary to mention that it is as inferior, when so taught, as any work of art is inferior to that of nature. The conjecture that at some uncertain period in past ages, in some vague manner, the dog's hunting and pointing were matters of education, should not be set against the fact of any individual, natural imperfections in the present. There is neither sense nor necessity in straining after far-fetched theories to prove that the pointing instinct had an educational origin, particularly when the same instinct is present in the pointer without any theory at all as to its origin.

A proper training is the result of honest, diligent effort and skill. Any system, professed to be a short, certain system, by which a dog can be taught thoroughly in a few weeks, by unusual methods, is either the result of a very imperfect knowledge of training, or an utter disregard of facts. Assuming the most favorable conditions, four to eight months, at least, will be required to complete the education, although, as a matter of course, every day of that time is not necessarily or desirably devoted to it; overwork is as incorrect and useless as any other erroneous method. Occasionally a dog performs well with a less period of instruction; on the other hand, there are dogs which require two full seasons. However, six months can be safely estimated as the average if the last three months of the training are in the open season, and ample opportunity afforded for field work. If all the training is done in the fall and winter in the South, the climate of the South being peculiarly favorable for such work, the training may be done in less time, the weather being cooler, the cover less dense, birds easier to find, the temperature more favorable for scent, and the dogs can work without distress.

Taking a finished field education as a standard, the progressive education, from start to finish, may be divided into three distinct stages, namely: First. The yard training, during which the dog is taught and comprehends certain acts with certain experiences, but does not understand their application in actual field work, such being obviously impossible. Second. The stage in his field work, in which he is learning to hunt, learning the application of acts taught in yard breaking, and the relation of his work to the purposes of the gun. This stage varies greatly in individuals according to their intelligence, tractability, and the skill of the trainer. It is the most difficult stage of training, and usually has distinct sub-stages—the dog at first has no knowledge of what is required of him, and, as is his nature, hunts impetuously, solely for himself. Partly by his own observation and partly by restraint, he next learns that by modifying his efforts so that they will act conjointly with the efforts of the shooter, there is a more uniform result and success. Gradually, with experience, he progressively learns the application and relation of every detail that has a bearing on capturing game. However, there are some parts which he cannot understand, consistently with the purposes of hunting, which is creditable to his intelligence. When the bird is killed he has the same feeling observable in the nobler animal, viz., to rush in and secure possession. Dropping to wing and shot are, to the dog, irrelevant acts. He can solve the relations of other dependent acts himself, but in this part he perceives no application to the purpose, and never learns it or observes it except as an act of arbitrary education. Third. The dog, after comprehending and applying the educational part, reaches the stage of *finesse*. He conducts all his work skillfully, with a view to shaping every part to the advantage of the gun; he contrives little arts and wiles to circumvent the birds; he displays intelligent management, schemes and acts which his trainer never taught him and of which he never thought him capable; besides exercising his inventive faculties and comprehension of details, he is on the alert to observe that the shooter is attentively performing his part, as may be observed when a dog slowly turns his head when on a point and looks out of the corner of his eyes to see if his master knows the situation; or when he abandons his point, when concealed, to go to his master and give notice, by his intelligent efforts to attract attention, that he has found birds. These stages of transition, while being distinct, are insensibly blended together in training, and are only perceptible when thoroughly established.

The training is not properly completed when the dog has merely reached a stage in which he is accurate and steady in all details of work and education. He may apparently be trained, but it has no permanency. He should be kept steadily at work till the discipline becomes *habitual*, and all the details permanently implanted in his memory; otherwise, after a rest of a few weeks, or when the next season arrives, he may forget or disregard his training entirely; thus it is perceived that a dog may have the appearance of being permanently trained when in reality he is not. In relation to making the work habitual, it should be noted as being of special importance that however obstinate a dog may be or however difficult to induct into any particular method, by long continued discipline it becomes so permanently established and habitual that it is second nature. Discipline, in the sense here used, signifies the regular and formal drilling which is necessary to permanently establish the training, and not in the sense which implies punishment exclusively.

Invariably one or more branches will be readily learned, while others, perhaps more simple, drag along to a wearisome length without any apparent progress; or the dog may be able to comprehend it imperfectly, or may have a faulty execution. Uniform progressiveness in each branch of training, by one individual, is an extremely rare occurrence. Even when a dog is trained in all other branches, there is usually one branch or other which requires days or weeks to finish. For instance, the dog may not back well, or may be faulty in retrieving, or may have some cranky notion, etc. The necessity of cultivating as much as possible such branches as the dog is backward in, is self-evident. The amateur, however, when the dog learns to point, is predisposed to give his attention to the shooting alone.

In the training, the dominant traits of character of the dog should be noted and used to advantage, if they are advantageous, or suppressed if they are the contrary. It is seldom that the training can be evenly conducted. The necessary functional powers are infrequently present in such naturally harmonious relations as to admit of each part of the education being equally progressive, one with the other. From natural aptitude and liking, the dog will have some special feature in his work that is superior to all other parts. The constant cultivation of the special part renders it the leading accomplishment. By diverting him from his preference and constantly drilling him in all branches, the weaker ones especially, the endeavor should be to make him as near an "all round" dog as possible. Due consideration, however, must be given to peculiarities of disposition and manner, the trainer adapting his methods to these as much as possible, instead of attempting to reduce all to an arbitrary standard. If a dog is allowed to indulge his special liking or faculty without any restraint, he is specially fond of it all his life, and may be inferior otherwise. Thus there are "covey dogs," which range wide and fast in search of coveys, but work on scattered birds with the greatest impatience, and are constantly on the alert to break away from such irksome work. Others are only useful on scattered birds, or in retrieving, etc.

In some instances, the apparent absence of any improvement will be very discouraging. Notwithstanding the diligent efforts of the trainer, long intervals may elapse before any perceptible advance is made in teaching certain parts. This backwardness may occur in any part or parts, or the dog may apparently be advancing when a relapse occurs, thereby necessitating further effort. Occasionally a dog will be met with which has a special proclivity for doing everything wrong. The attention and effort required to correct such idiosyncracies are very tiresome. Without any apparent cause, he may develop whimsicalities in parts of his work which will impede progress in all of it; or objectionable habits may be formed which may entirely obstruct training, or render the dog valueless. For instance, one experience which the author had with a dog of eccentric character will serve purposes of illustration. He was given to an inexhaustible display of cranky notions, and no sooner was one corrected than another, wholly new and unexpected, was sure to appear. The last one was final. He learned that, during the dry season, there were numbers of mice in the ditches, which are run in parallels and intersect each other at right angles, peculiar to the plantations in certain sections of Louisiana, thus cutting the plantations into squares, varying in size from an acre to several acres on different plantations, or different parts of the same plantation, according to the requirements of drainage. So thoroughly infatuated did he become in searching the ditches and digging for mice that he entirely abandoned hunting for birds. If removed from one ditch, he immediately went to the next one. If punished for hunting mice, he refused to hunt at all, and in time, instead of improving, he became wholly worthless for hunting. All this goes to show that training dogs is not uniformly successful, be the methods never so perfect, which is opposed to the inferences derived from the writings of many recognized authorities. It is beneficial to know that there are discouragements and failures to be met with; that there are parts of the education of a stupid, naturally inferior or obstinate dog that are unutterably wearisome, and with such the best efforts may result in failure. No trainer can wholly overcome stupidity, constitutional sulkiness, laziness, imperfections in nose, stamina, speed, hunting instinct, or physical infirmities. If a dog is worthless, a fine, long pedigree, the eminence of his ancestry, the merit of his ownership, avail naught against the fact of his individual worthlessness. The pedigree, while it vouches for the purity of the blood, kindly leaves the question of indvidual merit with the individual.

The importance of gradual progression has already been touched upon. This is particularly essential in the primary lessons. It is of transcendent importance to make the beginning of any new branch as simple as possible. One thing at a time, distinct and separate from all others, should be taught till the dog understands and remembers it; he will thus be saved much perplexity and confusion, constant advances will be made, and the trainer will save his temper. It may appear to be a dilatory system, but it is the quickest and the best in the end. Any forgetfulness should be treated kindly, a lapse of memory being excusable. Repetitions of the lessons will correct forgetfulness, while punishment is ineffective and injurious. In powers of memory, all dogs, except in rare instances, excel; but in the exceptional case, the infirmity should not be mistaken for obstinacy. It can be determined by the dog's apparent willingness to obey, but inability to do so from confusion of ideas, or when given an order to perform a certain act he may perform another entirely different act which he has been taught; his hesitancy and doubtful air at times under these circumstances indicate his feeling of uncertainty as to correctness. This confusion of ideas may be caused in dogs of good memory, by attempting to teach, hastily and imperfectly, several things during the same lesson—palpably an unskillful method.

While a small part of the dog's education is necessarily compulsory, the punishment required is much less than is commonly supposed. The trainer should endeavor to whip as little as possible. All beginners trust too much to force, regardless of the temperament of the dog. Generally the more experience a trainer has had, the less he uses the whip, although it can never be entirely dispensed with; but it can be reduced in its application to a minimum.

Due weight should be given to the important and pertinent facts that, in giving the lessons, the dog's attention can be held too long; that he can become mentally and physically weary; that he can be overworked; that he can become disgusted by bad treatment or can acquire a decidedly obstructive dislike to his handler; that he can be overfed or underfed; that his health and spirits are not always the same, and that he is not always bright and attentive. It should be remembered as bearing on the training as a whole or in part, and worthy of repetition, that unless a dog loves his handler he never performs at his best. For the master that he loves, a trained dog, properly handled and kindly treated, delights in his work; even when fatigued and hunting has ceased being pleasurable to himself, he will renew his exertions for his master's enjoyment. When a dog, which has no serious faults to be corrected, will run away or shows apprehensive or distrustful feelings with respect to his handler, there is something radically wrong in the system of training. The trainer, knowing the peculiarities and capabilities of his dog, should know precisely how to adjust his methods to be in harmony with them; but if his dogs all fear or ignore him, there is error somewhere.

To simply give the dog a lesson and then see him no more till the next lesson is also erroneous. The dog soon has only unpleasant associations of his handler, and his coming causes painful apprehension. Only by making a companion of him can he become truly affectionate and dependent, being happy in his master's presence, and anxious to please.

Every dog has a certain individuality in his methods, differing in some respect from those of every other dog, no two dogs being alike in either intelligence, habits or form. The amateur often attempts to shape the peculiarities of the dog to some ideal standard. Such efforts are futile. Do not imagine, because a certain dog carries a high nose and is a brilliant performer, that all dogs must perform with a high nose or that it is possible for them to do so. It is better to make the best of the dog's capabilities such as they are. If he carries his head low and roads his

BREAKING AND HANDLING.

birds naturally, it is better to encourage proficiency in what he can do than failure in what he cannot do. For this reason any artificial appliance, as the puzzle peg mentioned with much favor by some authors, is wholly worthless. This should not be confounded with appliances which are used to control his actions and not his manner of work, such as the checkcord, spike collar, etc. To attempt to make a dog into something other than he is naturally is to engage in dismal efforts.

It will be observed that, directly and indirectly, much importance has been attached to the dog's rational powers. In their powers of mind, dogs vary quite as much, making due allowance for the inferiority in grade, as the degrees and differences of variation in the minds of men, barring entirely those exclusively high cognitions of the nobler animal whereby friendship is valued according to its financial or social profit, or as an aid to ambition.

All these generalities are of the greatest importance in teaching particulars. The trainer, to be successful, must have a knowledge of them first or last, if he can do so. However, as in every other art requiring tact and address, there will be men who will excel all others.

CHAPTER V.

INSTRUMENTS USED IN TRAINING.—THEIR USES.

The spike collar has been the subject of the most unqualified praise and most unqualified condemnation; it has been claimed that it is applicable and efficient in every branch of a dog's education, and the most extravagant quickness and perfection of results have been ascribed to its use.

Much can be said for and against it, not from any inherent virtues or vices in the collar, but accordingly as it is used skillfully or otherwise. Unquestionably, men of uncontrollable temper and vicious propensities inflict terrible torture, and sometimes maim or destroy the dog with it, yet it is only a means to their brutality; in its absence, the whip or boot would more than probably take its place. For such men the collar is wholly unfit as a useful instrument in training, and the men are wholly unfit for trainers. Even in the hands of a novice whose temper and intentions are the kindliest, a great deal of unnecessary pain is inflicted from imperfect knowledge of methods and dog nature, awkward manipulation, and from failure to note the painful effects of punishment. The writer has seen the lesson abandoned and the most disgraceful barbarity exhibited from loss of temper. Such is not dog training in any sense of the term; and the vicious temper of the trainer cannot be ascribed to the properties of the collar. When used merely to gratify such temper, it ceases to be an instrument of education; and ill-natured punishment should not be confounded with training. The distinction is very positive; the two purposes are not even remotely related to each other. Barbarity, which justly excites the most intense indignation, is considered, by uninformed spectators, as being a necessary adjunct to the collar, if they have unfortunately seen it applied in a disgraceful manner, naturally inferring that such manner is the approved one of using it. The injurious effects of the collar, when used with unnecessary violence, are not transient. The terrible punishment never fails to cow the dog, or make him nervously apprehensive, or cripple him by breaking down his constitution, or by injuring his neck and spine from the violent shocks. Partial or complete paralysis may be produced by excessive violence; and many instances are known where dogs have been killed outright. Contrary to the general exposition of its advantages by its advocates, the spike collar will cow a dog if unskillfully used. There is less demonstration in its use than in the use of the whip, but it will have similar cowing effects in time. Dogs which are punished regularly and severely with it may not show positively disabling effects, but they gradually become more and more listless and less vigorous; and this broken down state may last for months or for life. The novice, observing the falling off in working capabilities afield, imputes it to the effects of field work or deficient stamina; he would be more likely to find the cause in the abuse of the collar, if he uses one. Many dogs have been completely ruined by it, but such effects were the natural consequences of ignorance of its proper use, and the injurious effects.

As between those who claim every advantage for it and those who claim every ill, its true place will be found to be intermediate. As a matter of fact, the spike collar should have but a limited place in a dog's education, namely, to make retrieving compulsory, to break bad cases of unsteadiness and to force a dog to come in promptly to order. It may be used transiently for other purposes, but such are merely incidental. When used skillfully for these purposes, it has no equal in thoroughness and effectiveness. A force collar should be used with spikes in it or not at all. The dog will not struggle against spikes; the force necessary to be applied to a plain collar so shocks the dog's whole system that positive injury is inflicted.

The great error lies in assuming that any man can take a spike collar and apply it to training purposes without prior experience. No man can use it properly in the beginning. The first dogs which, unfortunately for them, afford the experience always suffer for it aside from educational considerations. It would be as reasonable to assume that a novice could take a gun afield and shoot skillfully at his first attempt as that he could use the collar properly.

It is recognized by experts as a very effective and useful instrument in certain branches of the dog's education. When applied properly the advantages are great; the dog is more thoroughly obedient, the orders obeyed with greater perfection and precision; the control gained in one branch likewise affects all other branches; the effect of training is more permanent, and the general education is more uniform and perfect. Except in the case of obstinate dogs, there is no occasion to use sufficient force to shock the dog's system, and with them there is no need of inflicting permanent injury. The amateur should carefully note its effects, and proceed in the training with the greatest deliberation. It requires manual dexterity to manipulate the collar properly, which can only be acquired by practice. If there is a rope on the collar, it should be the proper length for the purpose used, and the trainer should endeavor to avoid getting awkwardly entangled in it. If he cannot apply the collar without becoming impatient and angry, it is better to abandon its use entirely. The collar is useful, but a violent man is out of place as a trainer with it.

In forcing a dog to retrieve, it is better to apply it with just sufficient force to punish the dog a little, and proceed with the greatest deliberation. The first advances may apparently be slow but they will be sure, and in the end will be more expeditious. By this course the dog is not cowed, does not acquire a dislike of his handler and is not injured. When the punishment is severe, it invariably causes terror, dislike, confusion of ideas, and from the pain suffered all kinds of erratic notions are exhibited. Much time is lost in correcting these eccentricities; in the gradual manner of developing the dog's ideas and obedience, all these are avoided.

The efficiency of the collar depends much on its construction. Many collars which are on the market are wholly worthless or nearly so.

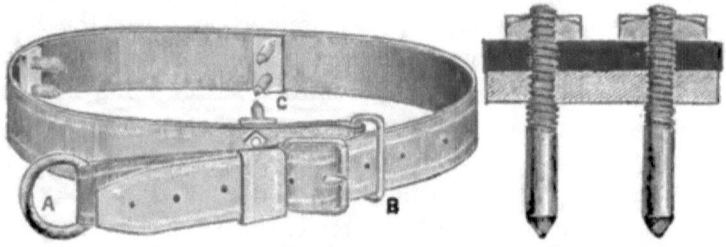

THE SPIKE COLLAR.   SECTIONAL VIEW.

Herewith is given an illustration of an excellent spike collar. It is very simple in construction, yet it is very effective, easy to carry in the pocket, and has fewer undesirable features than any other, and is not patented. As will be seen by the diagram, it is both a spike and choke collar. It should be made of the very best quality of harness leather, but the latter should not be over one-eighth of an inch in thickness. The long strap should be twenty-two inches in length and an inch and a quarter in width. The short strap, including both buckle and ring, should not exceed five inches. For obvious reasons the buckle should be square; the oblong, marked B, should also be square in the corners, thus preventing the collar from rolling and throwing the spikes' points upward, if the dog takes a few turns. This square should be made of tough steel rod, three-sixteenths of an inch in diameter, and in dimensions one and one-quarter inches by one-half inch in the clear. Having an oblong in place of a ring is a very important feature, as all those who have used a collar much will readily perceive. A ring allows the collar to twist, and this is a source of constant annoyance and obstruction in the training. The distance from the oblong B to the spikes C should be ten inches. The spikes nearest B should be one and three-quarter inches from the oblong, and the remaining spikes should be half-way between C and the spikes nearest B. The spikes should project five-eighths of an inch. The ring A should be one and one-eighth inches in diameter. The spikes should be one-quarter of an inch in diameter, and the points should be blunt and short. A very good illustration of the spikes is given in the sectional view of the collar herewith given. The spikes are screwed through a narrow steel plate, one-eighth of an inch in thickness. The diagram will show the remainder of the construction without further explanation.

Besides the direct uses of the collar in training, it has very advantageous incidental effects. If it is put on a dog's neck in field work, if he has had some training with it, he will be comparatively steady and obedient. He might refuse to retrieve a bird without the collar on his neck, and retrieve it nicely with it on. By taking advantage of this peculiarity, a great deal of unnecessary trouble can, at times, be avoided.

In forcing large, heavy, obstinate dogs to retrieve, it is much better to use both the spike collar and whip. A dog which weighs sixty or seventy pounds has so much weight that a severe jerk shocks the trainer as much as it does the dog. The trainer's shoulder or arm will be badly strained or lamed, particularly if he has three or four heavy dogs in training at the same time. The manner of conjointly applying the whip and collar is described in the chapter on retrieving.

A whip of medium weight is the best. The abominations which are heavily loaded with iron in the handle should be severely condemned. They are unnecessary and have a suggestion of brutality that is not in accord with the loving nature of the dog or the purposes of an education. There are too many novices who are disposed to use the wrong end of the whip. An ordinary one is severe enough. To gain an idea of its effects, the trainer may permit some friend to give him a middling sharp cut with it, and therefrom he will have a keener perception of its effects on the dog. A whip should be a whip, plain and simple. A combined whistle, whip, slingshot and dog lead, is a snare and a delusion. A snap on the end of the whip is useful to attach it to a loop on the coat, some sportsmen preferring to carry them thus on the outside instead of in the pocket. A better way is to have a small ring sewed on the inside of the breast of the hunting coat to which the whip can be attached. A pocket should be made, six inches underneath, for the lash, which can be rolled up easily, to rest in. It can be gotten at quickly, and has not the untidy appearance which it has when hanging loosely outside of the coat.

The whip is indispensable in dog training. Not that it is a constant necessity, but that at such times as its use is indicated, it is then required. The moral effect of its presence is a great governing influence with headstrong dogs. Timid dogs even will require a little application of it before their education is completed. By proper handling, a timid or cowardly dog can be whipped without cowing him. When they are sufficiently advanced to correct their offences, the whip can be used lightly on them, merely the weight of the lash without any force to it, if necessary. By also showing and cracking it occasionally, the dog becomes familiar with the sight of it, then it can be applied with the necessary punishing force. Obstinate dogs should also become familiar with the sight of it. There is no surer way to make an untrained dog whip-shy than to associate certain punishment with the act of taking the whip in the hand. After the timid dog has been whipped once so that pain is inflicted, merely cracking the whip will be sufficient warning to dogs of such very mild dispositions, for a time, for subsequent offences; indeed, a mere reproof is punishment to some dogs.

Hard-headed, obstinate dogs require much more punishment; and there are dogs which require good, honest thrashings frequently repeated; in fact, with some the occasion occurs with periodical exactness. The trainer can observe all the little premonitory signs that lead to the repetition of a fault, and, by experience, the dog knows equally well that he has committed the fault, yet will do it with a full knowledge that he has to suffer punishment. With such dogs the punishment should always follow the fault, and with every recurrence, it should be increased. Dogs of certain dispositions can be corrected by mixed reproof or punishment. Except with the dog which willfully and knowingly commits a fault, good training does not necessarily consist in punishing for a fault every time it is committed. It consists in developing the dog's capabilities by such system as accords with his capabilities and peculiarities. Many faults can be cured without inflicting pain; in fact many, such as false pointing, blinking, gun shyness, fear of the handler, etc., are intensely aggravated by it.

The whipping should be administered as nearly under the same circumstances, respecting any particular fault, as possible, to the end that the dog can properly comprehend and associate the punishment. Also judgment is required to determine the right juncture to give the proper quantity, and withal to retain control over him. It is injudicious to release a dog as soon as he has been whipped. Hold him till such time as he regains his composure ; and if he evinces an undue desire to get away, he should not be released if there is a probability that he will bolt. The trainer, knowing all his peculiarities, can easily forecast his purpose. A long cod-line can be put on him if there is danger that he will run away, and by this means he can be prevented. After punishing a dog it is better to refrain from giving any orders till he resumes his work. At all times the trainer's manner should be kind, but no frivolity should be indulged in.

Dogs will be met with which, from self-will and the absence of any of the natural affection which nearly all dogs feel for a trainer who treats them kindly, can only be controlled by reducing them to a state of fear. Fortunately dogs of such cold-blooded, self-hunting natures are very uncommon ; however, the trait varies from the mild degrees to the most intense, the latter being infrequent. To show the necessity of severe and regularly repeated punishments, the author will mention an instance which was in his own experience ; one of many, yet the worst one of all. It was still more remarkable from the fact that the dog was a pointer, he being of a breed which, when trained, is almost uniformly disposed to work to the gun. During the first two or three weeks he was given his head; he quickly learned the scent of game and how to point for an instant, but, inauspiciously for subsequent training, when he flushed and chased, he manifested the utmost indifference as to the whereabouts of his handler. He was a dog possessing wonderful powers of speed, wind and endurance. After he found the first bevy of chickens, his first experience being on the prairie, a chase ensued and thereafter an occasional glimpse of him would be caught as he galloped over a swell in the prairie a mile or more away. His nose was exquisitely keen; the manner in which he, carrying a high nose, would gallop to a bevy, was most admirable; but the subsequent proceedings were quite the reverse. A few whippings, such as would have beneficial effects on an ordinary dog, seemed to infuse fresh vigor and determination into him, he being quite willing to understand that the punishment was for failing to catch the birds instead of for attempting to catch them. He was going from bad to worse. The brief points were abandoned as being entirely too slow for his purpose, and punishment was exasperatingly ineffective. Chickens, at that time, were very plentiful, hence opportunities for a dog to point or flush were frequent. One day, immediately after the dog had had a tremendous chase, a large bevy was nicely scattered in long grass. A very long cod line was fastened to his spike collar, and he was not permitted to get beyond control. On the rise of the first bird, he started to chase with his customary vim, but the cod line held him, and he received a good thrashing. After the punishment, he would give himself a vigorous shake, not unlike that which a dog gives on coming out of water, and was then as calm and indifferent as if nothing had occurred. Briefly, he repeatedly flushed and was repeatedly whipped for about two hours in succession; his hide was completely checkered with welts, and a new whip was worn out on him; but before the afternoon ended he would point. It might seem as if such severity was unnecessary, but, severe though it was, its effects were transient. It was necessary to keep a checkcord on him all summer, and, had his merits been ordinary, he would not have been worth the trouble of training. The whippings had to be repeated day after day during the whole season, till at last he would work steadily through combined habit and fear, although he never did become reliable. Even when trained, in his second season, if one fault was permitted to pass unpunished, he rapidly thereafter became unmanageable. Whipping never cowed him, and only had transient beneficial effects. A good thrashing before he was cast off in the morning always had salutary effects; if not given then, it would be necessary shortly afterward. A dog of a colder nature never lived. He was naturally a self-hunter, and only hunted to the gun as a matter of arbitrary routine. Moral suasion would be as completely lost on him as would a puff of breath into vacuity.

In applying punishment with the whip for faults in field work, due attention must be paid to contingent circumstances, ones which perhaps may require the fault to be unnoticed. For instance, a dog might willfully flush a bevy, and immediately thereafter might point an out-lying bird; if punished then, he is quite as likely to consider that the punishment was inflicted for pointing as for flushing. Simple as this seems, there are many amateurs who will not consider such circumstances, notwithstanding the bad effects which ensue. By disregarding such essentials, or not even considering them, a great deal of unnecessary and injurious punishment is inflicted, and complications produced. Skillful trainers always use the whip or collar much less than amateurs. The latter are always disposed to apply excessive punishment from assuming that every fault shown should be visited with instant and severe punishment. Careful discrimination should be observed as to errors arising from inexperience, or accident, or design. With the average dog, mild corrections repeated with each recurrence of the fault will have much better effect than attempting to cure it at one effort. It is also worthy of note that heavy whippings, long continued, will have the some pernicious effects on the constitution that similar punishment has from the spike collar.

To such men as do not hesitate to kick their dogs (the number is not so few as might be supposed), there is but a waste of time in describing the worse than brutality of the act. Unhampered by the restraints of law and without fear from the known helplessness of their dogs, they simply show their real nature when free from restraint.

The whistle is a very important instrument in handling a dog when afield. It should have a full tone, of medium pitch, such whistle being easier to blow and more effective since it can be heard further than one which produces a shrill, thin tone, or a large one which produces a low, heavy one. A whistle is all that is necessary as a whistle. The metal double barreled affairs, with tones like a miniature fog horn, are cumbersome to carry, offensively noisy, and moreover are unnecessary.

A metal whistle is very objectionable for constant use. The oxide, which is sure to accumulate, is very disagreeable to the taste, and it will make the mouth sore. In frosty weather, from being full of frost, it is particularly disagreeable. The hardness and weight of the metal are also unpleasant to the teeth.

The best whistles are made of wood, deer horn or celluloid, the latter being very neat, light, and of good tone; and all are free from the objectionable qualities of metal whistles. Whatever kind is used, it should have a mouthpiece so shaped that it can be held easily in the mouth without the assistance of the hands. When in use, it should be tied to the coat near the collar by a strong string, about twelve inches long, thus being convenient for use. Nearly all hunting coats have a small pocket near the collar, purposely for the whistle to be carried in.

One whistle is sufficient for the purposes of handling or training a dog, although some good trainers use two or three, but the refinement partakes of unskillfulness, and besides it is unnecessarily troublesome. The tones of one whistle can be varied and modulated sufficiently to give distinct signals for all the purposes for which it is used.

No dog can be considered as being well trained unless he is at least passably obedient to the whistle. He can be taught to perform any act to it that he is taught to observe by oral commands, but in practical work it is commonly used to give the signal *Come in*, the signal to turn at the end of a cast, or to turn when he is going in a straight line ahead of his handler. It can also be used advantageously to give a signal for a dog to go steadily and slowly when working on scattered birds; a low note, softly modulated, just loud enough to be heard, is much better than using the voice when birds are wild. The whistle is also used to give a note to attract the dog's attention that he may see a signal of the hand. If the trainer has sufficient persistence, patience and skill, he can train his dogs so that they will work entirely to motion and whistle, this being more refined than the use of the voice; but such finish requires many working opportunities to educate the dog to such perfection, and the perfection is not attained till the second season. Continuous whistling is unnecessary, offensive, and defeats the purposes of a whistle. It loses all meaning and association when used in season and out of season. The habit grows, and eventually the trainer whistles unconsciously and perpetually, whether there is need of it or not. Such is insufferably annoying to a companion, particularly if he has a well-broken dog at work. Professional handlers are not all free from this disagreeable practice, as may be observed in the methods of the more unskillful while handling their dogs at the field trials. Hence it is evident that the whistle should only be used when necessary, and then should always have the correct notes on it to signal the desired order. If the trainer should make a mistake in the signal and the dog should obey it, it is better to let him continue, as two or three different signals only tend to confusion. The error can be corrected a few minutes later.

Nearly every trainer has his own peculiar signals, there being nothing conventional in this respect. At field trials particularly, it has been learned by experience that it is undesirable to have uniformity of signals, one handler, when like signals are observed, being able to slyly manage another handler's dog. It is also very undesirable, when hunting with a companion, to have one's dog minding his companion's whistle, or *vice versa*.

Many men acquire a bad habit of carrying the whistle in the mouth continually, therefrom frequently acquiring the habit of blowing it excessively. It looks much better to blow it when required and carry it in the pocket the remainder of the time; otherwise it will surely be blown unnecessarily, and the act will soon become habitual. When noise and violence once become a fixed habit, they are seldom cured.

The checkcord has many useful places in a dog's education. It serves to keep him under control if he is unsteady on point, back, or to shot and wing. It is of constant use in giving the preparatory yard lessons.

A braided checkcord is the best, it being more flexible and less liable to kinkiness. Different sizes are required for different dogs, and different purposes. For work in cover it is better to have it tarred. It is evident that a heavy, strong, obstinate dog requires a stronger line to hold him than a small or timid one; the larger line is easier to hold in the hands, and less painful also. A quarter inch line is large enough for all ordinary purposes with the average dog. In breaking confirmed cases of breaking shot or chasing, a three-eighth inch line is necessary. In teaching the first lessons in retrieving, a half inch rope is the right size, on account of less pain or injury to the hands. Long checkcords are seldom required. The shorter a checkcord is consistently with the purpose in view, the better. There is no occasion when one which is over twenty feet will be required, except the instances where it is desired to give a bolter plenty of room to run with a long checkcord, to give him a snubbing; then it can be used to advantage. In general field work, a long checkcord becomes tangled, awkward to handle, and inefficient. Expert trainers use them only in special instances in field work, the greater part of the education being given without them; however, it is always advisable to carry one so that it is available for use if needed. It should be neatly coiled and tied so that it can be used instantly. One which is tangled and snarled is but a short remove from none.

"Bolting"

CHAPTER VI.

COMMANDS.

All signals and oral orders, to which the dog is taught obedience, may be considered under one generic head, namely, commands. The chief distinction is in the manner of delivery, and not in the mental activities which they produce in the dog; considering the subject only as it relates to the dog's perceptive powers.

The commands, by the medium of sound, such as those delivered with the voice, the whistle, the gun, or the sound produced by the whirr of wings, are conveyed to the cognition of the dog through the sense of hearing; the signals, by the sense of sight; a touch, by sense of feeling. Identical meanings can be conveyed through the different senses by appealing to them under circumstances which come within their powers. Thus the order *Drop*, a command by voice, or the report of a gun, or the whirr of wings, is conveyed to the mind through the sense of hearing; the signal to drop is conveyed by the sense of sight; a touch of the whip on the shoulder, which signifies that the dog is to drop, is perceived through the sense of feeling; yet each one of these commands, distinct in form, yet the same in meaning, can be associated alike in the mind with the same ideas and the associated act of obedience. As these are all the senses which are directly appealed to in enforcing obedience, the others are not worthy of consideration in this relation. By thus tracing these similarities of principles in conveying knowledge, and similarity of cognition in acquiring it, a more orderly and systematic theory and practice of training are established. Ordinarily, every distinct branch, sometimes parts of the same branch, is considered and treated by authors as being not related either in methods or ideas, —a wholly erroneous conception. While the act of knowing is through the mediation of entirely distinct organs of sense, the principle of training is the same in all branches, namely, to associate certain forms of obedience with certain fixed forms of command, whether such commands are sounds or signals.

While it is necessary in training to associate the command with the required act of obedience, it should not for a moment be considered that the dog's powers of understanding are limited to a simple corresponding association of ideas. Such is merely the inceptive form of knowing and does not differ materially from the primary forms of teaching the infant human subject, as for instance, in object teaching; or the more complex forms in the adult, as associating certain ideas with certain words, certain sounds with certain objects, even if the objects are absent; certain ideas with certain other ideas, etc., which is abstract knowledge.

The words of command and signals in common use are as follows:

Come in is the order which denotes that the dog is to come directly to the handler without delay. A beckon of the hand has a like significance. A prolonged blast on the whistle is the order which has a corresponding meaning, although, in respect to the common use of the whistle, these are not constant or uniform signals.

Hie on or go on is the order to begin hunting. If the dog is at heel, a click with the tongue, or a slight motion with the forefinger, are equivalent signals.

Heel is the order which denotes that the dog is to

get behind his handler and there remain until ordered out. A slight wave of the hand to the rear has the same significance.

Drop, charge, down charge, denote that the dog is to lie down and remain in that position till ordered up. The right or left hand and forearm raised perpendicularly is the signal to drop.

Hold up denotes that the dog is to stand up. A click of the tongue, or a motion of the finger, has a like significance.

Dead, or *dead bird,* denotes that a bird which was shot at is killed, and that it is to be retrieved. It is generally combined in use with the order following.

Find, seek, seek dead, denote that the dog is to search for a dead or wounded bird.

Fetch is the order to retrieve. Some trainers use the order *Bring, or bring it here,* but it is not necessary to use more than a monosyllable in an order.

Steady, or careful, denotes that the dog is to shorten his pace, and pay more heed when working for dead or scattered birds.

To ho is the order to stop and stand still. It is now obsolete in field training and never had any practical use at any time, except in teaching backing.

Over, or *get over,* is the order to jump a fence.

Hi, or any other exclamation the trainer fancies, can be used to order a dog to desist from doing any undesirable act, such as chasing birds, rabbits or sheep, jumping a fence, etc.

Two or three short, sharp notes, or one long and one short note, may be blown on the whistle to denote that the dog is to turn and take another direction. As mentioned before, the trainer uses such notes as pleases his fancy. Care, however, should be taken to have a distinct note or notes for the different acts required. Some handlers teach the dog to drop to certain notes on the whistle, preferring this to using the voice, but such does not find general favor, and is unnecessary.

Every command should be given in a firm tone, but the greatest care should be taken to use the ordinary tone of voice; and the ordinary demeanor should also be observed. No other tone or demeanor will be required if the dog is broken in a proper manner. After a time the ordinary tone becomes habitual; also loud tones and excited exterior become habitual if practiced, hence the necessity of avoiding objectionable habits.

A dog can be taught to obey the slightest signals with the greatest nicety. When he is too far away to distinguish them, the whistle comes into play. The awkward, ungraceful style of delivering signals with the arms widely extended and the whole frame stretched should be avoided. Some trainers unconsciously put force enough into a signal to give the impression that they lifted the dog along by main strength. A light, graceful motion is every bit as effective and much less laborious.

It is surprising that a dog can be taught to obey a slight signal to such a degree of perfection. The common block trick which is performed by many trick dogs, illustrates the capacity of the dog to comprehend very slight signals. For the benefit of those who never have seen it, it may be mentioned in this connection to show the uselessness of very demonstrative signals. A number of blocks, having the necessary letters or figures printed on them, are placed in a row a few inches apart. A certain name or number is given, the letters or figures of which the dog is to pick out in the correct order of succession to spell the word or notate the numbers correctly. The dog walks along the row, stops, picks out the correct letter or number, one at a time, and carries it to his trainer. This trick never fails to mystify the spectators. The eye of his master, though apparently fixed, materially assists to direct him, and at a proper juncture, the trainer moves his toes in his shoe without moving the rest of his person, and the dog, observing the signal, picks up the block next to him.

The order, *ware*, signifying that the dog is to desist from certain acts or intentions, is not used in this country. Exclamations should be used as little as possible, as they are not an artistic accessory to handling a dog. When a dog shows an intention to jump a fence when it is not desired that he should do so, instead of bellowing *Ware fence!* or *Hi!* the handler should blow the signal on the whistle to turn, which is equally effective, if the dog is properly trained, and much more elegant.

Promiscuous, purposeless orders will detract from the dog's interest, and if, unwisely, he is deceived intentionally many times, he becomes disobedient and indifferent.

CHAPTER VII.

PREPARATORY TRAINING.

Yard training consists in teaching the dog the proper acts of obedience to the respective orders, and prompt submission to them. Sometimes the term house breaking is used erroneously as having a synonymous meaning,—this breaking, as the name implies, simply consists in teaching the dog correct everyday deportment and habits, when at liberty, in or about the house. In most instances, if a puppy is raised about the house, he, without any special training, forms correct habits from observation and association, keeping very intelligently within his proper sphere in the domestic economy. If he commits a fault, he is scolded or whipped for the offence, probably with no reference to his education; hence his house training is given unconsciously; however, by his powers of comprehension and imitation, he learns a multitude of details himself. So familiar to every person is the sensible deportment of a dog which has had the liberty of the house from puppyhood, and so gradually and easily is his education aquired, that its very commonness causes it to be unnoticed, or accepted as a matter of course. The difference, however, is very apparent when a dog which has been kept constantly on a chain or in confinement is allowed his liberty; then all things are alike to him; he jumps on the bed or table, or capers in the parlor or kitchen with equal *sang froid*, and naturally from his inexperience considers the house a superior kind of finely furnished kennel. He must then have experience to learn correct conduct; and when it is considered that this is learned in a year or two, it is very creditable indeed when compared with the length of time necessary to teach some of the nobler organisms, and when it is compared with the crude behavior of the untaught said organisms. It is true that some dogs are dishonest. They will steal, but this trait appears to co-exist with high orders of reason.

There are a few traits peculiar to the dog under domestication which are exceedingly disagreeable at times, and which should be corrected. One of the most irritating is the common habit of affectionately placing the fore feet on the person of his master or a visitor. It is a source of extreme annoyance to the latter, particularly if neatly dressed. In muddy weather, it is extremely offensive to have paws loaded with mud placed on one's clothing, no matter how many prizes a dog may have won or how royal is his pedigree. The owner should not permit his affection for his dog to blind him to what is due to courtesy. The habit is easily and simply cured without any violence or injury to the dog's affections. When he places his fore feet upon the person, grasp a foot gently but firmly in each hand, speaking to him in the blandest tones and the choicest pet phrases, the manner being the perfection of kindness, at the same time stepping on his hind feet just hard enough to pinch them. He will soon endeavor to break away, notwithstanding the kindness of manner; but the punishment should be continued for a few moments before releasing him. Soon thereafter call him up and repeat the lesson. Usually two or three of these simple lessons are ample—he cannot then be induced to place his feet on the person. Occasionally, at long intervals, he may forget himself for a moment; but the slightest reminder adjusts him to instant correctness. By observing this simple training the dog will be a more desirable companion, and will have more friends.

Another serious fault is the persistent and irritating habit of barking at passing strangers. Sometimes, when the owner is present, the dog will show a bravado spirit and will be louder and more violent, presuming on immunity, from his master's presence. From habit, the act often becomes malicious. The dog should be broken of the obnoxious habit by whipping him when he is caught in the act. Instances are not infrequent where the habit caused an abrupt termination to an otherwise useful career. Men are not always in a humor to enhance a dog's pleasure by being a subject for his barking—dull men are unable to distinguish between the bark of a dog full of blue blood and that of a common cur. The very little trouble required to correct these faults makes neglect of them inexcusable.

Yard breaking is very essential to satisfactory progress and skillful training. The advantages of teaching certain orders and acts, and establishing discipline separately, free from field complications, are obvious. If obedience is not taught to these orders in the yard, it must be taught in the field under much less favorable circumstances, and with much greater trouble, frequently to the injury of the dog's field work. The yard training should approximate as closely as possible in manner to that of actual field work, thus the transition from it to the other will be easily accomplished. Such training also avoids many objectionable and sometimes extremely troublesome faults, such as blinking, bolting, etc.

In yard breaking, a dog may be taught obedience to the following commands and their corresponding signals, namely: *Fetch, Find, Drop, Hold up, Go on, Come in, Steady, Dead* or *Dead bird, Heel,* and numerous incidental details, as will be more particularly described hereafter. If the trainer teaches these orders thoroughly and at the same time holds his dog's confidence and affection, he will have no difficulty in teaching their application in the field; on the other hand, if his dog is afraid of him or has learned to dislike him, he will have endless trouble and inferior results.

In giving a yard lesson it should be done seriously and kindly. Any attempt of the dog to divert the lesson into a frolic at any period should be promptly but gently checked. The demeanor should be such that the dog will neither be encouraged to play nor anticipate violence. If the trainer is emotional and demonstrative the dog will learn to anticipate his intentions, not always to the benefit of the training. After a lesson is finished, the puppy may be encouraged to play, particularly if at all downcast ; but if he exhibits no unpleasant memories he may be left to his own will. To play with a puppy does not injure his training in the least, if not permitted during the lessons. It is an objectionable practice, however, to permit children to play with him. In playing he learns to carry sticks, old shoes, etc., and is apt to develop a hard mouth, besides learning undesirable cunning tricks, such as running away, hiding, etc., which by no means add to the pleasures of training.

Amateurs always attempt to accomplish too much in one lesson. Usually they expect that a half dozen lessons ought to accomplish almost any educational purpose, whereas, with some dogs, that number of lessons will not make a perceptible beginning.

It often happens that a dog is willing to obey but is unable to comprehend what is required, from the absence of all method on the part of the trainer. Mixed or various orders for the same act, or attempting to teach two or three different things at the same time, or abruptly changing from one thing to another before any one is half taught, will make progress slow and unsatisfactory ; such course is confusing and unskillful. One thing at a time should be the rule. The elementary details should be taught separately and thoroughly impressed on the dog's memory, and as he progresses the details should be nicely graduated from the simple to the more difficult. Proficiency in one detail is a fair standard by which to judge his fitness for learning the next. Too much is expected of a dog in too short a time. Considering his natural short life it is wonderful what a variety of intelligent acts he acquires; yet amateurs often expect a dog to learn an act in much less time than they could learn it themselves.

The yard breaking should not be attempted until the puppy is at least eight months old; ten months old is better. He needs the freedom of puppyhood with its frolics and carelessness to gain common experience, and mental and physical development. It is not reasonable to expect much ability before the puppy approaches maturity. If the trainer desires to teach retrieving by the natural method, so called, he may begin when the puppy is five or six months old, and inasmuch as it is associated with playfulness, it does no harm.

The methods of teaching obedience to the different orders are described under the following appropriate heads:

Obedience to the order *Come in* is very easily taught if the lessons are given properly; the whip has no place in these lessons. By giving the dog a palatable morsel when he is called in he soon learns to understand and obey the order when there is a reward in sight. However, he must be taught to come in promptly to order, reward or no reward. Disobedience or indifference should not be tolerated. Put a spike collar with a rope about ten feet long attached to it upon him. Stand off a few feet and give the order *Come in;* pull him in simultaneously by means of the rope. Repeat until he will come in promptly to order alone.

When he comes in he should be petted and treated kindly. When he becomes fairly obedient a few lessons may be given in a securely inclosed yard, without using the collar unless necessary. Escape being impossible, he will soon obey promptly. A long checkcord can be used in giving him some lessons in the open fields if he is obstinate. They should be conducted so kindly and deliberately that the dog will not become shy or unduly frightened—this can be accomplished only by taking ample time, avoiding excitement, violent punishment, or loud orders. Make the dog feel that when he comes in he is safe. By the same means he can be taught obedience to whistle or signal. Extreme violence is an obstruction to progress.

Go on, Hie on.—The instances are very rare in which it is necessary to give any special lessons to teach this order. It can be taught while giving the puppy exercise in the fields, and in conjunction with which it is constantly used. The inclination of the dog is to range or run without restraint, hence the order, *Go on*, is usually in accord with his inclination, and he therefore soon learns its meaning and eagerly waits for it. By associating the corresponding signal with the order, he, after a few opportunities, comprehends its meaning, when the verbal order may be dispensed with. Or a click of the tongue is sufficient.

If two dogs are in training as a brace, either one should be taught to leave heel and begin ranging when the trainer speaks the name of one or the other, or his name accompanied with the proper signal to *Go on*. He can, if he prefers, teach each one a separate order; such, however, is unnecessary, as the dog's name when so used is equivalent to an order, and much easier to remember and deliver without confusion. Occasionally a sulky dog will require to be forced from heel with the whip, but this should be considered as a last resort. While it is an easy matter to drive him from heel, it is not so easy a matter to keep him from running away, therefore it must be applied with a great deal of tact. Just sufficient punishment to drive him from heel is all that is safe to apply. The whip, held threateningly in the hand, will deter him from returning. If left to himself without further interference, he usually trots about in a sulky or surprised manner for a while, then resumes work, the conditions being unfavorable for sulking. No orders should be given him after he is driven from heel till he regains his ordinary manner. There is a probability that if they were given he would bolt. If he is unusually cranky and obstinate, the method given under the head of *Turning to Whistle* may be advantageously used.

Obedience to the order, *Heel*, is easily taught, yet it is necessary to exercise a great deal of judgment as to what period of the training it is best to teach it, such, in many instances, being an important consideration. Dogs which are energetic and eager to hunt at every opportunity may be taught it during the yard breaking. No attempt should be made to teach it to timid, cranky, gunshy or lazy dogs until they are well advanced in training, having outgrown their fears or failings, as the case may be. It is always better to wait until the dog has settled to his work with interest and regularity. If the timid, gunshy or cranky dog is taught to remain at heel in obedience to an order, he improves on it by coming to heel voluntarily, and no efforts may thereafter induce him to hunt. Under such circumstances the trainer is powerless. He can do no more than to walk patiently along until time effects a change, or some adventitious circumstances, such as a rabbit starting close by the dog, or the fluttering of a wounded bird, may stimulate him to make an effort to kill, whereupon he may range, seeking for more. With such, there is no remedy save time, kindness and favorable opportunities to chase or kill. Lazy or sulky dogs, as aforementioned, can be driven from heel with the whip, yet it is frequently the case that they are not worth the trouble.

To teach this order, the trainer leads the dog about in the yard or in the fields. When the dog presses to the front, or to one side, which he is sure to do, a sharp tap or two with the whip will drive him to the rear. At the same time, the order *Heel* is given in the ordinary tone of voice. Every attempt to walk elsewhere than at heel must be promptly checked. If the dog struggles or sags back in an ordinary kennel collar, put a spike collar on him, not necessarily to jerk him about, but simply to hold him in place. The spike collar alone is recommended by a few writers as the proper instrument to employ in teaching a dog to heel, but it is unnecessarily severe, and less effective than the whip and spike collar combined. All punishment should be avoided unless it is a necessity.

After the dog comprehends the meaning of the order, the signal, a wave of the right or left hand downward to the rear, may be associated with it. When he will follow with any degree of certainty, he is sufficiently prepared for field work, as, in the primary lessons, there is every reason to avoid inculcating the act so thoroughly that it becomes habitual. Field training is the proper part wherein to perfect obedience to this order. The dog is sent out to work betimes, there is something to interest him constantly, thus differing materially from the conditions of yard breaking. It is no particular trouble to teach it in the field without any yard lessons. The same method is used, when so taught; it has the advantage, when taught in field work, that the trainer can always tell accurately how the lessons are harmonizing with the rest of the training, and can thus conduct them intelligently.

Drop.—A few trainers use the spike collar exclusively

in teaching the dog to drop, but it is an undesirable method, being unnecessarily severe in its effects, and awkward in its application. It being an inferior method, the manner of it is not worth describing. The spike collar, however, is valuable as an auxiliary instrument, and as such is especially useful.

It is not necessary to inflict severe punishment, or indeed much punishment of any kind to teach this branch. Regularity and thoroughness are the most important factors.

The proper position for a dog at the *drop* is to lie down with the body in nearly a straight line, and it is immaterial whether the hind feet are on one side of the body or one on each side; if taught to lie straight, he will eventually learn to drop squarely enough for all practical purposes, if properly drilled in his lessons. He should not be permitted to curl up or roll on his back, both being undesirable positions, easily corrected in training.

The painfully artificial attitudes which amateurs occasionally attempt to teach are extremely tiresome to the dog, and they are practically useless. The dog is required to lie with his fore legs extended straight in front of him, with head and neck in a straight line and resting between the fore legs; the hind legs being placed one on each side of his body, and resting squarely.

To teach the dog to drop, procure a light riding whip or very light rawhide, not on account of their punishing qualities, but on account of the quickness and ease with which it can be used, being in this respect incomparably superior to the ordinary dog whip. A checkcord about four feet long should be tied to his kennel collar to keep him from running away. If he struggles against the kennel collar, a spike collar may be substituted until the attempts to escape are abandoned. The rope should be held in the left hand, the whip in the right. Give him a light tap on the shoulder, and, at the same instant, give the order, *Drop*. Repeat the tapping and order till he lies down. If he tries to escape or is frightened, the trainer has hurried too much or hit harder than was necessary, for no severity is needed or desired. A distinct interval should be allowed between each order. When the dog lies down, the punishment should cease instantly, and the attitude should be maintained for a few minutes. If petted at this stage, he is very apt to rise, which is not desired. It is immaterial whether he performs the act with correctness, at first, the manner of doing it being then subordinate to teaching him the meaning of the order; yet he should not be permitted to roll on his back or curl up. The manner of doing it can be gradually improved upon as he comprehends the meaning of the command better. If he rolls on his back, give him a few sharp taps with the whip on his toes, giving only force enough to sting; he will then roll quickly back into the correct position and draw his toes under him for protection. If he attempts to bolt, the rope is always in the left hand to prevent him from doing so—the rope serves no other purpose. After two or three corrections he cannot be induced to remain on his back. If he curls up, a few taps on the toes will likewise make him lie straight. He persistently avoids these positions when he learns to associate pain therewith. It is worthy of repetition that the dog should be given time to comprehend the lessons. If he is frightened or confused, there is so much time and effort wasted, if no worse.

Forcing the dog quickly and repeatedly to lie down and stand up bewilders him so much that he comprehends nothing.

For special parts of subsequent training, it is worthy of attention, in teaching the drop, that the whip be applied to the same part when used, the shoulder being preferable. The dog soon learns that a touch on the shoulder is an order of itself; if so applied invariably, and instant obedience required, he can be taught to drop at a slight touch. This method is particularly useful in teaching dropping to wing and shot. Using the whip promiscuously and harshly always, naturally prompts the dog to run away if he possibly can do so; besides, it is more unskillful, troublesome and inefficacious than in following a systematic course which has every detail properly associated with the required act of obedience.

After he has a fair comprehension of the order, he may be then drilled in dropping to signal, the right or left hand raised being the signal in common use. This signal should be used for a longer or shorter time with the order. Gradually, as the dog becomes obedient, the order may be used less and less; at last the signal alone will be sufficient. The trainer should always take pains to stand a little in front of the dog, so that he can readily see the signal; and if he has been taught to drop to a tap of the whip on the shoulder, it will materially assist to teach obedience quickly, easily and perfectly. When the dog is fairly well trained, instant obedience should be exacted. If, at the signal, the dog does not drop on the instant, the whip should follow immediately; however, always be sure that the dog sees the signal.

Such is the method of teaching any dog of average disposition. But if the dog is obstinate or sour, the punishment may be applied more liberally, due regard always being paid to the purposes of the training. It is necessary to teach the order very thoroughly, as it is in constant use in field work while training and hunting.

Hold up.—As soon as the dog is fairly obedient to the order *Drop*, he may be taught obedience to the order *Hold up* in the same lessons, observing the same policy in respect to deliberation that has been mentioned heretofore.

The spike collar now comes usefully into play with some dogs. It should be put on, with a rope about four feet long attached to it. It is not required to inflict severe punishment; on the contrary, it will accomplish the purpose with less punishment than any other means. When the order *Hold up* is given, the collar should be jerked lightly with the left hand, which usually will be sufficient to force the average dog promptly to his feet. If he is sour and obstinate, apply the whip smartly to his toes with the right hand until he rises, which he will very soon do, then he should be petted till his fears subside, if he has any. He may then be ordered to drop, and the training in rising to order repeated.

He may obey the order readily if the handler is moving away from him, and refuse if he is motionless. Obedience must be given to the order whether the handler is in motion or at rest. The lessons should be regularly continued till the dog obeys either order cheerfully and promptly, without the need of either whip or collar.

A beckon with the forefinger is the easiest and most natural signal for the command *Hold up*. By associating the order and signal the latter is taught in like manner as described in teaching other signals. The dog is not sufficiently obedient unless he will drop instantly when the hand is elevated, or rise when the beckon of the finger is given. If the amateur cannot enforce unhesitating obedience when he has the dog in a position where he is powerless to evade obeying orders, he has very little hope of doing so when the dog has his liberty in field work.

The short rope should not be dispensed with till the dog is obedient. A few lessons may then be given in a room or yard from which he cannot escape; for when the rope is removed he may refuse to obey, and hence the precaution necessary to prevent the possibility of his running away. He then should be trained without the rope. No compromise is admissible. If he goes into a corner or sneaks up to the feet of his trainer, he should be taken back instantly to the place where he should have dropped, and a cut of the whip given; he should then be required to remain quiet till ordered up. If he is allowed to select his own place to drop, he has a feeling of security and immunity which is not favorable for subsequent discipline in the open field.

When he is obedient in the yard he may be given lessons in the open fields, yet he must at first be kept under some restraint to put a proper finish to his yard breaking. One end of a quarter inch line, about twenty feet long, should be tied to his spike collar, the other end tied to a stake firmly driven into the ground. Make him drop close to the stake. Walk away from him and if he attempts to follow, return him to his place and make him drop, giving him a cut with the whip. Walk away about twenty yards, then around him, and correct any unsteadiness exhibited by him. When he is trained so that he will remain steady while the trainer walks or runs, he may be considered as being trustworthy. These lessons should be given in different places in the fields; for a dog from the familiar associations may be obedient in the place in which he is trained, and disobedient in all others. Whether he will be run thereafter with a checkcord, or whether he will have all the training necessary at this stage, will depend on whether he is obedient or whether he evinces no disposition to run away, etc., which his trainer can determine.

One thing is certain, when the dog is put into actual work, the talent and industry or inefficiency of the trainer in giving the preparatory lessons will not fail to show itself; any imperfection adds just so much to the trouble of training in the field and under less favorable circumstances.

Very few dogs require all these formalities and training to perfect them in this branch; yet inasmuch as every dog differs more or less in temperament from every other dog, some parts will do for one, some for another, and an occasional one will require the whole course combined with the best judgment of his trainer; but there is one part that must be observed with all dogs, namely, regularity and deliberate training.

In teaching a dog to drop to shot, caps may be exploded, or a common 22-caliber blank cartridge exploded in a rifle or pistol. If the dog is at all gunshy, no greater folly could be committed than to attempt to teach him to drop to shot.

Just the same methods should be used as in teaching a dog to drop to an order delivered by the voice, the report of the gun having precisely the same significance. The other training, relating to the same thing, will enable the trainer to teach this part very expeditiously.

The orders Charge and Down Charge have fallen into disuse with expert sportsmen; besides, they are meaningless and inelegant.

Toho is the order which denotes that the dog is to stop and stand still. With expert trainers, the order has fallen into disuse, the improvement in methods and greater knowledge of the dog's nature rendering it superfluous. The old theory was that it served a useful purpose in teaching the dog how to point and back, or in restraining him when roading. Amongst an unskilled class some very efficacious powers were supposed to be inherent in it. Amateurs frequently use it; they will give the order *Toho* to an unsteady dog which had never been taught its meaning; yet it had about the same beneficial effect that it had on any dog, taught or untaught.

It is a wholly useless and superfluous order, as, if it is desired to stop the dog, it can be done more perfectly by making him drop. To perpetually and unnecessarily stop a dog when he is roading or drawing on birds, is the height of field stupidity or inexperience. The dog, if properly trained, understands his work and requires no mistaken attempts at assistance from his handler. It is extremely painful to be afield with a companion who is crying "*To-ho!—to-ho-o-o!—to-ho-o-o!!*" every time his dog scents game; the more so that the dog, from experience with the gentle failings of his master, ignores the tumult. If he is a timid dog, it balks him perpetually. Even if it had the benefits claimed for it, they are of no importance when compared to the trouble of teaching it thoroughly. The true method of training and handling a dog in roading and pointing, is described under the appropriate heads. For the benefit of those, however, who have a veneration for the customs and methods of the past, the mode of teaching it will be described. It is very simple. A piece of cord about five or six feet long is tied to the dog's collar. The rope is held in one hand, close up to the collar, during the first lessons; and a whip is held in the other hand. The first part to be taught is to make the dog stand still. A piece of meat or other tempting morsel is placed on the floor a few feet in front of him where he can see it. He must not be permitted to lie down or move restlessly. Nothing but the most rigid obedience fulfills the purpose. Hold him steady with the collar and tap him with the whip every time he stirs, repeating the order Toho as the occasion requires. He will claw and struggle to reach the meat at first, but his attempts must be defeated, and he must be forced to stand still. After he will stand without struggling, give the order *Go on* and let him spring forward and eat the meat. After he has a fair comprehension of his trainer's intent from repeated lessons, and will stand when his trainer is a few feet away from him, he may be taught to obey signals, the hand held forward in an attitude of caution (or any other signal the trainer chooses) being the signal to stand still; a wave of the same hand is an order to *Go on*. When the dog is perfectly taught, he, in conjunction with performing the act, can be moved forward five or six inches at a time and stopped instantly by signals, every movement being delicately responsive and sympathetic to the slightest signal of the hand. It is very pretty as a trick. When steady to orders in the house, it is then necessary to finish the *Toho* in the field without any reference to direct hunting; after this it is necessary to give him more lessons when working on birds. No matter how steady he may be to the order when no birds are present, he generally pays no attention to it when on game, unless he is of a very honest, submissive disposition, and such dog does not require it. Several weeks must be devoted to teaching it perfectly, and this labor greatly exceeds the labor necessary to steady the dog in a proper manner. If the trainer should persist in training obedience to it to the exclusion of the real purposes of a dog in field work, he will have to so completely subjugate him that he has no self-reliance, but simply and slavishly looks to his handler for instructions at every turn, the worst possible stage of over-training.

The author, in his early attempts at training, diligently taught the Toho, because it was after the methods prescribed by recognized authorities on training. The insufficiency of it in the field in contrast to the charming powers ascribed to it by the authors was difficult to reconcile; however, it was assumed that more experience would bring a better understanding of it. The writer was a long while in unlearning this, with a mass of other like rubbish which was learned with much trouble and practiced faithfully. It is simply a method which found favor when methods were crude and the dog's nature misunderstood; and the method has been perpetuated theoretically, by constant repetition. In an experience at field trials covering several years and an experience in field shooting with expert trainers, the writer never heard the order *Toho* used by them in a single instance. However, it can be used to advantage in steadying a dog in backing, although it is more trouble than to teach the backing.

The orders *Fetch*, *Seek*, etc., are associated with the act of retrieving, and are described under the appropriate head.

CHAPTER VIII.

RETRIEVING.

Different strains of pointers and setters respectively, vary greatly in their natural capabilities for retrieving; some take special delight in it, others are indifferent or dislike it; a few learn quickly and correctly, and such are usually willing retrievers during their lives. The greater number learn well by careful training; while a small percentage, either from stupidity, dislike or functional imperfections, such as poor nose, or all combined, never attain more than mediocrity.

Very obstinate individuals are met with in both breeds occasionally; but as between pointers and setters, the former will learn to retrieve much more willingly and quickly, a pointer of resolute obstinacy and self-will being very exceptional. However, owing to physical advantages of coat, and greater dash and powers of endurance, the setter, when trained, is the superior retriever—this comparison is in respect to them as a class, for there are individual pointers which are most excellent retrievers and individual setters which are worthless. Obstinate setters, ones of the most determined obstinacy and self-will, are not uncommon, and during their preliminary training, when they fully comprehend what is required of them and how to perform it, they will yield only under severe punishment; yet, when dogs of this character are once properly subjugated and comprehend the purpose and application of their lessons, they become thoroughly and permanently obedient, often making first-rate performers. Rarely will one be found which is wholly worthless, or which will not be taught.

Perfect retrieving can be established only by the greatest care and fidelity in teaching details, and punctuality in the preparatory lessons. If it is taught at all, it is worthy being taught perfectly, for it is an eminently useful accomplishment, it being a necessity in field shooting, and, when performed correctly, a source of pleasure to the sportsman. Poor retrieving mars the best of sport; indeed, if the retriever has acquired vicious habits such as mutilating birds, running away with them, etc., he is much worse than none.

Notwithstanding its indispensable value in successful field work, it at times in the first or perhaps also in part of the second season, is the source of objectionable traits in relation to other parts of field work which are more or less associated with it. This, of course, has no reference to such dogs as are used as special retrievers; but such, for upland shooting, seldom find favor in this country, sportsmen preferring that a dog is both a finding dog and a retriever. The objectionable traits usually disappear as the dog matures and gains in experience. One of the most annoying faults is when a puppy, from taking great interest in capturing a dead bird and delight in the act, develops an over-eagerness and a consequent disposition to break shot when a bird is killed; the necessary efforts to steady him may dampen his ardor temporarily. Again, he may be annoyingly and obstructingly persistent in searching for a real or imaginary dead bird whenever the gun is fired; so thoroughly determined are some dogs in this respect that even if led quite a distance away so that they may resume hunting for live birds, they will immediately return to complete the search to their satisfaction. This offensive habit is commonly associated with retrieving in the early stages of field work. It is particularly undesirable when practiced among scattered birds, as, when ordered on, the dog is wholly intent on finding the dead bird, and in his rapid, short casts to and fro never fails to heedlessly flush all the remaining birds. However, with experience, an intelligent dog will learn, from his own observation, whether a bird is killed or not, and will thereafter, with proper handling, work correctly according to the requirements. If he should, nevertheless, show no improvement from his own knowledge, the gun may be fired in likely places for birds, but when no birds are present, then permit the dog to search till he is satisfied, neither attempting to restrain nor encourage him. Repeat the deception as many times as are necessary, and generally he will soon learn to distinguish between when a bird is killed and when not. If he should be an exceptional case and persist in the habit regardless of this treatment, the whip must come into use; but it must be applied with great caution, and is rarely necessary at all. The handler should trust more to regular work and moderate restraint than to pressure by punishment.

If the puppy breaks shot to retrieve, the greatest caution must be observed in steadying him; his disposition and the effects of punishment on him should be carefully noted, and all treatment modified to harmonize with his peculiarities. Otherwise, the attempts to steady him may impair his retrieving, pointing or finding, or all, inasmuch as he may construe the punishment as relating to these acts instead of the act of unsteadiness. However poorly he may perform in any part, nothing should be done that will develop a fear of birds, or a blinker. This may be guarded against by conducting the training slowly, making the dog a steady retriever by imperceptible gradations of advancement. An aged dog, in some instances, from insufficient experience, dull powers of observation or bad handling, will have no comprehension of retrieving aside from the simple act of carrying the bird to his handler, which is but one detail which goes toward making a skillful retriever.

A first-class retriever must be intelligent so that he may have the capability of acquiring a full knowledge of all the details of retrieving, and its purposes; he must have a natural fondness for it; he must be steady to shot, must seek diligently for a dead bird when ordered to do so; must be prompt and obedient to commands whether verbal or by a motion of the hand or gun; he must have a keen nose and a tender mouth, and must work for his handler, qualities which in their entirety are rarely possessed by one dog. If the retriever is accomplished in addition to the foregoing, he understands his work so that he can conduct it without orders or assistance. He, whenever possible to do so, will mark the flight of a wounded bird, or the place where it fell, with wonderful precision, even though the flight was a long one. The slightest irregularity of flight, at times so slight as to be imperceptible to the shooter, is intently watched and noted with perfect accuracy; if the bird does not drop in sight, he estimates, with rare judgment, the fall of it, and by the aid of a keen nose, soon finds it, and retrieves cheerfully, quickly and tenderly, without any supervision. This degree of perfection is only reached when the dog has full experience and has not been hampered by bad training.

With dogs as a class, retrieving is usually the most difficult branch to teach to perfection. The amateur may succeed very well by devoting the proper attention to the yard lessons, but, from a passion for shooting, may neglect to give the proper attention to it in field work, hence it is rarely taught with the nicety it should be and is capable of receiving.

If the amateur should unfortunately have an obstinate

subject for his first attempts, he should not be discouraged, for persistency and skill will subjugate the most difficult ones. After one has been taught, subsequent attempts will be easier. Intelligent dogs usually learn quickly, but the first attempt, whether difficult or otherwise, should not be considered a standard for all. It requires an extensive experience to thoroughly understand dogs in general. Still, the amateur by carefully studying the disposition of the dog which he is training and avoiding that pernicious failing of all amateurs, namely, *hurry*, can apply his efforts with success if he has any talent for training. The professional trainer knows precisely what course to pursue with a dog of any disposition; the inexperienced amateur must make his advances by carefully noting effects. There is no part of training in which a calm exterior is more necessary than in teaching retrieving; and if the trainer cannot proceed with deliberation and consideration, he is misdirecting his efforts, and only very imperfect success can be attained. A dog soon learns to interpret any inauspicious expressions of countenance, and if he is at liberty he will bolt; if not at liberty, he is in such a state of perturbation through anticipation that his mind is entirely diverted from his lesson. It is noticeable that the amateurs who bring their dogs to a certain rough degree of training are always of the noisy, bellowing order, and if the dogs so trained could tell of their training, they would relate the history of a miserable life.

The retrieving of pointers and setters, if they are good finding dogs, should be confined strictly to upland work. Duck retrieving, if it is made partially or wholly the dog's regular work, never fails to induce rheumatism, deafness, stiff joints, or a broken constitution and premature old age. Many setters and pointers will retrieve ducks excellently well, but in cold weather they perform from pure courage and intense liking for the sport. Not infrequently they work simply as an act of obedience. It is requiring too much of them. They have not the strength of limb or hardiness of body or constitution necessary to withstand the effects of the severe labor and exposure. There is no more pitiable sight than that of a good setter or pointer, shivering violently between shots, fatigued from violent exertion and chilled to the marrrow from exposure to ice, cold and mud, water and raw winds. They have not the natural properties for the work that the Chesapeake Bay dog and Irish water spaniel have. The former is stockier in structure, heavier in bone and muscle, denser in coat, and is a much more powerfully built dog in every respect, as is necessary to meet the requirements of his special work. Extremely cold water, or work in mud and ice, does not have the distressing effect on him that it does on the setter and pointer. The Irish water spaniel has an extremely heavy, oily coat, and is very powerful in proportion to his size. Both these breeds are naturally water dogs, working in water from choice. The setter and pointer love water at such times as they are warm from exertion, but they do not favor cold water in cold weather. Too often the mere fact that they will retrieve ducks is taken as sufficient evidence that they are constitutionally fitted for the work. Aside from humane considerations, the value of the dog as a hunter is, by duck retrieving, first impaired and afterward gradually destroyed.

In common practice, there are two methods of teaching retrieving, namely, the forcing system and what is commonly called, or miscalled, the natural method. As these systems differ materially in details, they will be described under separate heads.

THE NATURAL METHOD.

This method is applied by taking advantage of the

puppy's natural inclination to frolic, and carry objects in his mouth from playfulness; therefore the best time in which the puppy can be taught after this system is in puppyhood. Puppies, when playing alone, often take an old shoe, bone, or other object, in their mouths, toss it in the air, and run about with it. With the staid, aged dog, this method has very little value, such dog being too matured in intelligence to be deceived into considering a dry lesson an amusement, particularly when there is such a very small element of fun in it.

Occasionally a very good retriever is made by the so-called natural method. The term is misleading in its meaning, as no dog retrieves naturally, although some learn with very little training. As applied in training, the term is used simply in contradistinction to the method in which force is applied.

A vacant room is the best place in which to give the lessons, it serving the double purpose of preventing outside incidents from diverting the puppy's attention, and restraining his freedom within proper bounds. It is decidedly desirable to have no spectators, it being self-evident that the trainer should have the puppy's undivided attention in his lessons, which he cannot have unless he is alone.

The whole method is comprised in training the puppy, by insensible gradations, from carrying an object in play for his own amusement, to carrying it to command, for his master's pleasure. All the different moods and peculiarities of the puppy must be carefully noted, taking advantage of those which are favorable, and guarding against those which are unfavorable. Simply by constant practice he learns the meaning of the orders, and obedience is established by force of habit. A matter of prime importance to remember is that, in the actual work of the dog which is taught after this system, since he obeys of his own will, and the trainer is entirely without any compulsory means to enforce retrieving if the dog once refuses, the most uniform kindness must always be associated with this branch of his work, otherwise when it ceases to be a pleasure, or when he resents punishment, he may quit permanently as a retriever.

The usual manner of beginning this training is to engage the puppy's attention to a ball or glove, at the same time, by little artifices commonly known, exciting his playfulness. Assuming that the ball is used, it is then thrown gently out; the puppy will, in most instances, run after it and pick it up. If he does not, his playfulness must be excited by tying a handkerchief to the end of a stick and waving it, or skim it along the ground in front of him; at all events, his playfulness must be developed by some means, else the matter there ends. For the same reason he must be permitted to have a great deal of latitude in carrying and playing with the ball, in the beginning, during several lessons. In these early stages, more effort should be made to amuse the puppy than to make him obedient, thereby gaining his permanent interest in the lessons, as a habitual diversion. After that is accomplished, the training can commence. When the ball is thrown out, the command *Fetch* should be given simultaneously therewith, and by many times repeating the order co-incidentally with the act, he will learn to associate the two, and from habit will obey. When he is proficient in this stage, he is ready for the next. When the ball is thrown out, hold him by his collar a few moments thereafter, then when he is released give the order *Fetch*. If he struggle to break away while being held, he should be held firmly without alarming him. He can gradually be held longer and longer, accordingly as his interest and fondness for the play will admit, till at length he will be steady and retrieve to order. If he is amused properly, he will have a passionate delight in the lessons, and by easy intermediate stages, he is trained from carrying and fetching, in play, to retrieving to command; still, he retains more or less playfulness in his work until he reaches the natural steadiness and sedateness of maturity. His playfulness, however, can be judiciously suppressed to a certain degree, *i. e.*, what the dog will submit to. When he shows the slightest alarm or indifference, the limit of suppression has been reached.

Important details must not be overlooked as the dog progresses. As soon, in the primary lessons, as he will carry the ball in his mouth with any degree of certainty, the efforts should be directed to training him to hold it gently in his mouth without tossing it in the air, rolling it in his mouth, or violently shaking or biting it. If he cannot be steadied in this part in the regular lessons without exciting his distrust, it can be taught in separate lessons in a different room; for a dog not only can learn to associate correction with a certain act, but he also learns to associate it with the place in which it was given, and will anticipate a recurrence of the unpleasantness if taken into such associated surroundings; hence it is obvious that no unpleasant associations should be established with the place wherein he receives his regular lessons.

To enforce steadiness in carrying the ball, a little mild severity is necessary. Tie a short rope, two or three feet long, to his collar. Make him stand still and check all efforts to frolic, for there is no amusement in this lesson. It is better to use a different object so that no impediment may arise in other lessons from associating unpleasantness with the ball. A glove may be used, and this will serve the better, as most dogs are predisposed to bite it. Place it in his mouth, hold the left hand gently but firmly under his lower jaw, and if he attempts to bite, toss or eject the glove, give him a tap with the whip. The whip should be used just sufficiently to steady him without alarming him. If it excites his resentment and obstinacy, he must be forced to hold the glove in his mouth, whether he will or not. If he drops it, put it in his mouth, and at every attempt to eject it, give him a cut of the whip, and the order *Hold*, or *Steady*. Make him stand up if he shows any attempt to lie down. If he persists in dropping it, apply the whip smartly. He must be forced to hold the glove, however much he dislikes it. When he will hold it steadily while standing still, he may then be led about the room. Any act other than carrying it with regular steadiness should receive instant correction. After several lessons, given with rigid formality, he will carry it steadily. The order *Steady* should be taught so that he will instantly desist from rolling the glove or biting it, when the order is given. Then by kindness his interest can be regained, observing, however, that he must not be permitted to presume on it, by attempting his old tricks. These lessons must be given separately, until thoroughly inculcated, and the dog carries cheerfully and reliably. So long as there is the slightest distrust or unpleasantness, the lessons must be continued. When he has reached the desired proficiency, these lessons can be given in conjunction with the regular lessons in retrieving. If the dog manifests any uneasiness in the new requirements, some little tact is necessary to cajole him into obedience. After the puppy has learned to fetch the glove to his trainer, he will be sure to display some peculiarities which add to the fun from his point of view, but which should be corrected. He will jerk his head to one side as the trainer reaches for the ball, or he will hold it tightly with his teeth, thus refusing to deliver it. He is not properly trained unless he will release it instantly to order. Many good trainers fail to finish the education in this respect. If the dog will not release the ball when the trainer grasps it, it should not, by any means, be pulled out of his mouth forcibly, or any force applied to it. Simply grasp it gently and command him to *Give*, at the same time stepping on his fore foot, pressing harder and harder until he will release it. Very little pressure will accomplish the purpose. It is astonishing how quickly a dog will learn the meaning of this order, when taught in this manner. After three or four orders conjoined with the pinching of his toes, he will release the ball instantly to the order, *Give;* thus by a very little care he may be prevented from acquiring a very disagreeable, harmful fault, which he would always retain. Only by observing and perfecting these little details is the finest training established.

In teaching retrieving by this method, the lesson should never be continued so long as to fatigue the dog, or impair his interest in it. The associations with each lesson should, so far as possible, always be pleasant, that he will anticipate them with pleasure and conduct himself with spirit, bearing in mind also that this method is dependent for its success on the pleasure or willingness of the dog; and if the affair at any juncture becomes too serious to please his fancy, it may then and there end, so far as it usefully relates to retrieving.

After the puppy is fairly proficient, he should be required to bring various objects which he can conveniently carry. If trained too long on one object, he may become partial to it, and refuse to bring all others. By neglecting this important consideration, the amateur will learn that, while the dog may readily retrieve a glove or ball, he, from having become habituated to them, will not retrieve any other objects. The transition from one stage to another, and one object to another, can be made gradually; for instance, if a dog will fetch a glove and will not fetch a bird, the wings and large feathers can be neatly attached around the glove, beginning with a few; then, as the lessons advance, adding more and more. In this manner the repugnance which some dogs have to grasping feathers will be overcome. Also, the glove may be increased in size and weight from time to time, by stuffing it with scraps of cloth; thus he will learn to grasp a larger and heavier object.

The most precise regularity should be observed in giving these lessons, since only by constant repetition and diligent attention can obedience be established as a habit. Regular discipline must be depended upon to bring his will into subordination. If the lessons are given in a desultory manner till the puppy reaches maturity, it is useless to attempt perfect training afterward by employing this method. Even by omitting two or three lessons, or conducting the lessons in a heedless manner, progress may be impeded.

As to the quickness with which the dog's fun can be graduated into steady obedience, much depends upon the temperament of the dog, and his interest in the work. The training does not always progress with uniformity even when all the requirements of skillful training are observed. The dog may be capricious and develop successive obstructive crotchets, and frequently progress is thus brought to a standstill. Under such circumstances it is impossible to progress faster than the humor of the dog will admit, if at all. It is very injudicious to attempt any compulsory treatment unless the system is entirely abandoned. Such would surely chill his ardor, and have a corresponding ill effect on the training.

Moreover, whatever care may have been taken in yard training, the greater number of natural retrievers soon acquire a slovenly manner of retrieving. He may come in in segments of circles; he may deliver the bird with reluctance or give it a vicious pinch as he releases it; he may toss or roll the bird in his mouth; he may drop it several yards from his handler and resume hunting, and no persuasion thereafter will induce him to touch it. If the trainer attempts to correct any one of these faults by punishment, it invariably results in the end of retrieving. The dog does not comprehend that the punishment is for the ill manner of retrieving, but he applies it to the act of having the bird in his mouth at all, the difference between a sound bird and crushed one being nothing to him; but he can readily perceive that he could have let the bird alone. So with other faults relating to retrieving. If he breaks shot to retrieve, from the dog's point of view it is simply a desirable effort to get the bird in possession, and if he is punished therefor, he associates it with the act of getting the bird and not with a failure to remain steady, as his handler intended it should be. Thereafter the dog endeavors to avoid punishment by refusing to retrieve, and such refusal is commonly permanent unless rebroken by the force system. A dog taught by the natural system will rarely retrieve more than one species of game well, and that is the kind which he has hunted most. One trained on quails will refuse to retrieve snipe; a chicken dog may refuse to retrieve quails, and *vice versa*. As in all other cases, there are occasional exceptions, yet such are retrievers more from their natural willingness to please, intelligence and comprehension of the purposes of hunting, than from any inherent merit in the system of education. The same peculiarities may be observed respecting retrieving on different kinds of game in dogs perfected by force, but there is this important distinction, the handler always has the means of soon forcing obedience.

The trainer should not expect to find any dogs which retrieve from inheritance of the trait. Instances are related of puppies which began to retrieve from the very first time birds were shot over them. The professional trainer is never favored with dogs of this kind, although they perfectly understand what is meant, and have many times seen the act which is mistaken for a retrieve. The puppy takes the dead bird in his mouth because it is a gratification to him, birds being part of his natural prey; if called at this juncture he may hold it in his mouth while going to his master, thus it may have a slight resemblance to a retrieve; but if the handler had waited quietly for the natural completion of the act, he would have noted that the dog completed it nicely by eating the bird. Sometimes by repetition in this manner, the dog can be induced to retrieve, but it is always very faulty. All experienced professionals attach no importance to an act of this kind. They perfect the retrieving lessons regardless of it.

In his first years of training when the author, by a little experience and a great deal of reading, had qualified to an imaginary degree of excellence as a trainer, having theories unlimited, and a performance inverse to the theories, he adopted the so-called natural method; and had an abhorrence of the forcing system on account of its reputed cruelty, although it was not then in general use. The natural system worked with average success, which was considered very good success, as no better method at that time had ever been practiced in that section. The beauties of the system and the cruelties of the force system were much descanted on; although the writer had never seen a spike collar at that time, it by no means impaired his powers of criticism on it; this, however, not being peculiar, as such powers relating to any subject appear to be innate in all true sportsmen. At length the writer applied the system to a sedate, mature dog which had neither fun nor frolic in his composition. He had a great deal of sense, and looked upon life as too serious to make room for levity. By sundry blandishments and many rewards for the little recognitions he would occasionally condescend to show, he was wrought up, through a painfully tedious series of degrees, to a point where he would exhibit a look of affected cheerfulness, and on rare occasions, when he had an unusually profuse flow of spirits, he would cut a mild caper or two, if a reward was in sight. By assiduous attention he was perfected to a degree, wherein he had the whole affair calculated to a nicety. If he was hungry, he would fetch a glove to order for a reward, but he performed with such *nonchalance* that it was hopelessly discouraging to all expectations of spirited work. Hunger would not improve the quality of his work although it would prolong it until his appetite was satisfied, whereupon he would declare the lesson off for that time, and his fiat, perforce, had to be accepted. Thus matters stood for several weeks, the dog knowing thoroughly just what profit there was in it to him; and he, like a rational animal, worked to get the most out of it that was possible for the least effort. At such times as he did not feel inclined to begin the lesson at all, it was necessarily adjourned until he recovered from his *ennui*. Seeing it stated that a bone was a peculiarly nice object to teach the dog to retrieve, he was practiced with it. When he learnt that the bone was not truly his own, he would sit and calmly contemplate it. His *insouciance* became so irritating that, sad to relate, a spike collar was procured and, one morning, his self-complacency was greatly shocked by a practical introduction to its application. Within a few weeks thereafter, a better retriever, so far as obedience, quickness and tender retrieving are concerned, could not be desired. This experience changed the author's views entirely in respect to the efficacy and cruelty of the spike collar.

However, it is a very beneficial experience to the trainer, and one to be earnestly recommended, to train a few dogs to retrieve after the natural method, as the knowledge of dog character and manner of holding his attention, so acquired, the necessary self-discipline in giving the lessons, and the tact in developing the dog's ideas, are all valuable and important adjuncts to the forcing system; precisely the same skill is required, inasmuch as, if the forcing system is properly applied, it is, in a great measure, accessory to this system, and not a distinct system by itself, as many imagine.

THE FORCING METHOD.

Establishing retrieving by force, particularly if properly done with the spike collar or the spike collar and whip, is the superior method of all methods. The dog's actions are constantly within the control of the trainer; and even the manner and force with which the dog grasps an object can be regulated. If, at any time in the dog's life, he should refuse to retrieve, there is always the means at hand to make retrieving compulsory; but when once *properly* taught, a retriever perfected by force is always a retriever. It is more difficult to apply to dogs of a certain disposition than the natural method, hence some trainers give the latter method the preference at times; yet it is never then as well done, although it may serve the purpose of satisfying a purchaser or owner.

It is established simply by associating certain acts with freedom from punishment, and the non-performance with punishment. The spike collar has advantages because it is handier and more efficacious. Pinching the tail, toes, nose, pulling the ears, or, in fact, any other punishment within proper limits, can be applied effectively, but some of them, particularly pinching the nose, are unnecessarily brutal. There is no method whereby the punishment can be so effectively administered conjointly with keeping the dog in hand and quickly impressing the desired associations, as with the spike collar, or spike collar and whip.

A few trainers use the whip alone, but it is unnecessarily harsh and has many undesirable results when so used, although there are dogs of such obstinacy that the whip is none too severe to accomplish the object; with such it is the proper instrument. When used, however, to supplement the spike collar, it has special advantages; and they can then be applied with far less punishment to accomplish the purpose than if either were used alone. The other forcing means have nothing worthy of notice save their novelty, forcing a dog to retrieve through the instrumentality of the spike collar or spike collar and whip being the approved method with the greater number of expert trainers. As in all other branches where force is used, to teach successfully by this system requires a careful study of the disposition, different temperaments and the effects of punishment on the individual dog at different stages of his training. Forcing a dog to retrieve is not jerking him promiscuously and violently about from the very beginning till he, as many suppose, fetches the desired object. It is a system of distinct stages of advancement, nicely graduated into each other, and each stage requires some peculiarities of treatment differing more or less from the others. Instead of being a mass of coarse, unreasoning violence, it is simply punishment intelligently inflicted in small doses, to establish perfection, detail by detail. To do this in the best manner requires experience and knowledge of the best methods, but the novice who will take time enough and follow directions carefully can make a passable success if he has any talent for dog training; if he has none, neither experience nor instruction will avail.

Now there is a great deal of dexterity in the manner of jerking the dog, and equally as much judgment required as to the degree of force necessary, and the correct instant at which to apply it. The jerk should not be a long, sweeping one which will carry the dog along with it, but a short, quick, positive jerk, which will hardly stir the dog from his place, or permit him to do so even if he wishes. A fair degree of manual strength and dexterity are necessary quite as much to avoid giving unnecessary punishment as to punish. Without some dexterity the trainer cannot manipulate the collar with the force, promptness, skill and correctness which are required. He must be ever watchful to modify or change the application of the collar according to the peculiarities exhibited by the dog, and no two dogs require precisely the same treatment. Jerking a dog about violently from loss of temper is the height of brutality. By no possibility can such acts be considered a part of intelligent training; on the contrary, they defeat the purposes of training by cowing the dog, breaking his spirit, or wrecking his constitution. The punishment should not be so severe at any time as to terrify him. When terror stricken he is wholly incapable of understanding anything, and such severity is never required to accomplish the purpose. Rarely will the trainer have need to exert himself violently if the directions herein given are observed. The novice usually begins by telling the dog to fetch, and begins thereupon to punish violently with the collar; immediately he is terribly angry, perspires profusely, gives commands at the top of his voice, and continues the violence till man and dog are exhausted, and the neighborhood disgusted. Unless such weakness can be overcome, the trainer would do well to abandon the lessons. No experience or instruction has any value when the trainer's temper is uncontrollable.

Before beginning the retrieving lessons, the dog should be accustomed to the collar, which is readily done by putting it, having a rope eight or ten feet long attached to it, on his neck. Let him struggle as much as he will, holding him steady the while, and keep perfectly passive. Frequently he bites at the collar and attempts to fight it; let him do so without hindrance until he is satisfied that his efforts are futile and an injury to himself. The flurry generally is very brief. Permit him to rest and collect his ideas, then pull gently on the rope and let him struggle again if he will. Let him have his own time, for there is no occasion for hurry, or gain by it. Repeat this as long as he will struggle, which is rarely over three or four times; at all events it must be continued till he will lead promptly and easily with the collar; if it is done thoroughly it will save trouble at a later stage of the lessons. If the dog is not in good health, his lessons should be held in abeyance until such time as it is good.

Next, the dog should be taught to come in promptly to order from a short distance, say ten feet. This will be the outside distance that he will be required to be away from his handler in the early lessons. Give the order, *Come in,* and jerk at the same time with sufficient force to hurt him a little; continue this till he comes in, then pet him and let all punishment cease. After awhile, walk away to the length of the rope, and repeat the lesson. When he will lead easily with the collar, and obeys the order *Come in,* the first direct lessons in retrieving may be given. For this purpose select a vacant room, or some secluded, quiet place where they can be given free from interruption. The hands should be protected by heavy gloves, a precaution that should never be neglected. They prevent the rope from chafing the hands, and protect them from abrasions, bites or scratches. If the lessons are given in the summer time, early in the morning or awhile before dusk in the evening being coolest, are the best times for the purpose. If given during the heated part of the day, the dog becomes distressingly warm and listless, and he is then in no condition to train; in fact, if heated during any lesson, it should end, or else permit the dog to rest till he cools off sufficiently. When the dog is panting severely, it is painful to him to keep his mouth closed, and he has neither the power nor inclination to hold anything in it for other than the briefest period of time; hence he is incapable of receiving his lesson in a satisfactory manner when in that condition. A yard, for obvious reasons, is much better for summer training. After the lessons are begun once, they should be given punctually every day. This is specially necessary to teach thoroughly, and make proper progress. Frequently by neglecting the puppy for a few days, he may develop some whim, crankiness or objectionable trait, when the lessons are recommenced, which will add greatly to the trouble of teaching him; furthermore, a puppy's memory is not always retentive, therefore it is pleasanter, better and quicker to observe precise regularity. Nevertheless, if the dog is cowed much by the use of the spike collar, suspension of the lesson for a week or two, or until his confidence and spirits are restored by the kindest treatment, providing he has been trained to a stage in retrieving where little punishment is required, is frequently very beneficial to timid dogs, and sometimes to obstinate ones. If, in this interval, the trainer can secure the affections of the obstinate dog, he may, by flattery and kindness, induce him to take an interest in retrieving without much punishment. The trainer will have to rely on his own judgment as to the propriety of giving the dog a rest. The resolutely obstinate, sulky, churlish, or ill-natured dog will not be benefited by it.

One lesson in the morning and evening respectively are sufficient for one day; and the lesson should not be long, say fifteen minutes, unless the dog is unusually stubborn or vicious, when it may be longer. When he does nicely it may be shorter. It is well to make the lesson end with some little act of pleasant obedience. Pet the dog for doing well, and learn to stop without attempting to force him through the whole course at once. The true system is to teach the simple elements one at a time, perfecting the dog carefully in one stage before advancing to the next. His knowledge then will be uniformly progressive, the different details will be thoroughly understood, his confidence will be retained, and a great deal of unnecessary violence will be avoided. Remember, that this branch always tries a trainer's fitness, and loud tones, turbulence and intensity of feeling detract from the training; if present, they are a fault which indicates that the trainer needs training.

A corn cob is a very good object to begin the lessons on. It is light, neat, not disagreeable, and can be easily replaced when soiled. A pine stick, about the same shape and size, is also good. A roll of tightly wound cloth, about six inches long and an inch in diameter, is frequently used, but it absorbs the saliva readily, collects dirt, and hence has undesirable properties.

A piece of half inch rope about eighteen inches long, fastened to the spike collar, is sufficiently long for the first lessons. A smaller rope would cut the hands. The free end of the collar should be placed on top of the dog's neck, the longer part running from the hand along the side of the dog's neck nearest to the handler. Grasp the end of the collar close to the dog's neck with the right hand and hold the pad in front of him with the left. The dog should stand on the right hand facing to the left, nearly at right angles to the front of his tutor. If, during the lessons, there is any moving about, the same relative position should be maintained, or resumed if it has been disturbed. In this position the dog can be handled better and more effectively than in any other; and by always assuming the same position, uniformity of conditions is maintained—the force is always applied in the same manner, the pad is held in the same place, and the dog and handler are in their relative positions. This is very important to note, and no deviation should be permitted. To show the importance of main-

THE FIRST LESSON IN RETRIEVING.

taining fixed conditions it may be mentioned that, even when the dog is half trained in the primary lessons, if the trainer takes the collar in his left hand, thus reversing the positions if he is right-handed, the dog will become as confused and incapable as an average man who is right-handed would be, in wing shooting, if required to shoot from the left shoulder. A light jerk should be given at first to test the dog's temper and the effects of the collar, there being a variety of effects produced on different dogs,—some will cry out at the slightest pain, others become apathetic, others again become obstinate or vicious, or frightened or sulky. Every different phase requires a special treatment. The timid dog, or the one which will cry out at slight punishment, should be forced to retrieve with the greatest deliberation and gentleness. The others must be forced to obedience, always noting the effects of the punishment, and modifying or increasing it according to requirements.

The first punishment is merely to make the dog open his mouth. If he will cry out at slight punishment, that is all that is necessary or desirable in the beginning. Immediately, when he opens his mouth, place the object in it, giving at the same time, in a quiet tone of voice, the order, *Fetch*. The very instant that the corn cob is in his mouth, a cob being the best to begin on, the collar should be slackened and punishment should cease; however, he should be forced to remain steadily in place and hold the cob. In the first stages it is better to retain a hold on the cob with the left hand to prevent him from ejecting it, any such effort meeting a warning pull on the collar. The instant cessation of punishment, when the dog obeys or has the semblance of obeying, holds good throughout every stage of retrieving. If the dog will not cry out when the collar is jerked lightly, it is unwise to jerk him severely. Catch the collar close to his neck with the right hand, give the hand a firm twist to the right backward, thus drawing the collar very tightly around his neck and shutting off his wind; his mouth will open instantly; place the cob in it, at the instant loosening the collar. After two or three punishments of this kind, the most obstinate dogs will open their mouths when they feel the collar tightening. Thus the beginning is a light jerk for those that will cry out easily, and a choke for such as will not. The latter is less painful and terrible to the dog than violent jerks which he cannot possibly comprehend. Now, the amateur should make a firm stand to avoid the fault which is common to all amateurs, and which has the most pernicious effects, namely, he should not begin the next stage before its preparatory stage is completed. Keep the dog in the first stage until he will open his mouth, without punishment, when the order *Fetch* is given. If it requires five or six lessons, or five or six dozen lessons, give them faithfully, for it is self-evident that, if the dog cannot perform the simple parts, he cannot reasonably be expected to perform the more complex.

The greatest consideration should be shown the dog at this stage. Remember that he is wholly ignorant of what is required. Even if he does not perform any part of the act perfectly, he should be excused, providing he shows any willingness to please. Nothing is so worthy of supreme contempt as punishing a willing dog which from ignorance cannot obey. Such dog should be shown how to perform, and repeated lessons are necessary by which to teach him. Remember that force is purely an accessory, to be used only when needed. The amateur may think that so much pains with details are unnecessary, and he may force the training unreasonably fast. If the dog happens to be of the right temperament to endure the punishment, the amateur may make a success; but for one success of this kind, he will make a dozen failures if he should attempt to train many dogs.

After the cob is placed in the dog's mouth, in the first lesson, speak kindly to him and allow him a few moments to collect himself. Make the contrast between holding the cob in his mouth and refusing to hold it, as distinct as possible; the former by kindness and approval, the latter, by disapproval and punishment. If properly managed, he in a few lessons learns to open his mouth at the command *Fetch*, without any punishment.

However, at this stage, certain dogs may develop some traits which will complicate matters and seriously obstruct progress unless they are corrected promptly as they develop. The amateur pays no especial attention to them, but proceeds as if they were a matter of course. The following is a common one: The dog, when the collar is pulled, may lie down; in this position, no progress can be made in training. The lesson should be entirely suspended, and the efforts devoted to making him stand on his feet, which is distinctly a lesson by itself. Shift the rope into the left hand and take a good light whip in the right. Do not attempt to jerk him into position with the collar, for while the object can be attained by that means, it can be attained much easier in a greater number of instances with a light riding whip or very light rawhide. Tap him smartly on his toes, at the same time giving the order, *Hold up*. As he pulls one foot under him to avoid punishment, immediately apply the whip to the other feet and deliberately, but persistently, apply it thus until he stands up. The retrieving lessons may then be resumed. Any repetition of the fault should be invariably corrected in the same manner, thus it soon will be overcome.

When he will open his mouth voluntarily when the order *Fetch* is given, he is prepared for the next stage, which is to make him walk one or two steps to the object which the trainer holds in his left hand in front of him, and instead of placing it in the dog's mouth, he is taught to step forward and grasp it. Hold the cob about fifteen inches in front, conveniently for him to see it and grasp it easily. Then give the order *Fetch*, jerk the collar in a line with the object to be retrieved so as to impel the dog toward it and make him grasp it himself, yet assisting him a little by putting it nearly in his mouth if he is awkward about it. At this stage, as at all others, the moment that the dog has the object in his mouth, all punishment should instantly cease. Gently stroke him on his head, and speak to him kindly. Make him perform the act repeatedly during several lessons, and perfect him so that he will step forward and grasp the object instantly, without punishment, when the order *Fetch* is given. The most disagreeable trait which may be exhibited at this stage is jumping backward and sagging in the collar, a serious fault that must be thoroughly corrected before progress can be made. When he jumps backward, grasp the rope with both hands and give him a sharp jerk, so timing it that it will catch him at the end of his backward movement; repeat the punishment until he comes forward to place. Every time that he repeats the fault, repeat the punishment, for he must be forced to step forward when the order *Fetch* is given, instead of going backward. If the dog is vicious and attempts to bite, which is a rare case, put on a rope about five or six feet long so that the trainer can stand far enough away for safety. Hold a good heavy whip in the hand with which to keep him off if he attempts to close in to bite. If the trainer is not strong physically, or if the dog is very vicious, another rope can be tied to his collar and the other one tied to a tree, post, etc. If the dog attempts to rush on the trainer, the rope will prevent him from following him up. The sooner a dog of this kind is subjugated, the better. Apply the whip liberally and severely until he surrenders. Once subdued, he is permanently conquered.

When the dog has learned to grasp the object, he may have other disagreeable traits when he walks in. He may run behind his handler on the right side or the left, and do this repeatedly. This is faulty. He should be required to stand squarely in front of his handler. When he runs behind, the handler should not change his own position. Meet the dog with a cut of the whip from the opposite side to that which he ran by, and whip him back to his place. If this is repeated a few times he will learn to refrain from running behind. Speak kindly to him when he is in his proper place, thus making correct acts pleasant, and faulty ones unpleasant. The whip should be convenient to hand, either lying close by on the ground, or placed under a belt on the person.

Other faults, some of which the amateur is predisposed to treat with severity, should be indulgently considered. In his first lessons the dog will grasp the object awkwardly and will sometimes drop it from this cause, in which event he should be permitted to again grasp it without punishment if possible. When punishment can be avoided, it is so much gained. By continued repetitions the dog will learn to grasp it correctly, however backward he may be in the beginning. He does not fully comprehend at the beginning that he is to grasp it, as is shown by the fact that he will simply rest his nose on it, thinking that he has complied with the order, although some obstinate dogs will do the same thing when they know precisely what is required.

If the dog crouches and crawls between the feet, close the ankles on his neck and give him several cuts on the nose with the whip from behind. Two or three corrections will cure this very common fault. The most difficult part of the system is in teaching the beginning, and if pains are not taken to correct these obstructive faults, they are a drag to progress, and may entirely prevent the trainer from achieving success. When once corrected, they are permanently cured.

When the dog will step forward and grasp the cob to order, without hesitation or awkwardness, he may be taught next to take it from the hand when it is lowered two or three inches. He may refuse to lower his head or grasp it in the new position, but he can be taught this part as before. Thus he is perfected in each successive stage till he will take the cob from the hand on a level with the ground. With some dogs which are willing to obey, these successive stages may be overcome much more expeditiously. As the dog moves forward to grasp the cob to order, it can be moved forward and at the same time gradually downward; he will follow it with his mouth in trying to grasp it. This should be done with tact, sometimes requiring him to follow it a few inches, sometimes nearly to the ground, and other times simply to grasp it when held at a level with his nose. Now, at this stage, or even an earlier one, if the trainer is artful, he may induce the dog to retrieve without further punishment. If the dog has a good temper and is willing to obey, the trainer may induce him to play by moving the cob teasingly to and fro in front of him, all the other conditions of collar, position, etc., remaining the same. If he springs forward and grasps it, and shows some interest and pride in his success, permit him to carry it, and praise him. The spike collar has been applied sufficiently to accomplish all that is necessary to make him always obedient and to establish all the necessary rudiments for a finished retriever. The collar, however, may be left on him during many successive lessons to enforce the necessary promptness and to suppress any faults which may show signs of developing, such as a hard mouth, refusal to come in, etc. This playfulness can only be developed in comparatively few instances. The greater number have to be drilled through each successive stage, with painstaking formality.

When the dog will grasp the cob from the hand when it is on the floor, there is usually next a troublesome stage to teach, *i. e.*, to pick the cob up off the floor. This is caused by the awkwardness of the dog in grasping the cob, he not being conscious of the proper manner of doing it when under compulsory teaching, as when he does it voluntarily. If he experience any difficulty in grasping it when it is on the floor, the hand can be lowered to the floor, the backs of the fingers resting on it, then let one end of the cob rest on the floor, the other on the ends of the fingers, thus he can get his lower jaw under it without difficulty. Mr. N. B. Nesbitt, an eminent expert trainer, uses a very ingenious contrivance which fills the requirements of this stage admirably. A piece of soft wood, about the size of a corn cob, has a couple of small pieces set cross-wise at right angles in each end, thus forming an object having some resemblance to a miniature saw-horse. When it rests on the ground there should be space enough underneath it to readily admit the dog's under jaw. As this stage is the most difficult to teach, any contrivance which is valuable should not be omitted. If, at this stage, he should become confused, it is better to re-commence at a previous stage, and by degrees work him again to this stage. It will thus often save punishment or avoid confusing the dog so much that he does not know what act to perform.

In exceptional instances the dog may absolutely refuse to lift the cob or other object off the ground and may sit down and throw his nose high in the air. No progress can be made until this fault is corrected. Hold the whip in the right hand, the rope in the left, whip him lightly over the nose till he lowers it. There is no need of hurry or severity. Every time he raises his nose, repeat the punishment. An expert trainer can hold both the whip and rope in the right hand and can manipulate one or the other as the occasion requires.

Another very objectionable trait may be exhibited by an obstinate dog, at this stage of his lessons, namely, he may deliberately walk or crawl past the pad although well knowing where it is and how to pick it up. Some cunningly pretend not to see it. Prevent him from crawling by or passing it, by tapping him over the nose with the whip, thus punishing him for avoiding the object and driving him back to his proper position. This fault is discouragingly obstructive if not corrected, but is easily cured in two or three attempts by this means.

After he will pick up the cob willingly to order, it may be thrown a short distance, two or three feet away, gradually increasing the distance as he becomes more and more proficient with each succeeding lesson. A lighter and longer cord may now be put on him simply to keep him in subjection as, if he has been properly taught, he will need very little punishment thereafter. When the cob is thrown out, if the dog does not start promptly to the order *Fetch*, catch the collar close to his neck, hold the cob in front of him, give the cob a toss, the dog a jerk after it and the order, *Fetch*, all at the same instant. Repeat till he will start after the cob the moment he is ordered.

When he picks up the cob, he may stand perfectly still or refuse to turn around facing his handler. If he is jerked with the collar, it will probably throw the cob out of his mouth. A better way is to hold him steadily with the rope giving him at the same time some light cuts with the whip on his hind legs; this will force him to quickly face toward his trainer, when he will generally obey the order *Come in*. At this stage he may be encouraged and given an incentive to action by giving him an occasional reward for good performance. Now the trainer can form a very good estimate of his skill by the degree of confidence which the dog has in him. Except in the case of an extremely obstinate dog, the trainer should be able to hold his dog's confidence and affection. If he has failed to do so his application of methods has been faulty.

After he will fetch the cob nicely, the dog may show a tendency to frolic, but all capers should be suppressed. Anything more than cheerful obedience is not required, and is not consonant with a finished education.

At almost any stage in the training, he may show an inclination to grasp the cob or other object with too firm a grip, or even bite it. When this tendency toward a hard mouth is observed, an object should be specially prepared for him to retrieve. Drive some slim, wrought tenpenny nails through it in various directions, clinching the ends so that the surface will be as evenly covered as possible. When he closes his teeth on such object once, he is very cautious thereafter, and may refuse to retrieve at all; if so, begin the lessons again from the first stage, and accustom him to it by degrees. The dog intensely dislikes to close his teeth on iron, and will retrieve any object, protected with it, with the greatest tenderness. No sharp points are desirable or necessary on the object which he retrieves. He should be regularly drilled on this object till a habit of grasping with a tender mouth is firmly established. It is worthy of mention in this relation, that a dog thus trained can be made a tender mouthed retriever to a certainty. There is no qualification to it whatever save the one of his trainer's skill and industry. There is no trouble to inculcate promptness, precision, and tender handling of the bird. However, the lessons must be repeated regularly, prompt obedience invariably required, and the dog's intelligence developed—once discipline is established, the rest follow easily.

He may next be given lessons in a yard or room from which he cannot escape; and the checkcord may be removed. If he refuses, a jerk on the collar usually insures obedience. Any attempt at evasion should not be tolerated for an instant. Do not attempt to coax him. In this system the praises and rewards only come when the performance is completed. No repetition of orders should be given after the dog understands them. One order is sufficient. If a dog can be taught to drop instantly to shot and wing, he can be taught equally prompt obedience to all orders.

He may next be drilled in retrieving a dead bird. Some dogs retrieve it without any further effort on the part of the trainer, others have to be in a manner rebroken from the beginning. If the dog shows any disposition to bite or pinch the bird, some tenpenny nails can be tied about an inch apart around the body, and parallel with its length; or the nails can be sewed to two small loops of elastic, one at each end, which can be quickly slipped over a bird. This will force him to grasp the bird with the greatest tenderness, and will be a lesson which he will never forget. Sharp pointed wires driven through the body of the bird are unnecessary. Repeat the lessons, with the bird as the object to be retrieved, until he will obey with the greatest certainty and correctness.

Next the lessons may be repeated in the open fields. If the dog has been properly trained, he will not need either checkcord or collar at this stage to prevent his running away; but if there is any danger of bolting, it is better to take the proper precautions against it. It is better to guard against running away if he evinces the slightest inclination to do so, for if he runs away once he will be constantly on the alert for another opportunity, and it may require weeks of discipline to correct the carelessness of a moment.

After each lesson, when the collar is taken off, the dog should not be released immediately, but should be held and petted until he has regained his self-confidence and cheerfulness. A short run, giving him perfect freedom, will serve to keep a good understanding between handler and dog, particularly if the dog is kindly noticed betimes. No training in actual field retrieving should be attempted between lessons before the dog is reliably obedient; it never fails to end in trouble or failure, frequently it causes the dog to bolt.

Thus we have followed the dog's progress step by step through the simple act of fetching an object; we now consider some accessory acts which are necessary to give it an approximate resemblance to the manner of field work. When the dog will fetch in the early lessons with a fair degree of certainty, the cob can be thrown out and the dog held by his collar for a few moments, then give the order *Fetch*. This should be repeated a sufficient number of times in a sufficient number of lessons till he is familiar with it. If he has been taught to drop, which as a matter of course should be done in separate lessons, he may be required to drop and remain steady when the cob is thrown out, until he receives the order *Fetch*. It will be necessary to use the checkcord in these lessons. They should be continued until he is perfectly steady to the drop when any object is thrown out, and will not stir till ordered to retrieve. If he is over-enthusiastic and willing, do not destroy his confidence by severity. Restrain him mildly with the checkcord, and it is an easy matter to keep him at the drop, without violence. When he understands what is required, he will gradually submit. Hence it is apparent that jerking the dog about is unnecessary.

When he is given the order to *Fetch*, do not balk him by immediately afterward commanding him to drop. It confuses him and is no part of field work in any relation. When a puppy is sent to retrieve there are no half way measures about it. This is a very common and vicious fault with amateurs, and a very obstructive one in many cases.

It is desirable that the dog retrieve with a high head, or at least delivers the bird to hand in such manner. He can be habituated to this manner by giving him a reward when he fetches the bird or by petting him, and refraining from taking the bird from him until he holds his head up.

Some sportsmen prefer that the retriever will assume a sitting posture while delivering the bird; such has no special value, but is considered as being more elegant. To make it a part of the act of retrieving, it should be taught in separate lessons at first. Tie a rope to his collar, tap him gently over the hips till he sits down; the trainer can prevent him from lying down with the rope. A snap of the fingers is all the order that is necessary at first; later he can be taught to obey a slight motion of the hand alone. The lessons should be continued until he is obedient to the signal. While in a sitting position he may be given rewards, and will soon learn to be seated for them. When perfected, it may then be added to retrieving.

Even when he will perform accurately, the lessons must be continued during some weeks to establish a lasting discipline. His powers of observation by cultivation are also improved, and by association he becomes affectionately attached to his trainer. The lessons can be given under different surroundings, such as different places in the fields while giving him a run, different places about the yard, and different objects. He can be trained to retrieve a piece of steak, an egg, a bunch of keys, or other small objects, but these partake of the nature of a trick. If the trainer lives in a section where he can procure quails, snipe, woodcock and prairie chickens, he can make his dog a finished retriever on each kind. The lessons under different surroundings should not be neglected. As intimated in other places in this work, obedience may be given to orders under the conditions and surroundings which prevailed when the dog was taught, and he may absolutely refuse under all other conditions, except force is used.

In the preparatory yard and field lessons, it is beneficial to give the dog some discipline in carrying the bird steadily for several minutes, while following his trainer. Also drop the bird slyly in such a place that the dog will come across it. If he picks it up without any order, after he carries it a short distance relieve him of it, and praise him generously. This lesson should be repeated until the dog will pick up the bird without any order, and without feeling his trainer's eye upon him, for the eye has a great controlling influence over a dog. It is advisable to repeat this lesson betimes in the field. It has an application in regular shooting; occasionally the dog will find a dead or wounded bird which the shooter shot at, but was not conscious of hitting. When the dog finds a bird some distance away from his handler, he should retrieve it without orders. If trained nicely, he will take a great deal of pride in so doing, knowing well that it is commendable. Occasionally a dog of superior intelligence will voluntarily retrieve a bird which he accidentally finds; but a few lessons while training are not injurious or troublesome, and they should not be neglected when they so particularly enlarge the scope of a dog's ideas and usefulness.

In introducing him to the first actual retrieving to the gun, some precautions are necessary to insure a correct beginning. If the dog is gunshy, excessively timid, birdshy or unsteady to wing or shot, he is not ready for field retrieving until these are cured; otherwise objectionable complications are sure to arise which may require weeks to cure. Notwithstanding all the care expended on his preliminary training, under the excitement of the presence of birds, the smell of blood and the instinctive desire to kill, he may show a determination to crush his birds and may entirely forget about retrieving. This transitionary stage is the troublesome one in field retrieving, and it is very brief if managed skillfully. Leave the spike collar on him during the first few retrieves. No checkcord is necessary. Walk up with him to the bird and make him fetch it properly. If he evinces any intention to bite it, put on the elastic bands and nails hereinbefore mentioned, throw out the bird and let him rush on it without restraint. When he closes on it, he receives a lesson which he never forgets. He may then refuse to retrieve it to order, but can be easily forced to do so. When he retrieves the first few birds they should be thrown out several times, and the dog required to retrieve them. Rigid formality in details is necessary in the beginning; at a later period it is not so necessary. By starting him properly in field retrieving in this manner, he is a tender-mouthed, obedient retriever for life, and by a little care in handling, the quality of his work can be improved by experience, or at least maintained at a uniform grade of excellence at all times.

Hunting him in company with badly trained dogs will be sure to injure his retrieving. Under no circumstances should two dogs be sent at the same time to retrieve a dead bird. From jealousy or rivalry one will attempt to take it away from the other, the bird is mutilated, and the dog has learned something he ought not to learn. An expert trainer can make two dogs search for a dead bird, but the moment that one dog finds it, the other is dropped to a signal or quiet order; but few amateurs have their dogs so perfectly under control as to justify them in attempting this performance. Bad tricks are acquired with wonderful quickness, by imitation and natural predisposition, hence the constant need of guarding against the company of half-broken dogs. Mutilating the birds is perfectly natural to the dog, birds being part of his natural prey, therefore mutilating is only bad in so far as it is against the purposes of the handler; yet this shows the need of taking precautions against circumstances which may unnecessarily excite his destructive propensities.

A few individuals learn readily to mark the fall of a dead bird, or the flight of a wounded bird. A retriever having this accomplishment is incomparably superior to one which needs assistance at every retrieve. The one goes directly to the bird, the other has to search tediously for it. A little assistance can be contributed toward developing this accomplishment, by standing in an open field a few yards away from the edge of some timber, which is not so dense as to entirely obstruct the view. By throwing objects into the timber for him to retrieve, he may learn to mark their flight and fall, if due care is taken to have him see them when they are thrown. Such lessons will materially assist to develop intelligent dogs, but there are dogs which never learn more than the mere acts of seeking and fetching.

The proper time to begin the lessons in retrieving after the training has begun varies greatly according to the dispositions of different dogs. An obstinate dog can be benefited by making retrieving his first lesson. The subjugation which always results from skillful use of the collar is general in its effects—he is more thoroughly obedient in every part of training. The timid dog should be permitted to gain courage and assurance by freedom in the field before being forced to retrieve. The trainer will do wisely to note all the peculiarities of his dog, and if there is any reason for or against forcing the dog to retrieve at a certain time, the trainer should defer it accordingly. If the amateur is not pressed for time, it is better to simply give the yard lessons in retrieving in the first season and finish the field retrieving in the second season. By this course many of the undesirable features which casually appear in the puppy's first field work are avoided.

To recapitulate, do not hurry; teach one detail at a time; hold the dog's affections; be governed largely in the application of force by the dog's disposition; give the lessons punctually and repeatedly, to the end that obedience becomes habitual; correct all casual faults as they appear, and remember that the collar is simply an instrument to make the dog pick up a bird and carry it, a very small part of perfect retrieving. The comprehension of its purposes, the knowledge of all details concerning it, can be acquired only by experience and skillful handling when afield. When it is applied properly, it is a combination of the best parts of the two systems, *i. e.*, the natural method and the force system. The compulsory pressure is only required in the beginning; if the trainer does not succeed in dispensing with force after that period, he has failed to understand the application of the art.

The manner in which a dog is trained to retrieve when working as one of a brace is described under the head of Brace Work.

Find, Seek, Seek Dead. These commands are used incidentally with retrieving. They denote that the dog is to search for a dead or wounded bird which has fallen to the gun. The trainer teaches him obedience to one or the other of these orders, but such order should be given to the exclusion of all others, when once taught, different orders tending to confusion.

The preparatory training in this can be given in early puppyhood, it being an adjunct to the natural method of teaching retrieving; still, there is no special advantage in teaching it so early. It being made pleasurable and profitable to the puppy without being fatiguing, it is easily understood and readily learned. Punishment is inadmissible and unnecessary. It is one of the few methods that, from its simplicity, has not been susceptible of improvement, the old methods therefore holding good.

The lessons may be given in any suitable place, in the house, yard or field, according as the state of the weather or the inclination or convenience of the trainer dictates.

The trainer provides himself with about fifteen or twenty small pieces of meat, weighing each about a half ounce or ounce. He takes but one piece in his hand at a time while giving the lesson, the rest being placed in a position where the dog cannot smell or reach it. If all of it is held in the hand, it will wholly engage his attention, thus impeding the lesson.

If in the fields, place a piece of the meat on the grass, permitting the dog to note the proceedings, since it is desirable that he should know where the first few pieces are concealed, so that his interest will be excited. Lead him three or four steps away, then give the order *Find*, releasing him at the same instant, whereupon he will go directly to the meat.

After a few pieces have been given in this manner, he knows that, when he hears the order, there is something desirable to search for. The method is then slightly changed. He is required to find the meat without any previous knowledge of its whereabouts. Place one hand over his eyes, or throw out the meat when he is not looking, then give the order, *Find*. If he is backward in his attempts, or gives up the search quickly, assume an air of interest and pretend to search for it yourself, engaging his attention also in it. By observation and imitation, he will soon learn to search keenly for it, particularly if the trainer takes the precaution to give the lesson when the dog is hungry. With an indolent dog it occasionally is beneficial to pretend to find the meat yourself and withhold it from him, thus he will be stimulated to greater eagerness to find it himself at the next effort. These lessons should not be practiced too long or too frequently; once a day is sufficient for training purposes.

When the dog comprehends the meaning of the order and will search for the meat with more or less diligence, it should not be concealed on the ground thereafter, else he will thereby certainly acquire a habit of putting his nose to the ground when searching, and if the habit is confirmed, he may continue it in actual field work. In the fields, a piece of meat can be placed in the fork of a bush, or other object, low enough for the dog to reach with ease. In the yard, small nails can be driven into convenient objects, as, for instance, posts, barrels, the corner of a building, etc. A piece of meat is placed on one and he is required to search till he finds it. The piece must be changed from place to place with each successive attempt, else he will remember each place accurately and go directly from one to the other. By practice he will grow wonderfully cunning and successful in his search.

As he improves, he may be taught to obey signals of the hand, a wave to the right or left denoting that he must search accordingly. Generally, from observing that it assists him to success, he quickly learns the meaning of the signal. It is unwise to drag the meat on the ground to have him trail it, and also to conceal it so securely that the dog will have unnecessary difficulty in finding it. If the act closely approximates to that required in actual field work, it is sufficient.

When he is diligent and obedient, the transitionary stage between working for his own profit and working for that of his master may be commenced, although the dog must still have some incentive; his love of approbation should be cultivated, and rewards given betimes. A glove may be shown him; then throw it behind some object that will conceal it, a clump of bushes, rock, etc., preventing the dog meanwhile from seeing it. The order *Find* is then given. He may see the glove but not lift it, thinking that there is some palatable morsel to find. Show him by your actions that the glove is the object of the search, order him to fetch it, and praise him when it is retrieved. By repeated efforts he will soon learn to seek diligently, and retrieve it out of a desire to win applause. The lesson can be varied at times, giving it in one place, then another, thus changing the surroundings. If he will search diligently, obediently and intelligently for any object, that is all that is necessary. Training him to return to a long or short distance after a glove, handkerchief, pocketbook or other object is no part of field work. It has been said that such is a useful accomplishment inasmuch as the shooter might lose his pocketbook, powder flask, or other valuable articles. The trouble and skill required to teach the act are worth more than the average pocketbook; and a little precaution, in any event, would obviate the need of a retriever for such purposes. Training dogs to hunt for possible lost pocketbooks is becoming a lost art.

If the dog in his early training has been judiciously permitted to break shot to retrieve, he has learned to mark the fallen birds with more or less accuracy, and will not therefore need to search for them. Care should be taken to cultivate his powers of observation in this respect, such being very important in a good retriever. When the bird falls, if the shooter notes that it is winged, which he can in most instances do if he is an experienced field shot, the dog should be sent for it without delay to guard against possible loss, or unnecessary hard work in searching for it. Many birds are lost by neglecting this course. If the dog has been taught retrieving by force, he can be trusted to retrieve wounded birds as well as dead ones; if taught by the natural method, the greatest care must be observed during his training, in this respect.

Occasionally, the trainer teaches this order during field work, without giving any preliminary yard lessons, but such has obviously many special disadvantages, and is not so certain or uniformly progressive as when there is a course of proper preparation. While the expert trainer may accomplish the necessary results without so much formality, it is unwise for the amateur to attempt any training in such manner. However, in yard training the experienced trainer, simply by arousing the dog's enthusiasm and praising him, can teach this branch perfectly without any rewards.

STEADY.

This order denotes that the dog is to shorten his pace at such times as it is necessary to do so, as when searching for a dead or wounded bird, or for the scattered birds of a bevy.

Many dogs learn this without any assistance, if given a reasonable time for experience. A few from impatience or stupidity will not work at a slow gait unless forced to do so. With such, a long course of training is sometimes necessary. When it is desired that an impatient or headstrong dog should go slowly, a checkcord can be put on him, thus affording a means of forcing him to a slow gait. The order *Steady* should be repeatedly given every time that he is checked. If he will not work well with a checkcord, two pieces of wood, sufficiently long to reach to his pasterns from his collar, may be tied one on each side of his collar. If he attempts to go fast, they will play so lively on his forelegs that he will be forced to go slowly. A self-willed, obstinate dog may need a liberal application of the whip to subjugate him permanently. Persistent and long continued effort will accomplish the necessary obedience to the order in all cases, and its importance is such that it should not be neglected.

CHAPTER IX.

PREPARATORY FIELD TRAINING.

The first informal field work of a puppy may be given when he is sufficiently developed, mentally and physically, to have unlimited curiosity, and strength enough to run without excessive labor and fatigue, which is generally at about the age of eight months and upward; at least, it is not specially advantageous to attempt any training at an earlier age.

Contrary to the common practice and the teachings of many writers, no training, in the sense in which it is commonly understood, *i. e.*, to the gun, should be attempted in the preparatory training. This training, given during a longer or shorter period, according to the requirements of the dog, is simply an opportunity to learn to use his hunting functions, and is very important, it being the foundation on which the training to the gun rests, as is specially described under the several heads of Pointing, Roading, and Ranging.

It will be assumed that the training is to be conducted on quails, they being the birds which are most commonly sought for the purpose, as they are the best, most numerous, and widely distributed. However, if the dog is to be trained on other kinds of game, the course to pursue would be the same in manner, but with ruffed grouse or woodcock more restraint would be necessary in training at all stages.

Before methods can be applied in regular training, the dogs

must have some knowledge of field work; indeed, skillful methods assume such pre-existing knowledge when applied, the true system being merely to train the dog's natural efforts to the use of the gun. There are ever varying complexities in field work, which cannot be reduced to any rules, and which must be left to the intelligence of the dog. The amateur who will recognize these elementary principles has made a great advance toward success. It is incomparably better to permit the dog to exercise his intelligence at first, after which train him to observe formal methods which subserve the purposes of the gun, than to attempt, from the beginning, to reduce every detail and act to artificial rules. As between the dog which is forced to observe formal methods, from the beginning, because they are methods, and the dog which works intelligently and only has methods as they relate to the purposes of the gun, there is no comparison. While a dog cannot possibly be developed to a greater degree than the limit of his native capabilities, it is equally true that his capabilities may be injured or kept dormant by unskillful training.

If the puppy, at the start, flushes, chases, runs riot and is wholly without system, do not imagine for a moment that such will be his manner perpetually, even if his handler should refrain from interfering. The dog learns and improves from his own experience, and after awhile settles down into uniform regularity in his work, although at this period his efforts are all wholly in his own interest. No concern need be felt as to training him to steadiness. Remember that the dog does not live that cannot be worked to a standstill. The time required to gain the preliminary experience varies greatly with different dogs. Some require a few days, others as many weeks, while timid, cranky, or indolent dogs may require months. The preparatory fitness of the puppy can be determined by observing whether he is hunting for game or merely running about from excess of spirits or vitality. When he ranges and hunts resolutely, roading his birds quickly, pointing, flushing and chasing with determination, he is in very good trim to begin his training.

It is worthy of special note that the manner of beginning the experience with the gun often determines whether the dog will or will not be gunshy. Gunshyness is frequently the fault of the trainer, although amateurs are prone to consider it a fault of the dog. Any dog, however courageous, can be made gunshy. There is no greater mistake possible than to assume that a dog has an inherent knowledge of the gun and its uses, or a hereditary love or fear of it; a knowledge from inheritance which the handler himself reaches by education, for man has no intuition of the gun and its uses, and frequently the report of a gun is very startling in its effects to himself, hence he should be more considerate toward the dog. By observing the disposition of the dog, whether timid, cowardly, distrustful or courageous, and whether he is intelligent or of weak mind, the training may be conducted in a manner which will not run counter to his peculiarities, thus much loss of time and the occasions for trouble will be avoided.

It is of the utmost importance, in all branches of training, but rigidly so in this instance, that the trainer has the dog's confidence and affection before he attempts any training that may alarm him, such as firing the gun, etc. If the dog is shy from whippings or premature attempts to restrain him, all efforts to accustom him to the gun or to train him must be held in abeyance until such time as his confidence is restored. This can be accomplished by giving him his head and treating him with uniform kindness.

The best juncture at which to give the puppy his first experience with the report of fire-arms is when he is ranging in the fields a hundred yards or more away, and is in good spirits, is not afraid of his handler, and is interested in hunting.

A small pistol, for special reasons, is the best for the purpose. A percussion cap or .22 caliber cartridge should be snapped at first. If the puppy is at all startled at the report, the handler should continue to walk deliberately in his course, affecting the greatest unconcern, and taking no notice whatever of him. Usually the puppy, when he perceives that there is nothing to excite his fears, resumes his hunting. However, if he shows a suspicion of something wrong or an apprehension of danger, as he may do for several moments, refrain from shooting until he is again thoroughly interested in hunting and unobservant of the handler. If he is a dog of a nervous or timid temperament, an old steady dog may be taken to accompany him, and the calm exterior of the latter will do much to reassure the puppy. Under no circumstances should two or more green puppies be experimented with at once; if one runs, all will be apt to run, and mischief will be done in quantities.

The greatest care should be taken to avoid haste in shooting or in shooting at inopportune junctures. At any time that the puppy is expecting the report, which can readily be perceived by his expectant look and distrustful actions, the handler should not shoot or show other than the most placid demeanor. Gradually, the puppy, from observing that the reports are not injurious or related to himself and excite no apprehension in those about him, becomes indifferent to them. Then they may be judiciously increased in volume and frequency, from the lighter powder charges first used to heavier and heavier ones by easier gradations, always, however, noting the effects on the fears of the dog, if any, and retarding the efforts accordingly. When the dog exhibits no alarm at the report of the pistol, a gun may be introduced.

A bird or two should be shot under favorable conditions for him to see them, so that he may learn the purpose of the gun, which if he has no fears, will be done readily in one or two lessons, and thereafter he will always be keenly interested in its use. A pistol is better to begin with for many reasons; it is easier to carry; it can be concealed from the dog; the reports are light; and if the dog sees the pistol and becomes afraid of it by perceiving that it is instrumental in the frightful noises, there are not then the same objectionable results as when the gun is used, namely, he learns very quickly that bringing the gun to the shoulder is an act which precedes the discharge, and naturally, from the anticipation of the report, he flinches from this mere motion as much as from the report itself; in fact, this act may cause him to bolt. It has the further disadvantage that after he has outgrown his fears of the report, the act of raising the gun to the shoulder, being associated with past fears may excite his fears for weeks; thus the preparations to fire the gun may cause more lasting fears than the report itself.

In the beginning of field work, the trainer can be of no assistance in training the puppy aside from taking him to such favorable places as afford opportunities to exercise his hunting instincts. All the awkwardness and ignorance he displays, qualities always displayed by an inexperienced puppy, are gradually overcome by experience. It is impossible for the puppy to understand the application of methods before he has had sufficient experience in working on birds; prior to this, methods are simply so many incomprehensible obstructions. In the greater number of instances the amateur conducts his training on the theory and practice that the puppy must be controlled and taught even from a very tender age, such being, in times gone by, the approved method; as a consequence, the puppy is whipped, balked and perpetually restrained, the things he must not do, but wishes to do, ever recurring. It is not strange that this course pursued assiduously spoils the dog by unconsciously teaching him that he is not to hunt at all, instead of hunting in a formal manner as the trainer desired.

The puppy, which is naturally so subdued in manner that he is capable of hunting steadily to the gun at a very early age, has done nothing to excite hopes of superiority in his future performances. The precocity of youth rarely foreshadows pre-eminence at maturity, the period when the real struggle occurs.

The most skilled and intelligent workers are those which are strictly self-educated so far as finding birds is concerned, this superiority being the result of self-hunting, either alone or with other dogs; in fact, many expert trainers give their puppies full freedom to hunt, particularly if they are at all backward from timidity, slow development of hunting instincts, gunshyness, etc., with the most beneficial results. It is the only way in which a puppy can be developed to the highest degree of his working capabilities; and it accords with his natural instincts, and is quicker and more thorough; it is the best. When permitted to go with another dog, he is not hampered by any feelings of constraint which he feels in the presence of his trainer. He learns to comprehend the actions of his companion, learns the meaning of a point and back, learns how to road quickly and accurately, and how to mark the flight of birds and follow them; in short, he devotes his whole undivided energies to his work. To the novice, the wild pursuit appears ruinous, is against cherished traditions, and he cannot refrain from interfering with more or less turbulence and violence; yet, to develop a field dog, this experience is what he must have whether he acquires it quickly by freedom, or slowly and imperfectly under the continual balking and meddling of his handler. Many dogs are ruined for want of opportunity to develop.

The dog can be broken from hunting, either wholly or partially, quite as well as from any other act, and he very naturally interprets constant restraint and frequent punishment as being inflicted for the act of hunting, and not for the manner of it. When permitted to self-hunt, the progress is not obstructed by arbitrary rules.

The amateur is disposed to think that if the puppy points, the greatest difficulty has been overcome, and the main part of the training completed. The act of pointing, while indispensable, is but one of several equally important. Dash and range, being essential, should be cultivated from the first, which cannot be done if the dog is not given his head. Pointing will be established in due time almost to a certainty; however, without the ability to range and find birds, the mere ability to point well is of little value.

In giving the preparatory work, the puppy should be taken afield in the morning hours when the birds are out in search of food, when the scent is good, the temperature cool, and therefore when the conditions are most favorable, if the training is in fall or early spring. Rarely is it advisable to run two puppies together, their mutual jealousy prompting them to repeated errors, or the mutual confidence inspired, prompting them to willful disobedience.

When the dog's field work is begun, the trainer should note the condition of the dog's health. If he is not in good health and physical condition, he is wholly unfit for work. Dogs which have been in close confinement should be started to work very gradually. Also the greatest care should be taken to avoid overwork. When the puppy has had enough, let him rest well or quit for the time being.

Thrashing a dog at this stage, for mistakes, conveys no profitable educational experience; he derives no knowledge therefrom which will enable him to perform better at the next opportunity. No expectations need be entertained with respect to good work if the dog is not afforded ample experience.

For training purposes, grounds should be selected which are at least fairly well supplied with birds. If a puppy is worked day after day with only a find now and then, he ceases to hunt, or runs about carelessly as he would in a highway; indeed, an aged, experienced dog will become careless and indifferent under similar circumstances; and a hunter takes but little interest.

If the puppy is soft in flesh and thick in wind, it is very unwise to work him in a hot sun. If he is of a nervous, excitable disposition, he may become excessively overheated which may induce distressing fits, or in fact, he may die. The trainer should shape his route so that there will be opportunities to give his dogs water. In many sections of the West and the South, the streams dry up in the summer and fall, and the scarcity of water then becomes a great inconvenience. At such times it is well to carry a quart flask of water along, which will afford two small drinks for two dogs; and it can be re-filled at some point on the route. If hunting from horseback, it is then an easy matter to carry a sufficient quantity. If the trainer has not a drinking vessel along, the crown of the hat, if of felt, canvas, or corduroy, pressed down, will hold water sufficiently long for the dogs to drink it.

While all dogs have an affection for their master, working, when properly trained, to suit his pleasure, they vary greatly in their mental and physical powers, and therefore in their capability and usefulness. Occasionally one will be met with which can hunt well for his own interest, but cannot readily be taught to work to the gun; however, in hunting for birds, the dog is merely seeking his natural food supply, and until he has had the necessary experience to learn to work conjointly with his handler's efforts, he cannot reasonably be expected to abandon his natural methods; nor should more be expected of a dog than he is naturally capable of performing. It is also worthy of note that all dogs, good or bad, have off days. When not working up to their usual form, they are frequently treated inconsiderately, errors of work being ascribed to sulkiness, carelessness, or indolence, whereas the dog may be unwell, his powers of scent impaired for the time being. When a dog is known to be an honest, reliable worker on most occasions, any temporary incapacity should be treated with indulgence. This inexplicable irregularity will be exhibited more or less by all dogs. The dog is highly nervous in his organization, therefore liable to irregularities in his special performances quite as much as his master who breaks down, at times, in his shooting, without any appreciable cause, and no effort for the time being can overcome it.

It is well for the amateur to know that deafness and the consequent inability of the dog to obey commands may be mistaken for obstinacy, which it very closely resembles in effect; indeed, many experienced sportsmen have been deceived in their judgment respecting it. If the deafness is only partial in each ear, or in only one ear, it is very difficult to detect. When the wind is favorable for the dog to hear commands, or when the sound ear is toward the handler, he may hear well and be promptly obedient; at other times he may apparently be willfully disobedient. By noting such actions and his actions about the yard, the owner will be able to determine whether his dog is deaf or not. When lying down or standing about, he may apparently ignore his name when called, till it is repeated in a louder and louder tone, when he suddenly starts, looks about with a surprised air, sees that his master requires something and hastens to obey cheerfully, thus showing a functional imperfection in hearing. This infirmity is much more common than is generally supposed, and may be induced by excessive exposure to wet and cold. It is frequently caused by the promiscuous shooting of too many guns over one dog without any regard to his proximity. Two or three men about a pointing dog, one standing six or eight feet behind him, and shooting over his back, and one or two on one side or on each side, can do the mischief thoroughly. For the benefit of those who have not experienced the sensation, it may be explained that a gun fired from a position eight or ten feet from the rear, and the line of fire from three to six feet from the ear, has about the same sensation that a blow in the ear would have if delivered with a sand bag. The concussion may impair the hearing or completely destroy it. Many sportsmen have had their hearing impaired temporarily or permanently from this cause. Hence it can readily be imagined what effect two double guns fired behind and above a dog would have on his hearing, his head being near the ground. When all the crude methods of education and all the unknown pains the dog suffers from mismanagement are considered, the wonder is not that there are occasional gunshy puppies, but that both young and old dogs do not become so oftener. The amateur's theory of gunshyness generally places the dog in fault beyond question, but if the dog could tell the real cause, it would appear very simple and rational in most cases.

As mentioned in another part of this work, the dog is extremely jealous, and this trait can be taken advantage of to accomplish certain objects, but it has annoying disadvantages in field work. The dog cannot endure any rivalry from strange dogs without attempting to defeat them. The jealous dog prefers flushing to permitting a rival to get the point, and may break shot to prevent his retrieving. Also, this trait may be exercised against his handler, for from fear that his handler may get the birds from him, he will break his point and flush as he hears him walk up. This trait should not be aggravated, or cultivated, by working the dog possessing it, with a dog which is also excessively jealous, or has irritating faults, such as failure to back, stealing points, breaking shot, etc.

The dog should be so treated that when his handler is ready to go afield, he shows unlimited delight and eagerness to join. If he shows fear, there is something decidedly wrong in the training.

The sportsman who can spare but two or three days, or weeks, each year for shooting, makes a serious mistake if he takes a green dog along with the expectation of doing some training and shooting, although the mistake is not infrequent. In the greater number of instances the trip is a disappointment so far as shooting is concerned, and from attempting to make a puppy do in one day what he required a month to learn, the training is almost uniformly a failure. Shooting and training cannot be done at the same time consistently with the pleasure of the shooter and the development of the puppy; much more is it impossible when the shooter may not know even the elementary principles of training.

CHAPTER X.

POINTING.

Some of the commonest powers of organic beings are the most wonderful in nature, yet their commonness and the resulting familiarity reduce them to the level of the matter-of-course. Of these, none are more marvelous than the faculty which the pointer or setter exhibits in pursuing his prey by the delicacy of his scenting powers. The pressure of tiny feet for the briefest instant leaves an impalpable roadway which the dog follows with ease. So exquisitely keen is this function of smell that he readily discriminates between the direction taken by the birds and the back track, and between the body scent and foot scent. Also, by some difference in the intensity or quality of the scent, he can accurately determine his distance from the birds when he is on a hot foot scent or body scent, and can distinguish that of a dead or live bird.

Pointing, standing and setting are terms used synonymously to denote the peculiar, rigid attitude of pointers and setters when in the act of standing near birds of which they have the scent, although the act may be imperfect at times from pointing falsely, or on the foot scent. The style and intensity of the act varies greatly in different individuals; some are rigid and statuesque, others are slouchy or indifferent; and there are all kinds and degrees of variations between the best and poorest acts.

The two breeds, pointers and setters, do not materially

differ in their attitudes on point in any respect. The general characteristics of the act are precisely the same in both, the only difference being in the peculiarities of individuals, no two assuming precisely the same attitude, in the same sense that no two run or walk precisely alike.

As the exercise of the instinct is dependent, in a great measure, on the powers of smell, it is not strange that certain external appearances of the nose have come to be considered an indication of the degree of those powers. Many sportsmen and authors attach undue importance to wide, expansive nostrils, inferring very plausibly that such must give a corresponding increase in the scenting powers. This assumption is not founded on any tangible physiological data. With respect to the functional powers of the nose, a wide or close nostril is not of the slightest importance. In practice, no difference which could be ascribed to its external form is observable in the average scenting powers of large numbers of individuals. Every experienced sportsman has seen dogs having light, snipy, contracted noses, yet possessing exquisite delicacy of scent, and dogs having expansive nostrils which had dull scenting powers. The dogs which have the imaginary broad, expansive nostrils are rare indeed. The anatomical structure of the nose indicates that the exterior form is of no functional importance. The inner recesses have a very extensive, irregular surface of mucous membrane, which much increases its capacity of sensation. The olfactory nerves are therein widely and intricately distributed, yet comparatively few of them reach to the end of the nostril, although it has keen tactile sensibility. Undoubtedly the functional powers of the nose depend on the abundance and delicacy of the olfactory nerve plexus, therefore not on the size of the ends of the nostrils. It would be quite as reasonable to assume that the senses of taste, hearing and seeing are dependent on the external size of the mouth, ears or eyes.

The common explanation of the origin of the pointing instinct is, that when the setter was a spaniel or an improved spaniel, which is simply a conjecture, he was hunted on partridges and forced to lie close to the ground when he recognized the scent of them, whereupon a net was drawn or thrown over both the dog and the covey, which latter was patiently submissive and conveniently near to the dog in a favorable place for the net to cover both, and thus the birds were captured. No attempt is made to explain why the dog hunted the partridges instinctively, that part being a matter of course. As arms improved and greater skill was coincidentally developed in their use, sportsmen becoming expert wing shots, there was no occasion for the setter to lie down when he scented the birds, hence he stood up to his points, whereupon pointing, which previously was a matter of education, spontaneously became an instinct—at least, so say the historians.

Instincts are invariably for the benefit of the individual himself, or the perpetuation of the species, they being subservient to self-preservation. That, therefore, a dog should point a bird instinctively for a man to shoot at, is one of the many beliefs that exist and are perpetuated on the flimsiest of assumptions.

The pointing instinct is known to have existed in the pointer so far in the past as there is any history or tradition of the breed. It was particularly strong in the old Spanish pointer, yet no theory is advanced in respect to its origin in him.

It is more reasonable to suppose, and the supposition is supported by analogous characteristics in other animals, that pointers and setters had the hunting and pointing instincts implanted in them by nature as a means to secure a food supply than that they became permanently fixed by an imperfect education conducted by a few skillful trainers and a multitude of unskillful ones, through a comparatively brief period of time. Pointing is merely supplementary to the hunting instinct; merely a detail of it. Any explanation of the origin of the instinct other than that it is natural is rendered still more trifling when it is considered that the dog's teeth, digestive organs and instincts denote that he is a carnivorous animal, therefore a hunter; hence hunting his natural prey in his natural manner cannot be the result of education. This view, as aforementioned, is confirmed by analogous natural methods of hunting prey pursued by other animals. The fox roads, makes his casts to and fro, stops to locate the birds and makes his spring in a manner very similar to that of the pointer and setter, and all this without having had his ancestors taught to drop to command and have a net thrown over them while on birds. The same characteristics are observable, although in a lesser degree, in the manner in which a common house cat will steal toward its prey and, when at a proper distance, crouch and spring to capture and kill. Cur dogs will draw stealthily, by sight, to a rabbit, woodchuck or other quarry, and spring on it if they can approach without alarming it. But the most convincing property is that the dog exercises the pointing instinct for his own benefit when left to his will. Only by persistent training are his instincts made subordinate to the purposes of the hunter. As to the origin of pointing, it may be said, briefly, that it is unknown, and the cherished conjectures respecting it are poor ones, even for conjectures; moreover, it is as idle to advance any theory regarding its origin as it would be to attempt to explain all the instincts peculiar to the human race or lower animals. Its presence in an abnormal degree or its entire absence is not necessarily any evidence of impure breeding. Instincts frequently vary in intensity in different individuals. Even the strongest of all instincts, the maternal instinct, which is most uniformly present, is nevertheless entirely absent in some individuals, and present to an abnormal degree in others.

The point is simply a preliminary pause during which every faculty of the dog is keenly intent on accurately locating the game preparatory to springing on it. There is nothing cataleptic in the act, contrary to the often repeated assertions that it is so. Neither the senses nor volition are suspended, as can readily be perceived when an untrained dog is pointing, or when the birds run from the point of a trained dog; in either instance, every motion is indicative of consciousnesss and an intelligent intent to capture. Every sense is alert, and every muscle at its highest tension ready for the spring. Nearly all experienced sportsmen have seen a dog bound from his point with wonderful rapidity and capture quails, or prairie chickens, or ruffed grouse, such being his natural manner of obtaining a food supply. By duly repressing this natural inclination to spring, and preserving the steadiness of the point, man subjects the instinct in a useful manner to his own purposes; thus, while primarily the instinct is hereditary and for the dog's special benefit in gaining a food supply, it does not become a mechanical act when exercised for the benefiit of man. However, there is a transitionary stage during training, when the dog is insufficiently experienced in the purposes of the gun, wherein he may prolong his point merely as a matter of compulsion; yet the dog's perceptive and reflective faculties are such that when his judgment and experience are mature he intelligently and zealously applies his hunting powers to assist the gun. Many intelligent acts on the part of the dog, acts which have been observed by all sportsmen of extensive experience, prove this beyond question. For the information of those who may not have had an extensive experience, a few of the acts which are commonly known will be adduced in support of the dog's intelligent application of his efforts conjointly with the efforts of the hunter. When a dog, in roading an old cock prairie chicken, a bird which is a fast and cunning runner, suddenly abandons the trail, and taking a circular course whips in ahead of it to stop its running, then holds and points it until the shooter flushes it, such act is palpably applied to assist the gun. An act of a similar nature is when a dog, roading a running bevy down wind, perceives that he cannot pursue with any certainty of securing a point, backs out a safe distance on the back trail, takes a circular cast and comes up wind on the birds, thus stopping their running and pointing safely. An act of still greater intelligence is when the dog points birds at a distance from his handler, and, being concealed from him, abandons his point, returns to his handler and by every sign which he is capable of making, conveys the information that he has found birds. If the handler understands his dog, the latter leads him directly to them. This accomplishment is not generally observed, first because very few dogs are permitted to exercise their best intelligence; second, because very few sportsmen would comprehend the dog's actions if he did attempt it; and lastly, only dogs of great experience and intelligence acquire such a finished comprehension of details.

A common act, which shows reference to the gun, is when pointing running birds, a dog will turn his head slightly to see if his handler is approaching, and he so directs his acts with consummate skill that they are wholly in the interest of the gun. Many other acts could be enumerated showing that the dog applies his hunting instincts to the service of his master in a higher degree than the mere mechanical; but sufficient is mentioned to show that, with experience, he does so.

There are individuals in which the pointing instinct is

THE FIRST POINT.

very imperfect or absent, and less frequently ones in which the hunting instinct is also weak or absent, yet these instances are extremely rare and are not race characteristics; they are freaks of nature mentally as others are freaks physically. Except in infrequent instances, the instinct is displayed at some period during puppyhood, although different families and individuals vary greatly in respect to the age at which it develops. Occasionally it is dormant until a comparatively late period. Many dogs, remarkable for their superior field powers, showed no pointing instinct before maturity; however, in most instances it is exhibited in the first year, commonly the first months, if proper opportunity is afforded to exercise it. The pointing capabilities vary in the same individual at different times, undoubtedly attributable to the effects of cold, or other bodily indisposition; for the dog, like his noble lord and master, has his hours or days of depression when, consequently, his work is irregular in quantity and inferior in quality.

On the mistaken assumption that the instinct is due to education or that it needs intensifying, it has been said that it is a very beneficial act to take a pregnant bitch on birds, even when she is near the last period of gestation, so that the instinct may be strongly impressed upon the puppies. The hunting instinct of the dog is not dependent on any trifling efforts of man for its perpetuation. Disuse for a short period does not impair it to the extreme degree laid down by theoretical writers, many of whom evolve a theory from their imaginations; then the theory, by repetition, rises to the dignity of a fact in popular estimation. As a case in point, the instinct to hunt rabbits is quite as strong in the pointer and setter as the instinct to hunt birds, simply because both are their natural prey. This instinct has been restrained and forcibly repressed by sportsmen and trainers through an unbroken number of generations. Constant pains have been taken to prevent the exercise of it, and equal pains have been taken to afford opportunity to intensify the instinct to hunt birds; yet the instinct to hunt rabbits is just as strong in the dogs of to-day as in those of bygone ages. The desire to hunt rabbits appears to be, in fact, stronger than the desire to hunt birds, for dogs will hunt them from an early age and, if left to themselves, will often do so as a matter of choice. Even dogs posssessing indifferent merits of physique and poor merit in work on birds will hunt rabbits voluntarily with great dash and determination. Their fondness for hunting them is often so strong that severe punishment is required to break them of it. This leads us to the point that no breeder would entertain the proposition for a moment that it was necessary to hunt a pregnant bitch on rabbits to perpetuate the instinct in her progeny; nevertheless, the instinct is precisely the same in both instances, and has no reference to a man and gun, but to a food supply in a state of nature. Birds are but one part of the dog's natural prey; by education he can be taught to hunt birds and entirely ignore rabbits, or *vice versa*, but his instincts are not changed thereby in the slightest degree.

The early exhibition of the pointing instinct is often paraded as a decisive sign of superiority. The assumption is fallacious. Some puppies will point when very young, even when a few weeks old, yet such early exhibition of the instinct is of no material advantage. Until the dog has some maturity and working powers, pointing has no value. If there is no manifestation of it within the first year, or year and one half, the puppy should not be condemned if his other qualities are sufficiently meritorious to promise well. Probably at some period of the second year the instinct will develop. A dog of this kind may work weeks in succession under the most favorable conditions in respect to birds, grounds, handling, etc., and still not show the slightest indication that he descended from a race which pointed instinctively, and with the discouraging prospect that he would not point even with further weeks of trouble and work; nevertheless, the trainer should not be discouraged. In the human race, instances of the late development of the mental powers are not uncommon. Many boys who are stupid at school and simple at home show a superior intellect in mature years, far surpassing their more precocious companions. There will come a day when the dog catches the scent just right; when all the conditions are favorable, he will jump instantly into a point, straighten up and strike an attitude as if he had done the act for months. It will seem to be so easily done and such a matter of course that it will be a cause of wonderment why it was not done before. After a point has been made once, there is no difficulty in getting him to repeat it and establishing the act permanently in its proper relations, if the handling is done properly.

The failure to exhibit the pointing or hunting instinct, which is a very rare occurrence, is commonly ascribed to the entire absence of the race characteristic and often it is so stated as a fact, plainly a hasty and unwarranted conclusion as applied to all cases. Such may be the fact, and probably is at times, although, from the evident complexities of the subject, it is impossible to determine the cause accurately; therefore the most positive statement in regard to it can be but little more than conjecture. It is much more reasonable to presume that the sense of smell is functionally imperfect, or never was present, and the dog is thereby rendered incapable of pointing or pursuing by scent, from being wholly unconscious of the presence of game. This view is peculiarly plausible when it is considered that many congenital infirmities of the senses are not uncommon. Dogs are, in some instances, born deaf, or blind, or partially so. Certain diseases will sometimes impair the function of scenting or wholly destroy it, distemper being the most common. It frequently is very difficult to determine whether errors in work are due to carelessness or a poor nose. It can only be known by careful watching. A dog, possessing even a moderate nose, may do very satisfactory work providing he has good judgment, is careful, and free from excitement. If he will point tame chickens by sight, it is still more probable that his sense of smell is absent or imperfect, if the pointing or hunting instinct is not exhibited in the field by pursuing game by the powers of scent. It may be mentioned, by the way, that the pernicious practice of pointing tame chickens by sight about the yard should be discouraged. It does not, in the least, usefully improve the dog's pointing, and may, with some, be disadvantageous. If a puppy has persistently pointed chickens by sight, the habit of so pointing becomes fixed and still asserts itself in field work. When pointing game birds, the desire to see the birds is intense, and the consequent necessity to press too closely to effect the purpose may lead to aggravating and unnecessary errors. He should be required to depend entirely on his nose and judgment in locating and pointing his birds, which cannot be done by permitting him to point tame chickens by sight; besides the fact that such is detrimental to his field work, it ends in killing poultry sooner or later, when favorable opportunity occurs, and once acquired it is a difficult fault to cure.

Pointing is very easily established in the greater number of instances by actual field work on game, and all that is required is to afford an abundance of opportunities. When the dog makes his points naturally, they can be gradually established and prolonged by art. It is better to let him point quite a number of times before killing birds over him, so that the act may become confirmed and improved as much as possible; for when he sees a few birds fall, smells the blood and learns that the gun will kill, he may become, in a great measure, unmanageable and abandon all attempts at pointing. All his previous training, for the time being, may be entirely ignored. The determination to catch the birds or gain possession may be stronger than any fear of his master. Sometimes it requires a great deal of tact to get him by this period without developing other faults, such as running away, blinking, gunshyness, etc. If he is not wholly confirmed in pointing before birds are killed to his points, he may become so thoroughly unsteady that it will require weeks to adjust him so that he will again point with any degree of certainty, and the same method will then have to be pursued that should have been adopted at first, namely, let him point a number of times until he has some steadiness, only killing occasionally at such times as he can be kept under restraint, this part requiring the exercise of judgment; if he is earnestly intent on a bird being killed, shoot and miss. It is not at all essential that many birds be killed over a dog of such disposition in his early training; on the contrary, it may be injurious, since he may run riot, looking for a dead bird when the gun is fired, thereby causing complication and trouble. This is the maneuver shown by the average dog; but there may be timid and indolent dogs that can only be stimulated by shooting birds over them at every opportunity, and even permitting them to break shot betimes. Very little assistance can be given a dog to teach him to point aside from giving him ample opportunity, and if he will not show interest in birds, no assistance can be given. If he will road to a flush, he may be corrected just enough to make him wary of flushing, yet not enough to prevent him from roading; still there must be some indications of natural pointing, otherwise the dog is not worth the trouble of training. However, as explained elsewhere, it in many instances requires quite a long while to determine this.

When the puppy is drawing to a point, after he has learned how to point, he should be permitted to do so in his own manner. If there is danger that he will flush and chase, he may be given a word or two of caution; but the disgusting and interminable bawling out of orders, and the loss of temper common to amateurs, and a few who are not precisely such, are wholly unnecessary and accomplish no good; on the contrary, they do much harm. Such turbulence has its origin in the fears of losing a shot rather than in intense zeal in dog training.

Now, in steadying a dog to his point, it should be borne in mind that a short point, in most instances, will serve the dog's purpose, *i. e.*, to spring and capture when the birds are located; but by the art of the trainer, the point is prolonged and steadied to serve the purpose of the shooter. In place of flushing the birds, he is taught to avoid doing so. This, if properly taught, is done by slow degrees. If it can be done by repeated opportunities and kindnesses, such is the best method; if the dog is willful or heedless of his handler, the whip must be administered after every willful flush. In this connection, as with others where punishment is advised, the trainer must observe careful judgment as to the severity of the punishment and the disposition of the dog, for there is a turning point from the effects of punishment that must be carefully watched for; if passed, the most courageous dog may become cowed and blink, then there is trouble for the trainer.

If the dog is extremely difficult to control, a light checkcord should be attached to his collar. When he points, the trainer can step on the checkcord and walk along it to him. When the birds are flushed then, the dog is under control. If he struggles hard to chase the birds, a spike collar may be put on to restrain him. It will not only prevent him from struggling, but if he is specially headstrong or resentful, he may be given a little slack line and snubbed once or twice, which will deter him from chasing, in most instances. If he breaks the point and flushes the birds, when caught he should be taken to the exact place where he should have stood and then scolded well, or whipped if necessary. Keep him down for several minutes; if he manifests great impatience, make him remain until he is patient. If he is inattentive to scolding or his handler, a cut of the whip may be given; this part, as before mentioned, must be applied with caution, as, if overdone, there is a probability of more faults in a moment than can be corrected in a month. Timid dogs, particularly, must be steadied to their points with the greatest care and gentleness, and if they are at all whipshy, the whip must not be applied at all in connection with pointing. The trainer cannot be too careful in avoiding any acts which will cause blinking, and at the first sign of indifference or distrust with reference to pointing, he must withhold all punishment until such times as the dog's self-confidence is restored, if he needs it at all. There is no branch wherein it is more essential that master and dog should be on good terms than when pointing is being perfected; for if the dog dislikes his handler, it is simply a form of shyness—gunshyness, whipshyness, birdshyness or handler-shyness, all originating in fear. Unlike many other branches of a dog's education, there are several things to be accomplished at one time, the success of which is entirely dependent upon the dog's confidence and inclination. If he will not go to his birds voluntarily, there is absolutely no way to force him to do so; therefore it is evident that however badly he performs there must always be a certain amount of his interest preserved; he must not be punished so much as to destroy his interest in hunting, else the training ends. By various little arts, applied as opportunity offers, much can be done to establish stanchness with very little punishment. If the trainer can walk in from the front, or take a circular course and get nearly in front of the puppy while he is pointing, he will be enabled to catch the dog's eye and can easily check any signs of unsteadiness. No effort should be made to make the dog overstanch on his point. He should be permitted to maneuver and point his birds in an intelligent manner, and any stanchness beyond what is necessary is a fault, which will be shown by standing after the birds have run, or on a hot footscent, or by standing after the birds have flown away.

It is essential to train the dog to point at a proper distance from his birds—neither too far nor too close; in the former case he gives the handler a great deal of unnecessary trouble in beating over a large area of ground to flush; in the latter, he will make a great many unnecessary flushes; therefore, notwithstanding that pointing birds at a long distance is considered a desirable quality by many, since it is asserted that it denotes a keen nose, it is undesirable in practice. It does not necessarily denote a keener nose than that of a dog which points closer, but it denotes bad judgment in the dog or unskillful training in the handler. To correct the fault if he is well advanced in training, judicious punishment should be given for flushes caused by pressing the birds too closely. This will make him cautious to avoid flushing. The dog which stands on the footscent or points at too great a distance requires encouragement by kindness. Gradually he will acquire more boldness; and flushes which he makes occasionally may be overlooked discreetly. In fact, tact must be exercised in applying methods, it being quite as important as method itself. The intelligence and natural capabilities of the dog are important elements in training. If he is honest, but a bit stupid and frequent errors result from his working powers being inferior to his zeal, trust to frequent opportunities to correct it; if the dog is timid, encouragement is the chief reliance; if headstrong, the whip and kindness combined; if the dog is cunning, he is necessarily intelligent; the trainer can anticipate his schemes and checkmate him. He will learn to deceive a kind master in a dozen ways to accomplish his purpose; when he commits an error, he will affect a look of apparent innocence. A good whipping usually serves to sharpen his faculties. The dog which has a poor nose, or is mentally weak, should be dealt with leniently; he is blameless for his natural imperfections. In all cases the punishment is simply an auxiliary if properly used. The trainer, with all the punishment that may be necessary, can treat the dog kindly and make him understand that the punishment is entirely associated with certain objectionable acts, and aside from them there is nothing to fear.

If the puppy ranges well, it is better to hunt him alone, thus cultivating a spirit of self-reliance and making the pleasure of finding and pointing dependent on his own efforts; moreover, his efforts are not interrupted by any faults of another dog, for it frequently happens that the good work of one puppy is spoiled by the bad work of another, and the correction of one may disconcert the other. Two partially trained dogs generally show great ingenuity in working birds in their own manner, but it is not the manner that the shooter approves. One untrained dog is all that the amateur should attempt to control at one time. However, if it is desirable to give the puppy a great deal of experience in a limited time, as, for instance, when he is being fitted for field trials, an old dog which is steady, intelligent, and free from any acts of jealousy may be worked with him to special advantage. Wide, fast ranging is very fatiguing to a young dog, particularly if the weather is warm. The old dog is worked to find the bevies, while the puppy is kept at heel; when a bevy is found there is then an opportunity for the puppy to back; and afterward on the scattered birds of the bevy, he can have frequent opportunities to point. However, it is not advisable to keep him under constant restraint; let him range awhile so that his work will preserve its uniformity; special work in one branch to the exclusion of others is to their detriment.

No dog is properly trained unless he can be trusted to point his birds properly without any orders whatever. This proficiency can be established by experience and making him, as much as possible, rely wholly on his own judgment in pointing. He can be assisted prudently in subordinate details, as, for instance, if he roads on the back track up wind and loses the course of the birds, a little assistance will readjust him; also he can be prevented from running riot; but, if he has experience in his work on the birds, he should be allowed to attempt the point in his own manner, even if he is certain to flush. After he has committed the fault, if willful, he can be punished for it in the same manner as for any other fault, increasing the punishment with each repetition, if he will submit to it steadily, until he becomes attentive to correct pointing. Unintentional flushes, however, should be excused. If a dog is trained to constant supervision and prompting on his points, he naturally requires it in his work through life, and, at best, it is extremely faulty since the dog frequently finds game when out of sight or out of hearing, or beyond control. When trained to point honestly on his own judgment, he is just as trustworthy when out of sight as when in sight; or when a mile away as when within reach of the whip. Remember that the perfection of training is to educate a dog so that he will work to the gun *without* orders.

It should not be forgotten that the instinct to point is

sometimes present, in certain individuals, to an abnormal degree. Dogs having it to such a degree may be pointing perpetually on any strange scent, or by sight on any strange object, when taken afield, and at such times can only with difficulty be stirred; and then the next instant but to point again. A chip, stump, a bright flower, rock or likely place for game, all serve the purpose to point. Sometimes a dog, having this infirmity, will point immediately after being taken out of a wagon or taken into the field. Such dogs are wholly worthless for field work. The pointing instinct is sufficiently developed if present in a useful degree, and as it is so present in the greater number of individuals, it needs no intensifying.

Both setters and pointers stand to their points naturally, although some, having more caution than others, crouch more or less, while a small percentage drop to the ground, this manner being more frequent with setters than with pointers. With many it is only occasional, as when they suddenly discover that they have unconsciously drawn too close to the birds and are in danger of flushing, the act undoubtedly being one of concealment rather than one of inheritance. However, habitually dropping to point is frequently the result of too much discipline in dropping to wing, the training not remaining fixed at the degree which the trainer intended. At the first flutter of wings the dog drops instantly; as the habit becomes more and more fixed by constant repetition, he anticipates the rise of the bird, and drops too soon. Finally he will stand during a second or two and then drop, which soon ends in dropping to his points regularly. This is hastened if the handler, from fear of not having steadiness, as frequently occurs, drops the dog on his point before the birds rise; or if he is worked hard day after day, he may drop on his points from fatigue.

By far the greater number of expert breakers train their

dogs to perfect stanchness. Training the dog to flush regularly to order is not good training; in fact, this pernicious practice is not tolerated by experts. It is much more difficult to train the dog to perfect stanchness than to teach him to flush to order or signal, since in the former instance he is required to do an act against his will; in the latter, one in consonance with it. He may perform nicely during the first season or part of a season, but from being required to flush at first to please his master, he improves on the act, and at last learns to flush to please himself. In shooting woodcock, ruffed grouse, or quails in thick cover, it is sometimes necessary to order the dog on to flush, but it should only be done when absolutely necessary, and stanchness should be made imperative at all other times. It has been said that in some kinds of shooting it is a necessity; this in no wise affects the injurious consequences to the dog's work. There is no expert handler but what can easily teach a dog to flush to order, and probably there are none but what have so taught a dog at some time; yet, as a class, the handlers condemn it as being unnecessary, harmful and unskillful. Nevertheless, there are a few sportsmen with whom the method finds favor, and such should train in such manner as enhances their pleasure.

In teaching pointing, the training should be confined strictly to game birds. The amateur is disposed to think that it is a gain if his puppy will point field larks nicely. If the desire is to make the dog a true finder, larks should never be shot over his points. Hunting and pointing them should be discouraged as much as possible without punishment. The larks should not be shot at. By thus ignoring such work, he will eventually, in most cases, quit hunting them and confine his work to game birds. If game birds are scarce, almost any dog will point larks occasionally. If an aged, trained dog, from taking pleasure in hunting them, persists in pointing them to an offensive degree, the whip may be liberally applied at every repetition until he will blink them, the effects, however, being noted and governed with reference to the performance on game birds; for in being broken from hunting one he might be broken from hunting all. By showing approval and praising him when game birds are pointed, and disapproval and punishment when larks are pointed, the trouble generally may be avoided. Pointing rabbits can be corrected in a similar manner. Nearly all dogs will point turtles, snakes, etc., but so rarely, owing to the scarcity of such animals, that no notice need be taken of it. In teaching the dog to work to the gun, it is well to remember that the pointing instinct is not specially implanted in the dog's nature for the benefit of some man to shoot at the pointed bird with a gun; and that if the gun were not present the act would be incomplete and meaningless.

It is commonly supposed that false pointing is caused by an inferior nose. Dogs possessing the best of noses will exhibit the fault at times, particularly when excessively fatigued. It may be caused temporarily by severe punishment for flushing, in which event it disappears in time if the cause is not perpetuated. If a dog is naturally a confirmed false pointer, there is no remedy for it; such faulty act being probably from inability to distinguish between scents, or an abnormal development of the pointing instinct. If it is shown occasionally, ignore the point as much as possible. Punishment aggravates the fault.

The amateur invariably over-estimates the harmfulness of flushes in early training, generally because he is more intent on shooting than on dog training; many times the dog is punished, not for the flush, but for the lost shot. If the trainer wishes to know the true value of a flush, let him leave his gun at home, and thus the cause of his anxiety being absent, his judgment will be unbiased, and he then can see how the puppy, in his inexperience and awkward methods, was blameless. The flight of a bird consequent to a flush was not the unpardonable offence and irritating disappointment that it seemed when the gun was in hand. When the amateur can take his gun afield, take an interest in training and judge the merits of work as calmly and without prejudice as when the gun is absent, he has then attained a very correct frame of mind for conducting the training properly; but ordinarily it requires a long time to get the amateur past the stage where he feels a greater desire to kill birds than to train dogs.

Flushing is seldom a willful fault in a well-trained dog, although it occasionally is so, yet punishment is inflicted many times when the dog is wholly blameless. There are many conditions under which the dog is almost certain to flush. It is impossible for him to scent birds, with any degree of certainty, down wind. If after a bevy, he may cautiously road down wind, but unless he has rare judgment and experience, he will flush. If he stops to a point under such circumstances, he discriminates by the intensity of the foot scent, but he seldom points under such circumstances with certainty. An intelligent dog, if left to his own will, generally takes a cast around and below them to get the wind. Going across wind is practically as difficult for the dog to perform in as going down wind, if the birds are straight ahead of him. Any position which precludes the possibility of the scent reaching the dog's nose is sufficient to excuse him for any flushes.

Every sportsman of experience has seen a retrieving pointer or setter trot squarely over a dead bird, while searching for it, wholly unconscious of its proximity; yet if within fifteen or twenty yards of it down wind, the dog would scent and go directly to it. Under these circumstances, the novice invariably declares that the dog has no nose, for he cannot conceive how a dog can trot directly over a bird without scenting it. The breeze undoubtedly carries the scent with it and dissipates it over larger and larger spaces, much the same as smoke is wafted from a chimney-top by a gentle wind, although as a matter of course the scent is much more volatile; hence it is apparent that a dog, standing over a dead bird, could not scent it so well as when he was several yards down wind, and this from perfectly natural causes.

Flushes due to inexperience are also excusable, and therefore the puppy should not be punished for them. He may be held in check for awhile, and both voice and manner may show disapproval; and thus he is taught that it is a faulty act. So keenly can the dog's love of approbation be developed that he will exercise the greatest care to point so as to hold his birds; if a flush unfortunately happens, he will show by his crestfallen demeanor that he feels mortified at the failure. Some dogs show the same feelings when laughed at—dogs having such sensitive natures deserve to be treated with great consideration, and their sensibilities ought not to be abused.

The novice is also predisposed to blame the dog for flushes which he in no wise committed. A command given to a dog when near the birds may cause a flush, and the proximity of the dog is considered sufficient evidence to blame him. At certain seasons of the year when birds are wild, the sound of the human voice is sufficient to flush them instantly. Chickens on the prairie after the frosty nights of September, or after the high winds of autumn set in, are extremely wild. Quails, after a frosty night or a cold rain or wind, are very difficult for a dog to point, and it is rendered almost impossible if the handler gives loud orders, or a loquacious companion is present. This is particularly aggravating if such companion thinks the dog blamable for the flush, which is usually what he does think.

A puppy, in training, after he has learned to point, should not have birds shot to his flushes. Points alone are to be associated with the killing of a bird. Thoroughly trained dogs can have birds shot over points or flushes without injury to their training if kept within it, but such has no application to the proper manner of training a puppy; however, as in other cases, this is open to exceptions as in cases where it is desirable to encourage a timid or backward dog, etc., no rule in dog training being strictly arbitrary.

CHAPTER XI.

RANGING.

Ranging is the act of beating out the ground in a more or less irregular and informal manner, the dog in a great measure exercising his own judgment in conducting it.

It is a noticeable fact, and one frequently commented on by sportsmen, that the half broken country dogs, as a class, are wonderfully intelligent in working ground to the best advantage, and are also successful finders of game. This is not, as many suppose, from natural superiority; it is due to the natural and better manner in which they acquire an education. Their owners, in most cases, neither know nor profess to know anything of expert training. If the dog will point sufficiently long to afford his handler a shot, he does all that is expected or required, and in respect to ranging he is left free to suit himself, consequently he works almost entirely on his own judgment. Usually he is very quick to take advantage of all kinds of working opportunities. From unhindered experience, he learns to seek for the haunts of birds; and by cultivation his judgment becomes so excellent that he can tell a promising corner with as much precision as his master. Little sheltered nooks and thickets, which the comparatively inexperienced city dog would pass by unnoticed, he diligently searches; he knows all the wiles of the birds and how to circumvent them, taking advantage of favorable conditions of ground, wind and cover, with masterly skill. He learns the daily habits of birds, for during the feeding hours in morning and evening he searches through the cornfields, the stubbles, the favorable open grounds; during the midday hours he devotes special attention to the cover. He whips around the likely corners in the promising places, dexterously taking the wind of them, and he plans his work so well that the same ground is not worked twice, nor likely places left untried. He is averse to working in bare fields where there is no likelihood of finding birds. His range is irregular, wide or close, according to the peculiarities of the irregular grounds or promising places; withal the course of the handler is constantly observed as a guide and base of operations. He exercises his memory and profits by it, since, if hunted a few times in the same grounds, he learns the haunt of every bevy and will thereafter find one bevy after another with rare cunning and facility. He learns the variable habits of the birds caused by the changeable fall and winter weather, and the consequent changes in cover and food supply, and governs his efforts thereby; he learns to mark the flight of live birds and the fall of dead ones; thus by his superior knowledge, resulting from the experience unhampered by ceaseless training, he excels.

To hunt at his utmost capabilities, aside from all considerations of hunting to the gun, the dog needs no training by man; he merely needs natural opportunity to show that he is a fierce, intelligent and persistent hunter. When in pursuit of prey, he exerts every endeavor to effect a kill. Nor are his efforts blindly impulsive; when he has had experience, he pursues and captures with great address, and exhibits an admirable knowledge of means to ends. His knowledge, however, is acquired by degrees as his experience enlarges, and every experience adds more to his capabilities.

The young sportsman may have a dog which quarters

perfectly and is obedient to all orders, yet, when compared with a dog which knows how to hunt, he makes no showing as a finder, there being an important distinction between knowing how to quarter and obey orders, and how to find birds. The owner of the obedient dog is loth to believe that the self-educated dog is superior, and commonly ascribes the disparity of performance to pure luck; yet, if he could have noted carefully without bias, he would have seen that every act of the self-educated dog was performed with rare judgment, and that he was guided in his efforts by a full knowledge of the situation. Now, it is not to be understood that a strictly self-educated dog is a properly trained dog, nor that a dog which will obey all commands is such—the properly trained dog combines the excellences of both by blending the two acquirements in his education.

The fact that a dog learns by experience has been noted by many sportsmen, but comparatively few realize its importance in training. The expert trainers, however, were not slow to perceive its advantages and utilize them. A quartering dog is not in the competition with a dog which ranges well on his own judgment. While the latter is ranging from one likely place to another, after an intelligent plan to work all such places without unnecessary waste of time or effort, the former is uselessly hunting large areas, after a formal manner, where both handler and dog know there are no birds.

The method of developing ranging at its best is the same for all sections of country, although the manner of applying it in work to the gun will necessarily need modifying to meet the requirements of different kinds of game. It consists in the very simple and efficient way of giving the dog free opportunity to learn it himself, then training him to the necessary acts of obedience. The puppy, whether courageous or timid, needs a preliminary experience in ranging and chasing rabbits, roading and chasing birds within a certain period of time. In this manner he thoroughly learns the details of hunting, and this accumulated knowledge of details and art in applying it is the perfection of the dog's hunting abilities. To learn skillful methods of hunting, he must have an experience similar to that of the average country dog, thus when hunting there is no uncertainty in his purpose or actions. His energies are concentrated in determined efforts to find birds. If he has this kind of preparatory experience, which may be comparatively long or short accordingly as the dog is bold and quick to learn, or timid and backward, he usually is a diligent and efficient worker all his life. Timid dogs, particularly, require a period of self-hunting to acquire the necessary courage, experience, and self-confidence; indeed, with such, it in many cases is a necessity. With self-willed or courageous dogs, while they do not need encouraging, they need self-hunting opportunities to learn methods of pursuit and the wiles of the birds, for birds are very cunning in evading the dog, their natural enemy. The length of time required can only be determined by the progress of the dog. The opportunity to hunt without hindrance is not to be confounded with self-hunting as exhibited by a dog which ignores the gun entirely, hunting for his own satisfaction; in the former instance the dog is permitted to hunt by himself for his best development, but he does not abandon his trainer; in the latter, the dog is naturally averse to hunting under any restraints.

It is well to note the dog's gain in progress and confidence, so that he may be taken in hand at a proper juncture for field education, otherwise he may become obstinately headstrong and correspondingly difficult to reduce to submission.

The amateur generally reverses the natural order of education. He tries to educate him first, and give the experience afterward, if any is given at all. A dog improperly trained in his ranging by having been kept under perpetual restraint may, in working, appear to be ranging well, but is simply ranging without any intelligent plans. He is running on all kinds of ground, and not systematically going from one likely place to another. This is particularly noticeable when he is hunting with a properly experienced dog. The inferior dog, from a system of incessant suppression, has no motive other than to run while in the fields.

The ranging may be impaired by working the dog too constantly against the wind. The dog, from habit, becomes accustomed to guide his course by it, and cannot work well in any other direction. If the handler walks down wind, the dog turns up wind at the end of his fling, and may come close in front or behind his handler; or he may turn up wind, then turn down wind and resume his cast across, thus making a loop at the end of every cast. This vicious habit is also at times caused by over-training. A few dogs naturally turn in at the end of their range. Whatever the cause, it is important to correct it in the beginning, if possible. Often it will require the most persistent effort to do so. If the dog comes in, meet him with the whip, flourishing it, and drive him out to his work if his disposition will admit of the use of the whip without injury to his work; if not, he should be ordered to drop, then turn him in the proper direction. Another faulty method, one very annoying to the handler and damaging to sport, is the constant running out and immediately returning to the handler. If the running is done in a course parallel with the handler in a line ahead of him, it can hardly be called ranging, and is next to worthless. By a self-hunting experience the dog learns to hunt in any direction, regardless of the direction of the wind, or rather, he can take advantage of it, in any direction except down wind.

A dog must have a fair degree of speed which he can maintain at a uniform gait for a reasonable length of time, if he has any pretensions to ranging. The slow dog is only fit for woodcock shooting, or quail shooting in cover. The fast dog is the king of the field. He can be trained to work in an open country, ranging wide and fast, or he can be trained to work at a slow gait in cover or small fields. A dog having great powers of speed and endurance, when trained to go at half or quarter speed in a cover country, is unquestionably working with greater ease than a slow dog which is running nearly at the top of his speed; yet neither the fast nor the slow workers are necessarily good performers merely because they are fast or slow. If a dog has a good nose, he can perform going at a high speed quite as well as at slow speed. Some fast dogs learn to adapt themselves, with wonderful readiness, to different ground and different species of game; for instance, a dog may be a wide and fast ranger on quails, yet on woodcock he may entirely change his methods to harmonize with the changed requirements and surroundings. But whether fast or slow, no dog can perform well if his nose is functionally poor.

All amateurs are inclined to work their dogs too slow. When left to his own volition, the dog soon becomes a fast and accurate worker, as may be observed when dogs are feral. The abilities of the dog in respect to fast work are well exemplified in the performance of foxhounds in the chase. The hound soon learns to adjust his speed to his powers of scent.

As to what constitutes the proper scope of ranging, much depends on the character of the ground, and the habits of the birds. In the prairies of the Northwest, West and Southwest, when hunting for chickens, a dog is not ranging too far so long as he can be seen well, provided that he is working to the gun. Half a mile on each side of the wagon is not an unusual range for some of the best chicken dogs, and a quarter of a mile to an eighth is about the average. It is plain that the more ground a dog covers, the more birds he will find. On quails, the dog is necessarily forced to range more irregularly, the character of the country, the habits of the quails and their habitat, differing entirely from the corresponding ones of prairie chickens. In the East, and in some sections of the West and South where the grounds are rough and cover dense, wide ranging is inadmissible. Nevertheless, the methods of work are commonly slower than need be.

The dog, for any kind of ranging, is not trained properly unless he will range wide or close as desired. On scattered birds particularly, it is necessary to have him so that he is controllable within a certain range. If the dog refuses to work close, the checkcord, or checkcord and spike collar, may be put on him, thus affording means to control him. In hunting for bevies he should be taught to turn to a note of the whistle, or to look to his handler when he hears a note which signifies attention, and should obey a signal of the hand which follows.

To preserve the dog's ranging powers at their best, it is better, and, in the end in most instances, quicker, to bring the dog under control gradually. Too much violence and haste before the dog learns the purpose or application, is commonly the cause of delay.

Few sportsmen realize the dog's natural capacity to learn methods of pursuit and ability to solve perplexing combinations of circumstances. This capability of improvement and cunning in pursuit is common to all breeds of hunting dogs. The foxhound, when experienced, unravels the most complicated puzzles in trailing, which the fox, with his novel and wonderful store of resources, can construct. The foxhound in receiving his education cannot have, from the nature of it, much assistance from his master—probably to his advantage, for, if it were possible for his master to meddle, he might never attain such perfection. If several foxhounds are run in company regularly, as is commonly the case, they not only learn to do their utmost in the chase, but they learn to take special parts of the work which are mutually advantageous in promoting the general success. Also, they learn each other's capabilities, for a note from a leader, which they know by experience to be true, will instantly be honored with due attention. Some become so cunning as to cut across country and come in ahead of the chase, others drop out and wait in a favorable place for the pack to drive the fox back by them.

Probably no one peculiar act of intelligence is so commonly known as that of running cunning exhibited by experienced greyhounds. When two inexperienced greyhounds chase a jack rabbit for the first time, they run perfectly true, each exerting his utmost hunting powers in direct chase. Generally, if a greyhound is in good running condition, he is a shade or two faster than the jack rabbit, particularly at the start. The two dogs, in a straightaway course, will generally press the rabbit so closely that it is forced to use defensive tactics peculiar to it, namely, owing to its peculiar physical formation, it can stop suddenly while going at tremendous speed, dodging to the right or left, and quickly starting off at full speed again. The hounds cannot turn so short, owing to their physical construction, although some will turn in a wonderfully short space; in addition thereto, their much greater weight and consequent momentum works to their disadvantage in turning. If two hounds run together a few times, they perceive that it is a decided disadvantage and frequent cause of loss to be both thrown wide at the turns. They then learn a special method of directing their efforts in a manner which is easier, more successful, and mutually advantageous—one hound presses the rabbit at his highest speed from the start, the other hound running comparatively at ease several yards behind, with ears pricked up, and keeping a very critical eye on the situation. The hound which is forcing the running soon turns the rabbit; on the instant, the waiting hound cuts across the corner and in turn takes up the running and forces the pace; the other hound has been thrown a little wide on the turn, but in the general effort there has been a positive gain—one hound has cut across the corner, is nearer to the rabbit, and the other hound is running cunning in a commanding position waiting for the next turn; meanwhile the rabbit has been at his highest speed. This is continually repeated till the poor rabbit, bewildered and exhausted, turns shorter, slower and oftener, only to find that the prairie seems to be full of hounds. At last, with a hound playing within a few yards of it, one on each side, a cunning scheme applied near the end of the chase to drive it to certain death whichever way it goes, the poor rabbit makes a last turn, a hound springs forward, reaches out his long neck and head sidewise, gives a sudden twitch at the flank, trips the rabbit, and before it can regain its feet it is in the jaws of the second hound, a victim to misplaced confidence in the power of matter over mind. In the chase, all the different distances are gauged and the mutual play timed to a nicety. They not only learn a finished manner of running cunning, but they learn to estimate correctly and take advantage of the individual capabilities of each other. For instance, the hound which is running cunning will rear high in front at proper intervals, without losing his stride or speed, to see if any gain is being made on the rabbit. If he notes that his companion has made his best spurt without being able to turn the rabbit, he immediately spurts in turn and takes up the running himself.

The setter and pointer, from the peculiar nature of their prey, have to exercise even a greater degree of intelligence; yet their first attempts, from inexperience, are very awkward and ineffective. Two, in chasing the common rabbits in company, learn to run cunning like greyhounds; but, after a short experience, the dog learns that his nose is a useful organ, and he depends on it more and more. Dogs are very observing and imitative. If two dogs, one old and cunning, the other inexperienced, are permitted to self-hunt together, the inexperienced one by observation alone will soon learn all the cunning dog's tricks and their application. In the case of a timid dog, or one which is backward from any cause, a self-hunting experience with an aged dog is always beneficial.

The whole superiority of the expert handler, aside from his skill as a tutor, lies in permitting the dog to develop his powers to their utmost capabilities in a natural manner. Whether this preliminary experience requires a week or a month, or more, it ought not to be neglected.

In the South the greater number of trainers hunt from horseback. As a rule, dogs range wider when so hunted than when the trainer is afoot.

Until discipline is fairly well established, two untrained dogs should not be permitted to range together. The boldness and disobedience of one encourages like traits in the other. If one is jealous of the other, or follows him about, no good work can be expected under such circumstances.

The dog should be required to work on the right or left with equal impartiality as the peculiarities of the grounds require. The habit of ranging entirely on the right or left, to the exclusion of the other side, is very undesirable, and decreases the value of the dog's work.

If a sportsman wishes to work a brace he should endeavor to have them supplement each other in any weak parts of their work; for instance, if one is good on coveys the other should be good on scattered birds; if one is a poor retriever, the other should be a good one; if one is excitable, the other should be level-headed, etc.; but both should be as good as possible in all respects.

CHAPTER XII.

ROADING AND DRAWING.

Roading is the act of following the trail of the birds, with more or less quickness by the foot scent.

Drawing is the act of approaching the birds by the body scent. This manner of determining the location of the birds is commonly performed with much greater quickness and precision than by roading. Dogs which can draw in a superior manner, will scent birds at astonishingly long distances under favorable conditions of wind and temperature. Sometimes at a distance of several hundred yards they will draw straight, or nearly so, to a bevy, at full or half speed, with nose high in the air. There are dogs which perform poorly after this manner as after any other manner. The brilliant performers are not common; if a sportsman has not had an extensive experience with many fine dogs over a large territory, he may have hunted during a long life without having seen one which performed in a brilliant manner.

A dog which locates his birds by the body scent, probably does so in a less degree than is commonly supposed. Undoubtedly he has the power of recognizing the foot scent and discriminating between it and the body scent; and at times, can draw to large bevies by the body scent alone. The writer believes that a dog of this kind is not guided alone by the body scent in the greater number of instances. It is more reasonable to suppose that he follows the aggregate scent of all the tracks as if they were one trail, having thus an easy course which enables him to go with undiminished speed directly, or nearly so, to the birds. Sometimes, instead of going directly to the birds, he takes oblique lines to them, his course then being slightly zig zag, but the high nose and quick execution are always characteristic. That the dog can follow the foot scent with a high nose is sustained by the analogous manner exhibited by foxhounds when in pursuit of their prey. Every foxhunter has seen the hound run at high speed many yards from the true trail, yet following the course with accuracy by the scent in the air alone. However, it is unquestionably true that a dog which performs well by drawing apparently by the body scent, has very sensitive scenting powers and can detect the presence of birds a long distance by their body scent alone when the wind and temperature are suitable, as may be observed occasionally when a bevy is flushed, marked down, and the dog cast off to find them, there being then no trail to follow; but the phenomenal long draws are not then exhibited unless the dog has cunningly marked the birds down by sight, which some intelligent dogs will readily do; and the novice may mistakenly think the dog drew by scent when he really drew by sight; hence it is more reasonable to ascribe the greater number of phenomenal performances to the refinement of skillful roading, than to the powers of the marvelous, even if opposed to the common belief.

Many dogs have a manner of locating their birds which partakes both of the manner of roading and drawing. They road with a high nose but follow the trail by feeling for the scent, and progress with more or less speed; generally at a trot. When near enough to the birds to catch the body scent, they abandon the foot scent and draw directly to them. A skillful performer of this kind is an excellent dog to shoot over, and is next in merit to one that skillfully hunts for the body scent alone.

The dog which follows the trail slowly but accurately, picking out foot scent of single birds of the bevy, and plodding after them methodically by sure degrees, may afford good shooting notwithstanding his painful slowness. On single birds in warm, dry weather when the scent is poor, he will accurately follow a single bird, the trail of which would be imperceptible to the dog which carried a high nose. Still, the slowness is a great objection.

The most imperfect manner of roading is exhibited by dogs which place their noses to the ground, sniffing and pottering in an area of a few square yards. Such are wholly unable to determine the course of a bevy, but are usually zealous to do their best. Often they persist in sniffing in one place until the patience of the handler is exhausted. Punishment will not correct the fault. Undoubtedly the dog's manner of roading is governed by the sensibility of his scenting powers and intelligence, hence he is unable to exceed his capabilities.

Another very annoying and worthless manner of roading is when the dog, from extreme cautiousness, drops to the ground on a hot scent carefully swinging his nose right and left, close to the ground in the segment of a circle, sniffs the scent deliberately, and is loth to move. He walks or crawls with painful slowness, continually repeating the stopping and sniffing. His fault may be due to natural over-cautiousness or to excessive punishment for flushing. Birds in rainy, cloudy or windy weather, when they are not disposed to seek concealment, will run completely away from dogs of this kind. The dog cannot be called a good performer which cannot, at least, road nearly as fast as the birds can run. Slow roading may be successful when the birds are lazy and indifferent, but when they become wild or restless from unpleasant weather, the slow roader becomes a very poor performer.

BREAKING AND HANDLING.

Much can be done to assist a dog in training by letting him alone. More dogs have their powers injured by interminable meddling and punishing than from any other cause. A dog which roads his birds quickly and accurately should not be interfered with in any manner; unless he abandons the trail or runs riot, no dog should be interfered with in this respect—then the order, *Steady*, may be given merely to compel him to renew his efforts in a systematic pursuit, but the manner is his own. Throwing him on his own resources develops all the abilities in him; he improves constantly by experience, consequently is able to do more and better work from week to week; on the other hand, if constantly harassed and balked, he may become excessively cautious or a potterer, or both. A common fault with sportsmen and amateur trainers is in constantly asserting rigid supervision. When the dog is roading, he should not be checked and ordered here and there, even if there are a dozen places close by which are crowded with birds—in the imagination of the handler. The dog's nose and judgment in finding and locating the birds are always much better to depend upon than the handler's intuitions, yet it sometimes requires several seasons for him to learn this simple fact.

A dog which excels in an inferior method of roading is better than one which performs poorly after a good method; thus a dog which roads his birds accurately and fairly fast by foot scent is incomparably superior to one which carries a high nose, works for the body scent and makes a succession of blunders. The manner is excellent if the dog has the functional powers to execute it, but if incapable he will make wretched blunders. The best dogs will occasionally waver or hesitate when puzzled or foiled, but the dog, which does so habitually is naturally inferior or has been badly trained.

If the handler positively knows that the dog has made

one error in roading which he is unable to correct, he should under such circumstances give him the necessary assistance; for instance, if the birds have run straight down wind and the dog, mistaking the course, roads up wind, which even aged dogs will sometimes do, the handler can give him a cast down wind and around the birds, thus correcting the error; but it should be a fixed rule to let the dog learn all that is possible from his own unassisted efforts.

If a dog is too slow in roading, yet has good nose and judgment, he may be kindly encouraged to go faster, provided that he is trustworthy in pointing, in respect to which the trainer must observe due discrimination. At all events, special pains should be taken to guard against pottering, extreme cautiousness and irresolution, even if the dog has to be encouraged to flush and chase—such qualities greatly impair a dog's value, or render him worthless, according to the degree of intensity. The whip is wholly useless to make a slow dog fast, although it is very effective to make the fast dog go slow. A dog which naturally hunts with a low nose and potters will rarely be above ordinary merit at best. The whip aggravates the evil, it having the effect of making him desist from all attempts at roading, he construing it as a punishment for noticing the scent at all.

The puzzle peg has been more or less warmly recommended by some writers as a cure for a low nose, pottering, etc., they attributing all the faults to the manner and not to the dog's inability—inferring that if one dog performs well with a high nose, all dogs must do so, as illogical as to assume that if one dog can run all day in a certain manner, all dogs could do likewise. Theoretically, it is a very plausible method for forcing a dog to carry a high nose, thereby preventing pottering, etc.; but practically, it is a barbarity, and worthless. Inasmuch as it is never used by expert trainers and is wholly inefficient, besides being wantonly cruel, it is no part of dog training, and will not be described. Even when used, many dogs cannot road if forced to carry a high head, and they suffer many cruel falls from it. When the peg is removed, the dog immediately assumes his old style and habits, and as such are natural to him, they are the best which he has.

In giving the puppy the necessary experience in roading, it is better to work him alone if he is in training for regular shooting, in this respect not differing in principle from that of training in the other main branches. If two puppies are worked together, there is always a keen jealousy in roading, which is sure to cause a riotous flush or chase, or both. Even aged, experienced dogs are not reliable always under such circumstances, if in company with strange dogs. However, after the training reaches a stage at which the puppy is fairly reliable, he may be greatly benefited by experience with an honest, obedient dog. If he has had perfect liberty in chasing and hunting, as recommended in the preparatory field work, he in most instances has learned how to road quickly and accurately; he only needs training with a view to making him steady to his points, it being self-evident that the roading cannot be done too quickly if the dog can locate his birds and point correctly. On the other hand, if he has been constantly suppressed and completely subjugated, and therefore is without any knowledge of methods or possession of self-reliance, he learns but slowly and imperfectly, his handler holding all his attention and thus being a discouragement instead of an assistance.

CHAPTER XIII.

BACKING.

Backing, backsetting or backstanding, synonymous terms, is the act of stopping and standing performed by one dog when he sees another dog point, the attitude assumed by the backing dog being generally much the same as that which he assumes when pointing; yet in most instances the back is less rigid than the point. Many individuals, however, which point well, back in a spiritless manner; and there are occasional ones which will not back at all; others, which cannot point well, back in a satisfactory manner.

Backing, the writer believes, and has long maintained, is a purely intelligent act, one in no wise instinctive. This opinion differs from that of some excellent sportsmen who hold that the act is instinctive inasmuch as it resembles pointing, and puppies will back at a very early age; in fact, they hold that the puppy may back the very first time he sees a dog on a point, when taken afield. This is an extremely superficial view of the case, and also too great an assumption of what constitutes an instinct, as will be shown hereinafter; remarking, however, that it is doubtful whether the act of pointing itself is purely instinctive. The writer has never seen an intelligent dog which backed without any experience previous to his first back, although he has seen a few which backed in the first time they were taken afield; but such had invariably run at large with other puppies and had learned to back them, while hunting birds, without any training; but such cases are extremely rare. Even in pointing, the dog usually needs several opportunities before he will point, and several more before he can do it intelligently. Those who have watched puppies at play in the fields must have noticed that backing gradually developed with experience. The puppies gallop about, stopping to a point betimes on little birds. At first they point and chase together, then by degrees they learn to point or back alternately with more or less steadiness. The common explanation is that what was a matter of education through many generations in the past became fixed in the dog's nature, and became an instinct. There is no proof whatever that it was regularly a matter of education, nevertheless, that does not for a moment detract from the positiveness and assurance of the assertion. In the chapter on instinct, in the *Origin of Species,* Darwin remarks : " Domestic instincts are sometimes spoken of as actions which have become inherited solely from long continued and compulsory habit; but this is not true."

Matters which are purely educational, and which are to subserve the purposes of man, do not become instinctive however long repeated, as may be observed in the case of the horse which has been uniformly educated, generation after generation for centuries, either to the harness or saddle, or both; yet he is not apparently benefited thereby, so far as educational instinct is concerned. Undoubtedly, education improves the intelligence of the animal; but in respect to the dog, the field education is trifling compared to that which man unconsciously gives by association to each individual under domestication every day in succession, therefore it is more reasonable to suppose that all knowledge appertaining to domestication would become instinctive sooner than a few details of field work. It also is astonishing that if backing, by education through a long series of generations, became instinctive, the other educational qualities, most of which were more uniformly and thoroughly taught and practiced, did not at the same time and in like manner become instinctive. If backing were uniformly taught there would be more show of reason in the theory of instinct, but outside of the dogs trained by experts, backing is not generally taught. A multitude of shooters own but one dog, and hence cannot train the dog to back. Many, who own more than one, cannot enforce backing or do not attempt it; and such has been the case for many generations. Thus a large percentage were never educated to it, or never had the opportunity; hence it would be impossible for the so-called instinct to be so uniformly present in a race, by education, when but an exceedingly small percentage of the race was taught it. All sportsmen know that it is not present as uniformly in setters as the instinct to point; in fact, it is very irregular in all its properties. If it were an instinct, it would be more likely to be obliterated by disuse than to be originated and perpetuated by education. Nevertheless this is all by the way, for it has very little relation to the true nature of instinct. It is well known to scientists that a true instinct is for the self-preservation of the individual or the perpetuation of the species. The instincts of birds to build their nests, sit on their eggs, migrate, etc., are true instincts. The bird will build the first nest without any experience, quite as well as the last. The young of mammalia nurse instinctively. A multitude of other instances could be enumerated, but they would all show that instincts were strictly for the benefit of the individual in gaining a food supply or other acts of self-preservation, as in fleeing from danger, etc.; or in the preservation of the species. Hence it is extremely unreasonable to suppose that since animals do not acquire an instinct for the benefit of other animals, the dog would acquire an instinct which he could exercise very irregularly at the best, and in many instances not at all, for the benefit of a man who carries a gun; an instinct separate and distinct from any individual profit to himself, but solely devoted to not interfering with his master's sport.

It is equally absurd to assume that a trait so common, though irregularly developed under the artificial restraint of training, is meaningless. It cannot have its origin in transmitted habits under domestication, since it is not useful in that state; it could not originate as an instinct by education, since the latter is too fragmentary and is practiced during a comparatively brief period of the educated dog's life, and therefore could not affect the progeny; it is quite as reasonable to suppose that a man would instinctively know the meaning of a language because his ancestors had, during many successive generations, been educated in it. In fact, the theory that it is an instinct, resulting from education, offers a multitude of inconsistencies, conjectures and insurmountable obstructions.

By assuming that it is an intelligent act, all these difficulties disappear. There are many different phases which prove that it is the result of understanding. It should be borne in mind that birds are but a part of the dog's natural prey, an important fact in explaining his mode of pursuit. It should also be noted that a dog can change his methods more or less to make his pursuit of game more successful. Thus the method of pursuing a rabbit is different from that with respect to birds. A litter of half-grown puppies when following and pointing tame chickens about the yard show the purposes of the act. After a little experience, when one points, the others will stop and wait, and as the chicken runs to one side or the other, the backing puppies cut across the corner and cut the chicken off, thus acting jointly with greater success. This act may appear amusing, but the puppies are serious, and have an intelligent purpose; if left to themselves, they will kill the chicken. The act partakes in character of the "running cunning" of greyhounds, and adds to the chances of capture. Without doubt, in hunting rabbits, which are also the natural prey of pointers and setters, the manner of approaching and pursuing is as successful to them as analogous methods are to the greyhounds. They quickly learn that certain acts and indications, as drawing, half-pointing and feathering, denote that game is present; and they learn by a little experience that, by co-operation in the pursuit, they are more successful, as is also well established by the methods adopted by foxhounds and greyhounds. Thus by noting the purposes of the dog's acts when he applies them to his own purposes, their real use is known; at least it is more reasonable to so interpret them than as being for the use of man after forcing them to subserviency.

There are variations of the act which are purely and admittedly due to experience, namely, backing the gun, an act more frequently observed in wild fowl shooting by retrievers. The dog observes that certain cautious acts of the shooter signify the proximity of game, and thereupon follows at a safe distance, drawing and backing. A variation of the same act, due to the memory of the use of the gun and a knowledge of its purposes, is exhibited by some setters and pointers; if the gun is placed to the shoulder, they will back instantly; a few will back if the gun is held in the hand in a position as if ready to shoot. This trait was utilized at field trials occasionally on marked birds till the judges became too thoroughly informed, and trickery in a great measure became obsolete; however, it is only just to remark that trickery was confined to the few.

That both pointing and backing may be exhibited as an act of intelligence is established by many well attested cases, and is mentioned by several authors. In youthful years the author had a terrier, which was an excellent squirrel dog, and which, from his own intelligence, learned to back the gun. As further showing what a dog can learn in the way of correct methods from his own powers of observation, an intelligent act of this terrier will be described: He, by seeing an occasional ruffed grouse shot during the squirrel hunts, learned that they were also objects of pursuit. From learning to recognize the scent, he gradually improved so that he would follow the foot scent slowly and truly, stopping on a point in a manner that would not be discreditable to an average pointer or setter. He had all the characteristics of a small, pure bull terrier in size, form, pluck and general habits, therefore nothing could be attributed to inheritance from a chance setter or pointer cross. On the trail of a ruffed grouse, he was cautious, silent and attentive, which was entirely opposed to his manner of hunting squirrels, yet he learned both methods from his own experience. Here were precisely the same acts, exhibited by a bull terrier, which are commonly attributed to instinct in the pointer and setter, and which were performed as a matter of pure intelligence.

At all events, the amateur who expects to find that backing is a regularly developed instinct, or that the puppy will back within the first time he sees a dog point, is elaborately preparing numerous disappointments for himself.

Usually there is no disposition to back manifested until a longer or shorter time after the dog has learned the meaning of a point, which, by the way, is very quickly. He may learn then in four or five opportunities, or four or five months of opportunities, the uses of a back; this being dependent upon his powers of observation, freedom from jealousy, and the skill of his handler; for the dog can be materially assisted by education in perfecting this so-called instinct.

In teaching dogs to back, many different phases of character will be exhibited—some individuals have an intense desire to take the point from another dog; others never observe any advantages in backing, being incapable of solving complex details of hunting; others again know its purposes fully, but do not care to observe it—such may back when the trainer is in sight and steal the point at other times; others will back at the first sign of game made by the other dog even if the latter is roading, and some are unreliable, and a few cannot be taught at all; the latter can be taught to drop or stop to a pointing dog. However, the greater number of setters and pointers can be taught to back with a fair degree of uniformity, but there is absolutely no uniformity in the length of time required to teach it.

When the trainer is first attempting to teach the accomplishment, he should not, under any circumstances, work the dog with one which is a false pointer. Even if an aged dog, which will back honestly and well, is hunted with a false pointer, after backing two or three false points, he will thereafter entirely ignore the other's points, learning by experience that they are erroneous and meaningless—thus showing that if backing is an instinct, it is a very intelligent one. With trained, experienced dogs, a false pointing companion is not of any importance except for the time being, their judgment being so good that they learn what dogs to back and what not to back, according to the pointing dog's reliability. It might be shown here by innumerable citations that instincts do not improve by the experience of the individual having them, and that there is a close degree of uniformity in their exercise by each individual of a breed—one bird of a species builds its nest similar to those of every other bird of that species; all birds of a species migrate about the same time to the same latitude; bees construct their honeycomb of the same material and in the same shape, and all without knowing for what purpose these acts were performed. It might be shown that intelligent acts performed by one individual differed greatly from those performed by other individuals, being quite as variable as the intelligence of the individuals; but the subject is too voluminous to dwell on at length. Suffice it to say that the dog comprehends the purposes of backing since he distinguishes between a reliable dog and an unreliable one; that he improves in the application by experience; that the act varies greatly in different individuals; that opportunities are necessary to learn it; that it varies a great deal in different dogs according to their inclination or intelligence; that it is serviceable to him in a wild state, and that therefore it is not an instinct implanted to oblige some man with a dog and a gun.

Nevertheless, if the amateur has a veneration for tradition and honored beliefs, and hence believes it instinctive, it will not adversely affect the training if he follows the directions hereinafter given.

If the young dogs are worked together before a certain degree of discipline is established, they will probably be more or less unmanageable in all branches, although, singly, they may be good workers. It is very beneficial to have the puppy prepared to such a degree that he will work with regularity and is under fair control, before working him in company; with a timid dog this is indispensable. Besides being under better control, he then has a better comprehension of details. As before remarked, the first lessons should be with a dog which is not given to false pointing. If the dog cannot observe some desirable results from the act of pointing, it is meaningless to him.

When the dog is pointing, the handler should call the

puppy to an advantageous position to see the point; a few opportunities should be given him to learn the meaning of it. The first acts of the puppy are generally devoted to attempts to steal the point. These should be checked as much as possible without injuring his ardor. When he attempts it persistently, he may be dropped to command on signal; if he will not obey them with a fair degree of certainty, he is not properly prepared. If he is inattentive from his own experience, a mild process of compulsory training may be begun. Put a light checkcord on him. Expert trainers seldom use a checkcord in this branch, it generally being superfluous. When the dog points, the puppy should be kept to the rear, and the manner of the handler should be extravagantly cautious and deliberate, while walking forward slowly to flush. The puppy is eagerly observant of the extraordinary care and caution, and at the same time is greatly impressed by it; indeed, he may unconsciously imitate the cautious movements of his handler. When the birds are flushed and a kill follows, the puppy has observed what the point, caution and accessory details resulted in, and the next time, or few times thereafter, may stop to watch it of his own volition, which is a back, or the inception of one. If, when the handler walks forward to flush, the puppy leaves his place either with the intention of following his handler or stealing the point, the handler should return and place him in the exact spot which he left. If he will stand with any steadiness, looking curiously on at the proceedings, do not disturb him, for such is a very good incipient back. By repeating these lessons with a grave demeanor and great caution, the puppy by imitation and observation will assume similarly precautionary measures. It has been noted hereinbefore that the puppy is very imitative. This may be observed if the shooter while walking assumes an air of great caution and expectation in his movements; the puppy is immediately impressed by it, although the act should not be practiced as a deception.

With the average dog, this treatment will be sufficient to establish backing if the dog is afforded sufficient opportunity. Yet a few dogs will be found which are very backward, and the lessons may not have any visible effect in promoting the purpose; nevertheless, the lessons must be continued precisely the same as if each one was the last, and would effect the purpose. Other little arts may be introduced. When a combination of circumstances combine to favor it, the puppy may come running in while the dog is pointing. He then should not be interfered with in any manner. To caution him is sure to defeat the purpose. If he does not see the pointing dog until he is close on him, so much the better. When he does see him, his surprise is so great and his caution, from a comprehension of the purpose of the act, is so stimulated, that he may stop instantly and back with great perfection. He may hold it with steadiness or break it in a few seconds; but once done, it is easy to establish steadiness by repetition. This is the usual manner in which many dashing, high-spirited puppies make their first back; those which are backward in their lessons also frequently learn in this manner.

There are individuals which, notwithstanding a full comprehension of the act of pointing, will ignore all method from their intense jealousy or desire to get to the birds. With such dogs the whip is beneficial. If the dog presses forward when he ought to remain on a back, whip him. The same results are effected by fear of pain that should have resulted from experience. This method requires discretion in its application. Just sufficient to effect the purpose is all that is necessary.

The dog which has no perception or interest in respect to backing can be taught to drop when he sees a dog on point.

When it is observed that he sees the dog on point, drop him on the instant. By continually repeating this with opportunity, giving him a cut of the whip on the shoulder when circumstances are favorable to back, he will eventually learn to drop at sight of a dog pointing, the act having the same effect as a signal of the hand. However, if he is cranky, excessively timid, sour or sulky when crossed, and will not show indications to back, it is better, if he will work well as a single dog, to leave backing out of his education entirely. Instead of making him a reliable backer, he may be rendered worthless in other more important branches. At all events he can be taught to drop promptly to order or signal, which in most cases answers all the practical purposes of backing, *i. e.*; to keep one dog from interfering with another when pointing.

A dog which is used to train puppies with, besides being reliably true in his points, should have a cool judgment so that he will not get excited; and honesty, so that he will not take any mean advantages when his handler is busy. Certain individual dogs, if there are any unusual occurrences such as whipping, loud orders, etc., applied to another dog, will abandon the point, or press forward to a flush. Old dogs which are accustomed to seeing puppies trained learn to comprehend the situation perfectly, and will hold the point regardless of any orders or punishment the puppy may receive; yet they are perfectly obedient if they observe that the orders are directed to themselves

After more or less effort, with very rare exceptions, all dogs can be taught to back, but there will be very irregular degrees of proficiency in the results. With a few, as in pointing, the act can be intensified to an injurious excess. Dogs of deferential disposition will watch a self-confident dog with close attention, particularly if he is a skillful finder, and the moment he shows signs of game by roading or drawing, they back rigidly, and it is difficult to move them. After such dogs become fatigued, they devote their entire attention to the finding dog and back from a combined desire to see the dog point and stand still to rest. A dog which backs prematurely in this manner causes a great deal of annoyance or lowers the standard of the work when hunting with a dog which backs honestly and accurately. If the latter roads or shows the slightest indication of finding, he is instantly backed; then he catches sight of the backing dog, infers that it is a point, then backs in turn—thus they stand backing each other. After being sent on, the act may be repeated again and again with more or less frequency, much to the disgust of the hunter and prejudice to the sport. After awhile, the more sensible dog learns that there is no accuracy in his companion's work, thereupon he probably refuses to back him at all times. If he is of an impatient disposition, such experience may make him distrustful in his work with other dogs. Two experienced dogs, which work correctly, rarely back each other. Pointers are more predisposed to this fault than setters.

If a trained dog should at any time become unsteady on his backs, he should be whipped in precisely the same manner as for any other willfully faulty performance. However, if the slightest unsteadiness is corrected at its beginning, there will be comparatively little trouble. By neglecting little faults, the greater ones ensue, and the training is then irregular and less skillful.

CHAPTER XIV.

QUARTERING.

Quartering is simply ranging in an artificial manner. It is obsolete in this country. The different field trial associations recognize it to the extent of giving it small value in the scale of points, but in practice it is not considered. The writer has seen braces, in their heats at field trials a few years ago, taken into the open, after their finding qualities had been determined by the dogs ranging as they pleased, to test their quartering. If it had advantages, it would be diligently cultivated at all times.

In England it is said to be a very useful accomplishment, the fields, cover and habits of the birds favoring this formal manner of ranging. In this country it is wholly unnecessary in any section, and a downright injury to quail shooting. However, there are a few who still believe in its advantages for all kinds of shooting and all kinds of sections.

No attempt should be made to teach it until the dog has learned to take delight in hunting, and has established dash and range. If he is tied down to formalities in his ranging from the start, his enterprise is checked, he has no opportunities to independently exercise his judgment, or get the experience which he should have.

Before the trainer begins the lessons in quartering, it is necessary to give the puppy at least a fair comprehension of the signal of the hand waved to the right or left, and the note of the whistle which signifies attention. Such preparatory training is necessary to have some control over him; to turn him at the ends of his casts, to send him in the direction desired. It is absolutely essential that the dog be worked across and up wind. The wind acts as a guide to the dog, and quartering, contrary to the common belief, can only be practiced when the handler walks up wind. Under such circumstances, the dog can take his casts to and fro with the nicest precision. Any attempt to enforce the method when the handler is walking down wind is merely sacrificing the hunting for the sake of a useless formality. At the end of his casts the dog is disposed to turn up wind, hence when the handler is walking down wind the dog is repeatedly turning in the wrong direction, thus entirely disarranging his quartering. If the handler directs his course across wind the matter is still worse, as the dog must then range directly up and down wind to preserve the formality.

Theoretically, quartering is when a dog takes his casts at right angles to the course of his handler, each cast being parallel to all other casts, if the handler pursues a straight course. The distance between the parallels is supposed to be about the length which a dog can command with his nose; hence it is apparent that the parallels cannot be an arbitrary distance apart at all times—when the scent is good they may be wider; when it is poor, they should be narrower; and they differ with different dogs.

The method of teaching it is very simple, to wit: The handler walks up wind invariably; he casts the dog off to the right or left, giving the proper signal with his hand. When the dog reaches the end of his cast, a signal of the whistle is given to turn him; when his attention is caught, if he does not turn properly, give a signal of the hand to turn him in the right direction across wind. By also walking in that direction while giving the signal, it will assist to start him aright; when he takes his cast correctly, resume the course up wind. It would seem to be an easy matter to teach a dog to quarter, after reading the instructions of authors. The dog is simply required to go to and fro at right angles to his handler's course. As a matter of fact, the first attempts will be far from accurate, and will have very little resemblance to quartering; but with experience and unremitting attention, he will slowly improve. The training consists in holding him constantly as near as possible to these parallels, day after day and week after week, until from the very force of habit he follows them without any assistance or direction from his handler. After the dog is proficient, he must be hunted against the wind continually when at work—the quartering dog which will quarter or work well in any direction is so extremely rare that he does not affect the rule in the least.

Now, if the handler aspires to train his dog to such a degree of refinement in quartering that he can sit on a fence on the windward side of a field, cast his dog in a straight line to the lee side, then have the dog quarter the field back to him, as is described by some authors, he is leading a very forlorn hope. In about nine cases out of ten, when the handler seats himself comfortably, the dog does likewise; the tenth dog is generally deficient in sense or experience. About once in a lifetime the average sportsman who owns the average number of dogs may own one dog which will have consideration enough to hunt a field while his handler sits on the fence. However, it is hardly worth his while to attempt training the average dog to this accomplishment, for he will be disappointed.

In teaching braces to quarter, it is necessary to teach each dog singly until he is passably proficient, it being self-evident that if one dog is difficult to train to it, two at one time would be immeasurably more so. Some writers advise that an old dog be started with a young one to teach him quartering. It would be just as reasonable to suppose that an inexperienced man could learn wing shooting by simultaneously shooting with a crack shot. There are certain things which both man and dog must learn from their own individual experience.

When the dog is reliable, he may be run with a brace mate which is equally so. Here a variety of complexities may arise that could not appear when working singly. One or both may be inordinately jealous, and may flush or chase as a consequence; one may defer entirely to the other and follow him about constantly, which act spoils the brace work completely; one may be a much faster or wider ranger than the other, which also impairs the value of the brace.

A brace should work perfectly independent of each other, and theoretically their parallels must alternate, hence each must take wider parallels than when working singly, so that they will not be closer than their noses can command. Or one dog must quarter on the right side, the other on the left side of his handler, a line ahead of the latter in the direction of his course being the point at which the dogs turn. Theoretically, the dog does it to mathematical accuracy; practically, the handler should only strive to approximate to it; if he can do so he does well.

In quartering, as in ranging, the dog may develop a variety of idiosyncracies; he may take a short cast on one side and a long one on the other; he may turn up wind at one end of his cast and down wind at the other; he may come to his handler at regular intervals, perhaps at every cast; he may in the middle of a cast take a turn to the rear of his handler and repeat it regularly at each cast or at one particular cast; in fact, there are a great variety of whims which he may exhibit, but the aforementioned are the most important.

As mentioned under the head of Ranging, one should be

excellent where the other is weak, thus both combined should have all possible abilities and accomplishments.

The disadvantages incidental to quartering are as follows: If the quartering dog has hunted on certain grounds during a whole season, he must hunt them day after day in the same formal manner. Undoubtedly he has learned where the haunts of many bevies are, but the strict formality will not allow him to use his knowledge. Under any circumstances the quartering dog is at a disadvantage in comparison with an intelligent ranger, but after the first day's hunting on certain grounds, the former cannot compete with the dog which exercises both his memory and intelligence. In consequence of the irregularity of grounds or the varying haunts of the birds, the quartering dog must work over large areas of grounds which are palpably barren; moreover, from being constantly held down to set forms of ranging he cannot exercise his judgment independently, therefore he cannot develop it. In this respect he never can approach the performances of a ranging dog as described under the head of Ranging, although he may have equal natural capabilities. Forms are merely a substitute for intelligence, but in this case they are a failure.

CHAPTER XV.

DROPPING TO WING AND SHOT.

In teaching the dog to drop to wing or shot, the whirr of wings, the sight of the flying birds or the report of the gun have precisely the same significance as an oral command. When taught perfectly, the dog drops promptly at the first intimation with reference to these circumstances. The same care in teaching prompt and full obedience to any other commands would insure the same results. Dropping to wing or shot is an unnecessary accomplishment—in many respects it is disadvantageous and injurious. It is much overrated in the good qualities claimed for it, namely, that it prevents the dog from chasing or breaking shot when the gun is fired. Theoretical writers overlook the fact that if the trainer can teach the dog to drop to shot, he can teach him to be steady to order; furthermore, it is much more trouble to train a dog to drop to shot and wing regularly than it is to simply steady him. The real reason of its popularity is the ornamental finish which it is supposed to confer on a dog's work. Dropping a dog to shot or wing may be beneficial in his early training, but merely for the time being, and then only in obedience to an oral order or signal of the hand.

The act is a disadvantage if the dog is a retriever, for it is apparent that he, when dropped to shot or wing in sedge grass or cover, cannot mark the fall of a dead bird, or the flight of live ones. Some intelligent dogs compromise by dropping, then instantly **raising up** in front and peering over the grass to mark the live or dead birds—when they accomplish the purpose, they immediately drop and remain steady till ordered on. The act is particularly objectionable and injurious in cold, rainy weather, on marshy or muddy grounds, or in winter hunting, for the dog must then drop in cold water, snow or mud; if under the circumstances the act is insisted on, it is an abuse of a faithful servant, and a degradation to an intelligent companion. This accomplishment is usually insisted on by owners who have their dogs trained by professional handlers, it being considered both useful in results and elegant in performance; but the amateur, so far as usefulness is concerned, need not trouble himself with it.

If dropping to shot and wing is taught at a proper time, it must be taught during the latter part of the dog's training. There are many things which are necessary to consider and note before it is attempted, namely, the dog must not be gunshy, he must have learned to point birds steadily, and must have no fears of them, or the gun, or his handler. To attempt it earlier is to run the chances of having a blinker or a distrustful dog.

If the dog is properly trained so that he is not afraid of the whip and will drop squarely and steadily to a cut of it on the shoulder, no precautions need be taken against running away; if not, the same precautions may be taken as with a dog which breaks shot. The advantages of training a dog to drop to a cut of the whip on the shoulder are now manifest. It is all the order that is needed, and being trained to it, the dog drops properly without trouble. If not trained to it, the whip always has a tendency to make him run away, at least it distracts his mind from the real purpose, and has no more meaning than a whipping in general. Eventually the same associations must be established, but it will be done in a more irregular manner under less favorable circumstances.

There is no occasion for hurry in teaching it; in fact, it is harmful. The closest observation must be exercised to teach him to drop and not incidentally injure his other work; also to avoid teaching him unintentionally to drop on his points. It is true that some dogs drop to their points naturally, but it is equally true that the greater number do it from education, the latter of course not being so intended, but is so in effect, since the dog so understands and applies it.

Every time a bird is flushed to the dog's point, or every time he flushes one whether unintentionally or otherwise, the trainer drops him by oral command or signal. Frequent opportunities occur when the trainer can walk up beside him, give him a cut on the shoulder with the whip as the bird rises; this must not be done too frequently else the dog drops when he hears the handler walk up, and this may be the inceptive stage of dropping to point. If he has been trained properly in his preliminary yard breaking, he will drop instantly to a cut of the whip. He soon learns to further associate it with the rise of the bird; finally, he associates the act of dropping with the rise of the bird, and the intermediate element, *i. e.*, the whip, can be left out. By dropping him with unfailing regularity, either by command, signal, or the whip, he will, after a longer or shorter time, learn to drop voluntarily.

Occasionally sour, sulky or obstinate dogs will drop to wing when they know that the trainer has the advantage, and will refuse when they have it. Severe punishment is the proper treatment for such cases, making them drop repeatedly to impress it on their memories in connection with the punishment.

The training should not be so strict at times when the

dog is greatly fatigued. He may learn that it is a comfortable position, and for that reason alone may adopt it on his points. Under such circumstances, dogs often drop to their points without any teaching; furthermore, what with dropping to his points when excessively fatigued, dropping to the anticipated rise of the bird, and dropping to unintentional flushes, there is always a probability that the dog may eventually drop to his points habitually; and when he once does so, it is permanent.

CHAPTER XVI.

TURNING TO WHISTLE.

In most instances the dog learns readily to turn by observing the purpose of the whistle, if the same notes in the same connection are regularly used. When first teaching the dog to turn, the whistle merely attracts the dog's attention; the trainer then gives the signal, walking at the same time in the direction he wishes him to go; the dog will, at all events, turn to take the course of his handler. By repetition the dog at last learns the meaning of the note on the whistle. There should be a distinct note for him to turn and take a cast back again; there should be another note which signifies *attention!* so that the handler can give a signal by hand to order the dog in any direction he wishes; and there should be a distinct note which signifies that the dog is to come in.

But some dogs are self-willed, and will evade obedience when they can do so with impunity. The better way with one of that kind is to force him to instant obedience. Take him into a securely inclosed yard, put a spike collar and a stout rope about ten feet long on him. The trainer walks the dog back and forth. Each time he turns, he blows the signal to turn, jerking the dog around at the same time with the collar. Prompt obedience is soon rendered to the whistle, but the lessons, which should be about ten minutes in duration, ought to be given regularly each day until he will turn promptly without force being used. Then the collar may be dispensed with and the lessons conducted in the yard until he will obey the lightest note. If he refuses to go out to a signal of the hand, force may be used to compel him. The writer, by this method, has trained dogs to perfect obedience, which were both headstrong and sulky. To put them under restraint was to induce a spell of sulkiness. They were determined to either work in their own way or not at all. By taking them into a yard as above described, and forcing them to obedience, a superior finish was put on their education. If the dog goes into a corner and sulks, the trainer simply gives the signal to *Go on*, and thereupon drives the dog on with the whip. When he learns that he cannot be disobedient, his sullenness will gradually disappear.

After these lessons, it is better to leave the spike collar on him for a few days while in field work. The presence of it will cause him to be obedient many times when, if it were absent, he would refuse to obey; besides, it is ready for instant use if he should presume on changed surroundings to be disobedient. This is strictly a forcing method, and should not be used if dogs can be otherwise taught; but the setter or pointer does not live that cannot be forced to obedience by it, if it is properly and persistently applied. The trainer, if he applies it, should continue the lessons until obedience becomes habitual, and the demeanor should be calm, and no loud orders given.

CHAPTER XVII.

BRACE WORK.

Brace work, in the formal manner in which it is practiced in England, finds no favor with American sportsmen.

It is an utter impossibility to make good braces out of all dogs, be they ever so good individually. Necessarily a dog cannot show all his traits when working singly, therefore his capabilities for brace work can be determined only by actual trial. To be desirable, the dogs of a brace must be as nearly equal in speed as it is possible to have them, it being evident that an irregularity in this respect, or in ranging, will detract from their value, since one dog will be doing all the work. They should be nearly equal in style—if one is stylish and the other slouchy in his ways, the contrast is displeasing. A matter of prime importance is that they should work independently. As mentioned in Ranging, one dog should be strong in qualities in which the other is weak. It is a very rare occurrence to find, even among the best performers, dogs which are good in all kinds of work—good rangers, retrievers, good performers on bevies or single birds, having good judgment, speed, range, intelligence, endurance and honesty. Of course it is desirable to have both dogs as near perfect as possible. An inferior training may not be specially detrimental when a dog is worked singly, but for brace work the training must be thorough.

Each dog should be trained to turn to a different note of the same whistle, so that turning both will be avoided when it is desired to turn but one; and in a similar manner, with other commands. Some trainers use a separate whistle and note for each dog, thus varying both the sound and note; but this is hardly necessary since the dog can readily distingush different notes as well as different sounds; however, there are individuals which differ in their perception of sounds—if trained to but one whistle they will turn to the sound of any whistle or any variety of note. This trait cannot be corrected, and therefore somewhat impairs the dog's usefulness for brace work.

Each dog should distinctly understand his name, and none other. If one dog is called by name the other dog must not be permitted to respond to it if he is disposed to do so. Each individual of the brace ought to be as susceptible to distinct handling and undisturbed effort when working jointly as when working singly.

When a bird is to be retrieved, it should be made a permanent and unalterable law that only one dog is to retrieve and he not till ordered. If they are at all unreliable in this respect, a pin about twelve inches long, sharpened at one end, is useful when there is a lesson in correct retrieving. This pin can be pushed in the ground with the foot, and one dog tied to it with a check cord. If he stirs while the other dog is retrieving, take him back to his place and whip him, keeping him at the *drop*. One dog, then the other may be required to fetch the bird several times, the greatest steadiness being required of the dog which is not retrieving. This must be persisted in till the prescribed steadiness is established. When the dogs are finished in retrieving as a brace, by simply looking intently at one and quietly speaking his name, when a bird is killed, he will spring forward and retrieve while the other remains motionless. They can be trained to even greater nicety—either one which the handler looks at and gives the slightest signal to, with the forefinger or a slight inclination of the head, or other slight sign that the dog can see, if it has been associated with the act by proper training, will be obeyed instantly; the other dog will be perfectly steady. It is important, in giving a signal after this manner, to catch only the eye of the dog which is to retrieve; if unfortunately the trainer should catch the eyes of both dogs at the juncture when the signal is given, both would certainly bound forward to retrieve, and if not under the nicest control, would not stop until the bird was reached.

The dogs, when at heel, can be trained to the same degree of perfection as in retrieving. Calling one by name is a sufficient order to send him on. This can be taught so thoroughly that the handler can train a dozen or more dogs to remain steadily at heel, and go out, one at a time, as their names are spoken.

No neglect of any formality in brace work, such as backing, retrieving, etc., can be tolerated. If any fault is permitted to pass without a reprimand, it rapidly goes from bad to worse, and this loose work will adversely affect the work of his companion.

By far the best method of working the dogs in this country, at least where sportsmen are vigorous, all-day hunters, is to work one dog at a time, keeping the other at heel, thus by alternating in the work, uniform effort is maintained throughout the day with less fatigue than if both are worked constantly. In fact, a better average of shooting will be maintained by keeping one fresh dog working constantly, than by two which are run long after they are thoroughly weary.

CHAPTER XVIII.

SHYNESS.

Gunshyness, whipshyness, blinking, and, frequently, bolting, are all caused by fear, hence they are intimately related so far as corrective treatment is concerned.

Gunshyness, in some instances, is, by a few sportsmen, supposed to be hereditary, but the writer, in a somewhat extensive experience with gunshy dogs, has never observed any cases which could be said to have the failing from inheritance. The chief causes are errors in giving the dog his first experience with the report of a gun, a fault common to inexperienced amateurs, and a few who are not inexperienced; and it also may be caused by many inherited infirmities of the nervous organization of the dog caused by bad breeding. In cases where dogs have degenerated through many generations in this respect, they are timid and easily alarmed at any unusual noise; and being afraid of a gun or other noises is simply peculiar to the degenerated nervous system in each individual, and not to an inherited fear. If such dogs were afraid of a gun alone, therefore indifferent to all other alarming noises, generation after generation, it might then fairly be inferred that the gunshyness was hereditary; but with nervously excitable dogs such is not the case; they are fearful of all alarming noises. The writer has seen dogs which, when in a room where a clock struck, would bolt out of the door or window in the extreme of fright. The slam of a door, the fall of a broomstick, or other unusual sound, would produce the like result. It is hardly necessary to add that they were gunshy. The gunshyness, merely an incident of the fault, is mistaken for the fault itself. Unquestionably, dogs of such character are predisposed to gunshyness, but no more so than, from their infirmity, they are predisposed to many other annoying traits.

Frequently good dogs are unnecessarily made gunshy by mismanagement, and quite as frequently the fault is ascribed to the imperfection of the dog. Very few cases, if any, are known where the trainer was admittedly blamable. When puppies are handled properly, the fault rarely appears. It is a safe estimate that four cases out of five are caused by bad management, consequently could have been avoided. Often the first introduction the dog has to the report of a gun is under the most adverse circumstances. The owner takes the dog out, for the first time perhaps, to a strange place. When a favorable opportunity offers, he looks sternly at the dog, shouts *Steady*, and fires, not improbably with five drams of powder with a ten bore. The dog sees a flash, hears a dreadful noise, smells a vile smell of burnt powder, is panic stricken and bolts—the owner shouts loudly for him to come in; when the dog is caught sooner or later, the lesson may be gracefully finished with a lavish profusion of whip, spike collar, and imprecation. If then it can be learned that the dog had an ancestor which was gunshy, such affords ample material, with some furbishing of the imagination, for a learned and lengthy public letter on hereditary gunshyness, whereupon the production finds favor as a contribution to science, and the amateur establishes a reputation as a close observer and astute reasoner. Such a case may apparently be overdrawn, but in the main features it happens frequently, the hereditary failing not being in the dog. In view of the fact that a respectably large number of men have a strong talent for developing all kinds of objectionable traits in all kinds of dogs, it is a cause of wonderment that larger numbers are not gunshy; indeed, it is strange that more do not die violent deaths from the carelessness of some sportsmen. Gunshyness is not confined to the dog. An experienced shooter can be made gunshy, even if he has good nerves. Many men will flinch when a careless companion is shooting; in fact, when afield with certain men, a wholesome fear is both commendable and discreet.

Occasionally a dog will be met with which is so excessively gunshy that it will require weeks or months to overcome it. It is safe to presume that there is no case of incurable gunshyness in any dog free from natural mental infirmities. Many cases have been abandoned as incurable, but they were simply incurable so far as the trainer had made his efforts, hence were incurable only by assumption; if the trainer had persisted, or used other methods, there would have been no doubt of success. The writer never saw but one case of gunshyness which he thought incurable, although he had seen several that required weeks to cure. After working months on this case and exhausting every known means to allay the fears without the slightest visible improvement, it was pronounced hopeless and incurable. Had this view been favored by subsequent circumstances, it would probably have been something toward supporting the view that an occasional dog could not be cured. Fortunately, during the following season, the dog was kenneled on grounds where there was a great deal of trap shooting and in time was completely cured. The changed surroundings also undoubtedly assisted to promote the cure; for a dog can become habituated to expect certain disagreeable sensations under certain surroundings and conditions. Frequently, for this reason, a change of handlers and surroundings is beneficial, the unpleasant memories associated with the handler sometimes lasting long after the fears of the gun are gotten over.

The methods of treating cases which are more or less developed generally differ from each other with different dogs. Hardly any two dogs exhibit precisely the same degree of gunshyness, or can be cured by precisely the same means. Cases which seem to be simple and quickly curable may last with discouraging pertinacity, while apparently bad cases may end suddenly by some adventitious circumstances, such as the killing of a bird with the gun, where the dog can see it, etc. As may be surmised, the natural intelligence, disposition and observational powers of the dog are all important considerations in the method of cure. Such dogs as crouch and become apathetic, or oblivious to all externals, are very troublesome. With such, there is no method but to shoot persistently until they become habituated to the noise. There are individuals which are simply afraid for the time being; they may run away and return of their own volition, or remain away at a distance at which they feel safe. The severe methods are inefficient. No punishment should be given under any circumstances, except that a checkcord may be put on the dog to keep him from running away. It often happens that an amateur, who is not habituated to persistent and patient effort, loses his temper, then adopts the treatment sanctioned by immemorial usage, which is a sequence to his superior reasoning powers; nevertheless, it is plain that whipping a dog for being afraid is not a reassuring method. Every effort to gain the confidence and affection of the dog by the kindest treatment is sufficient, and his trainer should personally give him a run in the fields every day. Everything that tends to hold his confidence, or strengthen his self-reliance, is so much gain.

Shooting over the points of a gunshy dog is extremely unwise. While it might cure him in one lesson if he is not very gunshy, there are many more probabilities that it might cause him to blink his birds by associating their presence with his other fears, and then there is a discouraging combination of evils.

The correct demeanor of the trainer adds greatly to the success of any method. He should affect the greatest unconcern when the gun is fired. After a few moments the dog can be noticed, and spoken to kindly. Any notice taken of him at the time of the firing excites his apprehension, and he naturally thinks that the noises refer to himself. By this course the unpleasantness is disassociated as much as possible; therefore, looking intently at the dog and giving loud orders in connection with the report, only serves to impress it on him that he is the direct object of the proceedings. Running away is an aggravating evil which ought to be carefully guarded against. With dogs of good judgment and which are not excessively gunshy, the trainer can take some chances in this respect.

The dog which will curl up and become apathetic is the most difficult to cure. No persuasion will arouse his attention. Shrinking into a small compass, even on bare ground, appears to give a feeling of security. A dog of this kind should be tied in an open yard where there is not the slightest object to conceal him or give him a feeling of concealment. Then fire about one hundred blank cartridges or explode percussion caps deliberately and at regular intervals, at about a distance of fifteen or twenty feet away from him, taking no notice of him in the meantime. The lessons may be repeated day after day regularly until a cure is affected. A dog cannot remain in a state of perpetual fright; yet a great deal of time may be consumed in curing him; if he is not unusually promising, he might not be worth the trouble.

As the dog becomes accustomed to the noise and shows less apathy, he may be petted and given a piece of meat betimes to excite his interest. Later, taking him into the fields on a light checkcord will be a gain. By taking advantage of little circumstances he will gradually become accustomed to hear the report with indifference. If a small bird is shot in a favorable position for him to see it fall, it may destroy his fears, and the keenest interest may supersede them, thus effecting a cure. As mentioned in the directions for accustoming a dog to the gun, a pistol is the better arm to begin with.

A dog which does not become apathetic from fright is in most instances easily cured. Tie him in a yard as in the preceding instance. If he struggles at a report of the gun or pistol, put a spike collar on him to prevent his doing so. After a few lessons his fright will become less and less, when he may be petted and given pieces of meat or other palatable morsels. The lessons may be given in different places at different times. When given the lessons repeatedly in a certain place at a certain hour, he is frightened before a gun is fired at all, when taken to the place having the unpleasant associations. Constant deliberation, kindness and calmness are indispensable to the best success.

Discharging a pistol at mealtime has some benefit with certain dogs. If one of this kind refuses to come out of his kennel, do not disturb him; take the food away and do not give him any until the next regular feeding time. Continue this treatment until he will come to his meals, which he is almost certain to do after missing two or three. At first it is better not to disturb him by any more shooting, then he will soon learn that the shot is a signal for his meals. All amateurs hurry too much in this method. They shoot during the meal and between meals, promiscuously, thus keeping the dog in a state of constant fearfulness. The greater number of cases can be easily cured by deliberation and tact. If the dog is apparently cured by harsh treatment, it is by becoming habituated to it—he could have been cured much quicker by kind treatment.

If a dog is intelligent and free from nervousness, but little more than an opportunity to learn the uses of the gun is required to effect a permanent cure. A few small birds killed with light charges, shot under conditions favorable for him to see them, frequently allay all fears. A light checkcord should be kept on him at the start, if he evinces any disposition to run away.

If a sportsman does not intend to train his dog himself, it is much better to refrain from any partial training. Trainers much prefer to have a dog wholly free from any experimental attempts. If there is any good accomplished, there are always a number of objectionable traits developed at the same time, which overbalance the little which is taught. A trainer always feels disposed to charge extra for a dog said to be partially broken; and if he is not short of business, he will probaly refuse him if offered, experience having taught him that such engagements are far from satisfactory.

Blinking, or the act of avoiding birds, is not infrequently associated with gunshyness. Excessive punishment for flushing or chasing, or to make a dog retrieve in the field, also may cause it. The trainer thus effects unconsciously what he purposely effects with respect to rabbits, chickens, sheep, etc. In rare instances a dog will be found which is so nervously fearful that the whirr of wings alone as the bevy rises will cause fright and blinking. Instances are known where dogs would have fits under such circumstances, and others would yelp and bark in a delirium of fright. Blinking is simply bird-shyness—the dog is afraid of the birds, and avoids them as much as possible. There is a form of blinking which is extremely rare, although it can hardly be called blinking in the proper sense of the term. The dog, from impatience, great nervous energy, or fear of his handler, will not hold his points sufficiently long for his handler to come up and flush. He points well probably, but abandons his point and is off again with undiminished vigor, hunting for another bevy. If not due to bad handling, it denotes a faulty understanding in the dog. He would be benefited by overtraining to a certain extent so that he would defer more to his handler; also by working amongst scattered birds with a checkcord on, and making him remain until the birds were killed and retrieved. By making him so work in a formal manner till it becomes a habit, it may be cured, although when apparently cured, it may appear at times, therefore the dog having such fault is an uncertain performer.

Blinking is one of the worst, if not the worst fault in a field dog. It generally is cured slowly and with difficulty. At the first intimation of birds, the dog skulks or cowers, and any efforts to draw attention to them, however kindly done, excite more fears, aggravate the evil and accomplish nothing. In many cases where the dog is a confirmed blinker, he may be hunted all day, and apparently find no birds. Such is not the case, really. He is constantly on the alert and at the slightest indication of scent he cunningly avoids them. Only by some trifling momentary change in the demeanor of the dog can it be detected that he is blinking. He may change his course slightly, or sneak a few yards; or skulk and go faster or slower than ordinary; or he may stop, hesitate a second, then turn and take a different direction. Each dog has some act in this connection peculiar to himself that the handler must learn by close observation. When a dog is known to be shy of birds and runs all day without apparently finding, he should be watched very closely. Unless the novice watches with the most ceaseless care, he may not notice anything unusual, and would conjecture that birds were scarce or the dog had not found any. The dog could run day after day without making a find, unless he happened to run into a bevy when the wind was unfavorable. The most unremitting kindness must be shown. Sometimes encouraging him to kill a crippled bird will restore his confidence; sometimes giving him opportunities to chase rabbits, or to flush or chase birds, will have a like effect. Opening birds that have been killed and permitting him to eat the entrails will sometimes stimulate his desire to kill. If the evil is corrected, the subsequent training must be very mild. Constant work and association should be depended upon to complete it.

If the dog is excessively timid, take an unbroken dog with him and by imitation and rivalry he may learn to chase rabbits and birds. If the handler's presence is a source of dread, it is better to give him free opportunity to self hunt, or chase rabbits with hounds. Few dogs can resist the inclination to chase when they hear other dogs open on a trail. If the dog is persistently distrustful of his handler, a change to other hands will be beneficial.

The better way is to avoid the fault by careful training, which can be done in most cases. The trainer should not always consider what he applied the punishment for, but what the dog considers he applied it for. If the trainer whips the dog for flushing or chasing, and the dog, construing it as punishment for hunting birds, stops hunting them, the trainer necessarily must govern his methods thereafter by the dog's peculiarities. Usually an experienced handler can detect or anticipate the turning point between unsteadiness and blinking, and modify his treatment accordingly. Just one whipping too much, or a gun fired at an inappropriate juncture when the dog is more or less gunshy, may entail weeks of the most irksome training, since the dog must thereafter be treated with unvarying kindness without reference to the good or ill he may do. Perhaps he may follow resolutely at heel day after day, in which event he must have his own way until time and kindness assuage his fears. It may be necessary at last to give him whole birds to eat, or permit him to tear the head off while the bird is in the hand. This, as a matter of course, has a tendency to spoil his retrieving, but at times there is only the choice between a spoiled retriever and a spoiled dog. Errors in training cannot always be corrected, hence it is better to avoid them.

Bolting is the act of running away completely; the dog has quit hunting, and has no intention of returning, at least within a reasonable time; and the handler has lost all control of him. It is the worst form of running away. It is generally caused by gunshyness, fear of punishment, or from a desire to be disobedient. This fault should not be confounded with self-hunting, since in the latter fault, the dog has no intention to bolt—he simply hunts beyond control and returns at times to learn the whereabouts of his handler. When a dog runs away, he generally returns home; sometimes he hides at a safe distance from his handler and may return after awhile; sometimes he goes miles and miles, traveling day after day. In training there is a great difference in the dispositions of dogs in this respect. There are individuals which will run away on the slightest provocation; others will not run unless unreasonably punished, and then they may run entirely out of the neighborhood; others again will run to a safe distance and begin self-hunting, and may refuse to pay the slightest attention to him further than to keep in mind his general course; thus there are several distinct degrees of running away. There is no part of training that requires greater tact than catching a runaway dog, providing he does not bolt, this act being uncontrollable. It may safely be laid down as a rule that a hunter on foot or horseback, in a rough country, cannot accomplish anything by running after a runaway dog with the intention of stopping him. It is sure to increase his alarm or stimulate him to greater exertion, and in the chase it is easy to forecast the victor. When the dog runs, the trainer will succeed better if he assumes an air of unconcern, although he should watch the dog closely and covertly to see when he turns to look back, which generally he will do; at that instant the trainer turns and walks in the opposite direction. In most instances the dog will follow cautiously, and as his fears are dissipated, will come in or resume hunting. If he will not come in, the trainer must use a little artifice—sit down where the dog can see him and pretend to be busily engaged at eating lunch; or if there is another dog along, the trainer can make a great demonstration of petting him or playing with him, thus exciting the runaway's jealousy. So intense is this feeling and the desire for approbation that a dog will at times come in, even if he has just apprehension of punishment. If he will not come in for these devices, his curiosity may be excited by earnestly digging with a stick; or by chasing an imaginary rabbit in a direction away from him. Whatever method is being pursued, the greatest indifference and unconcern toward the dog should be affected. Any attention paid directly to him excites his suspicion and hastens his departure, particularly if he has run away before. At times when he keeps at a safe distance from his handler, yet will not run entirely away, some order, such as *Go on*, may be given, and the dog again started in his work; in this manner his mind may be diverted from running away; shortly afterward he may forget all about it. If the dog runs out of sight and does not return in a reasonable time thereafter, the report of the gun will frequently be efficacious in bringing him in if he is fond of hunting and is not gunshy. The same artifice is not to be practiced too frequently. If the dog runs home, follow him, put on the spike collar, and bring him back to the place he ran from, even if it is five miles away. Lead him back and give the collar a jerk betimes to make the return trip as unpleasant as possible. A few lessons in obedience to the order *Come in* can then be given. It is not advisable to cast him off again until his fears are thoroughly allayed. A long, light checkcord may be attached to the collar and he may then be permitted to run, if he will, and snubbed with the checkcord. Many dogs will not attempt to run if they feel the spike collar on their necks, hence it is advantageous to leave it on such when necessary. If a dog is cunning and will not run when he feels the checkcord and spike collar on his neck, he may be deceived by taking off his kennel collar and still keeping on the spike collar; when he runs he may be brought up to a standstill with the checkcord and spike collar. After the dog is restored to his ordinary humor, cast him off; but it is better to refrain from giving him orders until he has forgotten the unpleasantness. If he starts to run, he generally expects to be chased. If he stops to look at his handler, he merely wishes to see if he is in pursuit. If the handler appears indifferent, the manner puzzles him. A dog can read by his handler's actions what his intentions are, in many cases. In hunting on the same grounds, it is unwise to have an unpleasantness twice in the same place, as thereafter, at the slightest alarm in such place, he may bolt. The cause of running away in the field may be remedied by long continued yard breaking, if it admits of being so done. It is commonly a grave error to whip a dog for running away, such treatment naturally having a detrimental effect on the next repetition of the act; nevertheless, a professional trainer who knows his dog thoroughly may do so profitably; but the benefit accrues more from the general superiority of the discipline in all branches than from the transient punishment—it is not discreet for the amateur to attempt it.

On the prairie, the fault is not so difficult to cure, if the trainer has a good horse. The worst runaway dog alive can be cured, under such circumstances, in one or two lessons. It is advisable to take the dog out on the prairie where there is a clear course in every direction for a mile at least. Give the order which the dog usually refuses to obey, and which he considers sufficient provocation for bolting. The moment he starts, not sooner, begin the chase. The pace should be made as fast as possible from the start, for if the dog is not caught within the first mile he generally makes good his escape. It is useless to attempt it without a good horse. Generally, by hard riding, the dog can be caught within the first quarter of a mile. Put on the spike collar when caught, lead him back in a walk to the place from which he started, giving him a jerk with the collar occasionally to keep his mind on his business. When at the place from which he started, take off the collar, assist him to regain his tranquillity, then cast him off, repeat the offensive order, and let him run if he will. He may again bolt, but it is very doubtful; if he does, catch him and repeat the correction. The author, when in Louisiana and Minnesota, broke several, first and last, by this method. The fault was never repeated twice in succession. In most cases, one lesson was sufficient to effect a permanent cure. The second lesson was always all that was necessary. As soon as the dog hears the horse coming and realizes the situation, he extends himself to his utmost. The trainer should keep his course a few yards one side or the other of the dog's course. The dog may stop suddenly, roll on his back and beg, or stop to give up the race. If directly in his trail, the trainer might ride over him, thus injuring him; or horse, dog and rider might go down together.

As in many other parts of training, precautionary measures are the best. By avoiding as much as possible such circumstances as are liable to provoke a runaway, the dog may not learn that he can do so. When the general discipline is perfect, it is then much easier to correct any imperfection of detail. If the dog once learns that he can evade obedience by bolting, there is no limit to the annoyance and injury it may do to the whole training. He improves rapidly in his knowledge of it and may become, in a great measure, wholly unmanageable. Dogs, being very intelligent and cunning, quickly learn what measures are conducive to their safety or pleasure when punishment is imminent or distasteful orders are to be obeyed; but once learned, the handler should trust more to his finesse than to any punishment.

CHAPTER XIX.

UNSTEADINESS.

Breaking shot, breaking in, and chasing are all different forms of the same thing, namely, an effort to secure possession of the prey. It is, to a certain degree, the dog's native manner of pursuit and capture, but is incompatible with the success of the gun. If the dog is trained, the first manifestation of unsteadiness should be appropriately punished, except such cases as have other faults which may be thereby aggravated, such as a tendency to blink, bolt, etc.; with such, simply returning them to the place from which they started to break shot or chase, and giving a scolding, will be beneficial, and if repeated with each offence, will generally effect a cure. The fault, if not firmly repressed in the beginning, soon becomes confirmed, and is one which amateurs cure with difficulty, although it is one of the easiest if the handler can lay aside his shooting proclivities for the time being.

In skillful training, the intent is not to arbitrarily suppress unsteadiness from the start. The matter of making them steady, partially steady or wholly unsteady is one of expediency, as has been intimated in previous chapters.

When the puppy is in field training it is always better to correct the fault gradually. The puppy is not conscious of doing anything but what is perfectly right; in fact, if a novice wounds a bird, he makes a chase in a similar manner. There are expert trainers who not only give the puppy a liberal, unrestrained, preparatory course, but permit him to break shot more or less until well advanced in training. Unquestionably the mode is superior if applied by a skillful trainer, since it infuses dash, self-confidence, eagerness to hunt, and encourages the marking of the flight of birds. It is particularly superior if the puppy shows timidity; moreover, in such cases, it is the only correct one. The amateur, however, would do well to restrain the liberties of an obstinate, hard-headed dog as soon as possible, consistently with his peculiarities.

After the training to the gun has begun, chasing rabbits should be corrected as soon as possible, unless the dog has some peculiarities which will be benefited by permitting it; hence sometimes it is a fault, sometimes not. To break him of this fault when it is such, watch for a favorable opportunity, in a chase, to shoot the rabbit ahead of the dog. This opportunity happens frequently. For a moment the dog thinks the chase a grand success. Put a short cord on his collar and hold it and the rabbit in the left hand. Hold the whip in the right. Thrust the rabbit in his face, at the same time giving him a sharp cut with the whip, and give the exclamation *Hi! Hi!* or any other order which is commonly used to make him desist. Continue the punishment according to his needs and disposition. A few corrections, thus applied, usually cure the ordinary cases. When a dog is unusually resolute, he needs a correspondingly greater whipping. After a few corrections, he may forget himself for a moment, but the warning cry, *Hi!* will suffice to stop him. This treatment is sure to cure him in time regardless of his disposition. It is simply teaching a dog to blink rabbits in the same manner that the trainer sometimes unintentionally teaches him to blink birds. The punishment for flushing, breaking shot, etc., is very similar, hence the distinction in the matter is chiefly in the idea of the trainer; if persisted in to a certain length, the dog refuses to chase; if continued further, the dog refuses to hunt. In this connection, it is worthy of note that in enforcing steadiness to shot and wing, much more care and attention are necessary, since the lessons have greater complexities than those with respect to deterring him from chasing rabbits, therefore much more caution is necessary, and his love of hunting must always predominate over his fears. Any time that he shows symptoms of distrust or hesitation in his work on birds, a modification of methods forthwith is in order. It is always much the safer, and in most instances the quicker way to steady the dog gradually, effecting the purpose little by little. Timid dogs will often stop when they hear the exclamation *Hi!* it being well to remember that dogs of sensitive dispositions can be restrained without corporal punishment, in many cases.

In the case of an aged dog which has broken shot season after season, until it has become habitual, a more radical method is required. Such dogs usually have no fears, and very little respect with reference to the handler. In most cases, the better way is to make them afraid. In breaking one, leave the spike collar on his neck when he is hunting so that it is ready for use without loss of time, or disturbance when he is pointing. Have a light checkcord, one about three-eighths of an inch in diameter, twenty feet long, braided, with a snap securely fastened at the end. Have it neatly coiled so that it will run without snarling or kinking. Walk gently up to him when he is pointing; secure the snap to the ring in the spike collar; flush the birds and permit the dog to run without any caution to check him—let him run to the full length of the checkcord. Do not attempt to jerk him up short—such might break his neck. The lesson will be severe enough; if the handler eases the shock a little, it will have even then sufficient force. If he will not permit the handler to walk close to him while he is pointing, both the spike collar and checkcord may be left on him. To relieve his neck of any undue pressure from the weight and friction of the checkcord, tie it to the ring of the kennel collar with an ordinary piece of twine, leaving a section of the checkcord about six inches long between the two collars; this will then throw the strain on the kennel collar, yet when he chases and is snubbed, the string breaks, and the spike collar then pinches. Pull him back to his place with the checkcord, and make him remain steady for several minutes. If he still persists, the method is still more simple and direct. Go afield with a friend who has a steady, reliable dog. Leave your own gun at home—start with the intention of devoting a full day to dog training, if necessary. Put the spike collar and checkcord on your dog, and keep the checkcord in hand. When your friend's dog points, give your dog as favorable an opportunity to break shot as possible. At the report of the gun or rise of the bird, let him go to the full length of the checkcord; pull him back to place; make him drop, then apply the whip according to requirements. If he shows any hesitation to break, encourage him to do so, let him have his own way, but apply the punishment at every repetition. No dog, however determined, will persist in breaking shot during a whole day under such treatment if birds are plentiful, nor will it soon be forgotten. This method will cure the worst cases.

CHAPTER XX.

TRAINED AND OVERTRAINED.

During the period in which the dog is in training, he must necessarily receive many orders to the end that his work may be made to co-operate with that of the gun. By being kept to formality in certain parts of his work, the formal manner becomes habitual. The dog, if properly trained, thereafter is capable of working intelligently to the gun without any supervision. He roads and points on his own judgment, ranges intelligently, and steadily performs such acts as are necessary to assist the gun. He does not look to his trainer for any orders while ranging, the general course of the hunt being a sufficient guide for him. Continual orders and checks to a trained dog is the crudity of handling.

As to the *manner* in which a trained dog should work, the opinions vary with the sportsmen who live in different game sections of this country, owing primarily to the important peculiarities and requirements of each section, the difference in topography, climate, food supply, habits and habitat of the different species of game in each respective section, making natural reasons for different methods of work; nevertheless, sportsmen of the same section rarely concur in their ideas of what constitutes a perfectly trained dog. Whatever his manner of work, there should always be self-confidence and individuality in it. The trainer, as a matter of course, should train his dog to hunt after the methods that are successful under the existing circumstances; still, by the necessary diversity of work, a dog can be taught to hunt well on different kinds of game in the same or different sections. A dog which has not the most perfect self-reliance in his manner of work, and does not do it to the best of such ability as he has without any prompting, has been imperfectly trained if he needs prompting; and if he does not need it, his handler is unnecessarily officious besides cramping the dog's capabilities, if ordering him continually. Besides working in a formal manner, the trained dog has a comprehension of the general management himself. He marks birds, works entirely in the interest of the gun, and is not only a trained servant, but an intelligent one.

Overtraining is really more objectionable than insufficient training, although few amateur trainers can hardly believe that a dog can be overtrained, their ideas of training being governed more by the question of obedience than by the manner of work with obedience. It is usually the result of too early and ceaseless training, both in yard breaking and field work; this on the one hand; on the other, dogs of peculiarly pliable and deferential dispositions are easily overtrained from even mild supervision, if the trainer does not observe great care. Indications of it are also most commonly observed in dogs which are naturally more or less lazy, deficient in intelligence, or unobservant of their work; still, if a dog is as high-couraged and industrious as may be, by ceaseless training to orders, his will can be wholly brought under the domination of his handler. From looking to him when compulsory attention is required in obedience to an order, he by degrees looks to him more and more from habit; finally, he loses all individuality, looks to his handler for an order or signal voluntarily, and performs his work in the most perfunctory manner—he will stop at the end of every cast and watch for a signal by which to direct his course, and if in doubt may stop again for a repetition of it after going a few yards; he comes in frequently, when working in cover, to receive orders; he works or remains at heel with equal unconcern; he has no purpose beyond his handler's directions; his acts are all mere habits; his dash, spirit and enterprise, from ceaseless dictation, are completely destroyed, leaving an animated wreck of what might have been the embodiment of energy and spirit.

It is advisable to check this fault in its inception as with all others. When a dog is observed to habitually stand at the end of his beat waiting for a signal to direct him, or when he hesitates in roading, or other parts of his work, to receive orders, ignore him entirely; in fact, it is correct to affect that he is not observed at all. In this manner he is thrown on his own judgment. By not receiving commands he will cease to look for them in time. If the discipline has been so thorough and lasting that it has become second nature, he will be an overtrained dog through life.

Nearly all works on training enunciate that, when a dog looks to his handler for a signal, it should be given, thereby firmly fixing the handler's control. Such is one of the most pernicious and incorrect of teachings, if not given with proper qualifications. A dog should work entirely on his own judgment until he hears the note on the whistle, which is the signal for attention, or until he receives a command, oral or by signal. If a trainer has the ability to train a dog to wait at a certain juncture for an order, he certainly has the ability to enforce obedience to commands. Expert trainers consider overtraining a serious injury to a dog's field value, and nowhere does its inferiority show so by contrast as in competition, the dog which looks to his handler for assistance not being in the race with one which works independently.

CHAPTER XXI

CONDITIONING DOGS FOR FIELD TRIALS—HANDLING.

In no other place does improper training, insufficient experience, or poor physical running condition, manifest itself so quickly and perceptibly as in a field trial competition. A dog which is naturally superior, yet out of condition, may be defeated by his inferior which is in good condition. So expert have field trial sportsmen become, that if a trainer has several dogs, they can accurately determine whether he has given them proper experience, work, and training to the gun. If they have been trained under the pressure of the whip, in place of ample experience, it will show by blunders, and fear, or distrust of the handler. If they have not had sufficient work to condition them, they will be soft in flesh, imperfect in muscular development, and thick in wind; moreover, there is a general want of knowledge in details which is brought out in bold relief by contrast with performances of better trained and conditioned dogs. The excellence of any performance is due simply to a knowledge of accumulated detail with native capability, but the latter alone is inefficient.

The real value of a dog in a competition, so far as the trainer's or handler's skill is of effect, is in his preparatory work and physical condition. There is truly some skill necessary to handle a dog well in a competition, but the handler's ability to *help* a dog to do good work is greatly overrated. The common belief that there is unlimited room for sharp practice is wholly imaginary. Do not assume for a moment that all field trial handlers cannot handle and train a dog well. It would be an anomaly if many who make training and handling a profession did not know how to manage a dog skillfully. Do not enter the competition with some vague idea that the dog will be pulled through by your superior skill. Trust more to ample experience and good training and conditioning than to any element of possible handling superiority. Do not make the mistake, at a trial, that, because the handlers and judges may appear to be unobservant or apathetic, they do not know what is passing. It is better to attend two or three trials before coming to a positive conclusion that the handlers do not know what they are doing, that the dogs are inferior, and that the judges are incompetent. After about the third or fourth trial, the novice will detect a multitude of things which he did not know at his first experience. To a spectator, it looks very easy and simple to handle a dog in a trial; it is so if the dog is a good one and properly trained, if not, it is extremely difficult; but the amateur, by an experience therein, will learn many things that he could not as a spectator.

There is an error to which many mature and sensible men are prone, namely, they, or their friends, have a dog at home which can surpass anything they ever saw at a field trial. They would be astonished to find how many errors could be found in their dog's work if an expert were to keep a tally on them disinterestedly. In field shooting, few sportsmen consider a flush a demerit if it leads to a successful shot. Such errors, while not injurious to the bag in private shooting, would seriously injure a dog's score in public competition. The inexperienced spectator always has in mind the dog's work as he has seen it in its best phases several days in succession; if run on strange grounds for an hour, about the average length of a heat, he might make a poor showing for want of opportunity; moreover, a dog may perform excellently well alone, or with familiar companions, while with a strange companion in every heat, strange whistles and commands, he might become excited, or confused, or jealous. The change of food, water, kenneling and long railroad journeys sometimes throw a dog off his work. It would seem that of the great multitude of dogs that are not present at field trials, but which can, nevertheless, beat the field trial competitors, it would be an act of true philanthropy to take one of the multitude to some of the trials by way of a model of what a good dog should be, not to mention the lesser honors and winnings.

The advantages of a superior course of education are of prime importance. The dog which has been trained to work on birds correctly, but independent of any prompting of his handler, will far outclass one which depends on his handler for assistance and guidance at every turn. The one can be cast off with certainty of good performance on his own judgment, the other cannot do so if it would; while the latter is making preparations to do certain work, the former has it done. The system which requires the dog to do the hunting stands distinctly superior over the one which requires the man and dog to do the hunting.

In preparing any dog for field trial, he should not be worked so long at one time as to cause him to slacken his speed or quit work. Whenever it is observed that the dog shows weariness, it is time for him to have a rest, or that work should cease for that day. The aim is to establish a fast pace that he can maintain uniformly for a couple of hours; also he should be trained to work on birds as quickly as is consistent with accuracy. Quickness of execution always gives a decided advantage to the dog possessing it. However, no dog should be encouraged to run at his utmost speed, for when so extended, his attention is taken up with picking out his course, and he cannot use his nose so well as when running more at ease; besides, the pace is so exhausting that the dog usually cannot repeat well. In establishing the pace, due regard should be paid to the quality of the dog's nose; if it is good, he can work correctly at top speed, if inferior, he cannot; hence he will be an inferior competitor, whatever his training may be. This for short competitions. In a private match, a two or three days' race, it would be manifestly unwise to train the dog to other than an all-day gait. In such matches, it is purely a question of endurance; of which dog will quit first; the writer does not believe that the dog lives that can run three days from sun to sun—this after seeing many of the best dogs in public and private. By this it is not meant that a dog may not jog and nose about for three days, but good, fair hunting is meant. Most dogs will be run to a standstill on the second day.

The dog, regardless of his field trial performances or great speed, when worked regularly every day and nearly all day, at least with no reference to fitting him for competition, adopts a steady swinging gallop which he can maintain with ease. Some dogs trot, but such are good to present to a friend. By graduating the work, almost any intermediate gait may be established. Exceptional dogs will be found which, while having capability to work well one or two days, have not sufficient stamina to endure the conditioning, or a fast gait for a short time. Others have a regular gait which cannot be improved upon. Some will start the work fast but gradually shorten their pace and range to less and less limits. Fast work is very fatiguing. A dog may work all day at a slow gait, and still be unable to run an hour at a fast gallop. Many of the field trial dogs have more endurance than is commonly supposed, the character of the speed not being justly considered. Because the dogs are required to run only an hour more or less, such is no grounds for inference that they cannot run longer; on the other hand some are better adapted to short runs in field trial than to actual field work.

The dog should have regular work to keep him hard and in good wind and practice. No definite amount of work can be uniformly prescribed for all dogs; it can only be determined by the capabilities of the individual. Some require work every day; others, alternate days; or work in two days, then miss a day; or, if there is any tendency to fall off in quickness, an exercise run merely may be given, the trainer being guided solely by the capabilities of the dog.

A dog which makes little delays here and there in his work is heavily handicapped. If he stops to potter occasionally, even if slightly, he has no chance to win at a field trial. If he holds his nose to the ground during five or six seconds, his competitor, if fast, gains a moral advantage by contrast, and a real one by keeping ahead, thus coming first to the birds; if it is repeated at intervals, the relative qualities are very apparent. Thus matters which appear trifling when the dog is working alone assume a serious importance in contesting with a competitor which may be a shade better.

In his preparation, at such times as favorable opportunities offer, it is well to work the dog with strange dogs so that he will become accustomed to such work—the excitement, jealousy, or hesitancy shown when first worked in company may be thus overcome. Puppies in training for a Derby may be greatly assisted by having an old dog to help them find birds, the greater number of birds found giving a consequent greater number of opportunities to the puppy on scattered birds.

All field trial associations limit the ages of eligible entries to their respective Derbys, or puppy stakes, to on, or after, January 1 of the year prior to that in which the trials are run; hence a puppy which has the full age allowed by the limits may be about twenty-three months old when he runs. This concedes a very mature age to a puppy, but it has been found necessary to grant a very liberal limit for various reasons, namely, with young puppies, the running is a spiritless, wearisome affair; many puppies do not develop their instincts or working powers during their first season, therefore the test would be of no value, for they might be poor performers in their first season and good or superior in their second season; it is impossible, in extremely hot seasons, to give a puppy sufficient training, before the trials, to show his real merits; many good puppies cannot be more than half trained under these circumstances; and last, but equally important, a narrower limit to age would cut off an important number of entries. A puppy, whelped on or after January 1, will be too immature to run in the trials of the same year, hence it is a waste of money and effort to attempt to run him. He will be about eight months old, assuming a full age, when the open season begins legally; but nature, in the South, effectually closes the season till there are a few sharp frosts to kill the dense growth of weeds, grass, and other cover; and till the cool days of the fall begin, which is in October or early November, no training of any importance can be done—previous to this time, the hot, sultry days, scarcity of water and poor scent preclude all possibility of improving work. Puppies which are overworked under such circumstances cannot be gotten to the nice condition, the dashing spirit and energy, of a puppy trained during the previous season. The one season puppy must be worked to the extent of his capabilities to give him training and experience, whereas the two-season puppy needs only such field work as will develop him to the highest physical condition. An overworked young puppy cuts a tame figure in a public trial. In this immature and imperfect state, he will have to compete against dogs which had work the previous fall, winter and spring, with the further advantage of a better experience in the same fall, wherein the one season puppy is worked; also having the advantage of greater age and consequent more mature powers. It is always the puppies of full age and experience that do uniform work, show reliable capabilities and win the prizes, except in very rare instances; indeed, a dog at two years of age has all the fire and dash of youth combined with sufficient experience and maturity to run with remarkable brilliancy with aged dogs, as has been demonstrated at the trials when such puppies have run in All-age stakes, they being capable of competing on terms of equality.

In handling a dog at a field trial, it is the correct course to confine your attentions to your own dog. If the other handler's dog flushes, chases, or makes other errors, make no remarks about it. Nothing is more disgusting than for a handler to turn around and exclaim: "*That dog flushed, judges!*" It, besides being ungentlemanly and super-officious, is a direct reflection on the perception and knowledge of the judges; moreover, it does no good whatever, for the judges will not consider anything they do not see, and they will not ask a handler's interpretation of what they do see. A professional handler may submit to the indignity, a few times, of having his rights invaded, but he is very sure to protest against it sooner or later.

If there is any part which unfairly works to your disadvantage, have no words with the competing handler. Protest or ask for information of the judges. All rules justly permit it, and the associations as they now exist are opposed to any trickery or unfairness. Anything that is not frivolous or malicious will be given a respectful hearing.

The better way in handling a dog is to cast him off and let him alone. The best handlers are generally those who make the least noise. An amateur can compete successfully if he has his dog prepared properly; there is much more in this than in the handling, but both should be correct. During the general competition a competing dog should be carried in a wagon when he is not running. The perpetual dragging and hauling on a chain in the hands of some awkward attendant is not conducive to successful running. Dogs which have to wait two or three days or more before their running begins should be exercised well every day, otherwise they will get soft, thick in wind, and accumulate fat. It is a fact well known to experienced sportsmen that a healthy dog which has been worked until he is in fine running condition will accumulate a great deal of fat in three or four days, if fed on good food and permitted to be idle.

In preparing a dog for private field work, there is no need of extreme care with respect to preserving a fast pace. Regular feeding, however, is necessary as with the racing dog. Nine dogs out of ten, owned and kept by sportsmen, are fed too much and exercised too little during the close season, and consequently they have an accumulation of fat, are thick in wind, soft in muscle, and have tender feet— they are wholly unfit for any unusual exertion in that state. They suffer great distress, particularly at the opening of the game seasons in the hot months of July, August and September. The grossly fat dog suffers most of all; he can work but a few moments at a time before he is painfully blown and exhausted; and as his fat can be worked off but slowly under such circumstances, it is a wearisome task to the handler to condition him and a distressing experience to the dog. The excessive weight and resultant awkwardness induce sore feet and muscles, frequently preventing the dog from working at all for several days; or the dog, from distress, prostration or discomfort, may absolutely refuse to work when excessively fat, although he might be an energetic worker when in proper condition. If a sportsman goes shooting without paying any attention to the condition of his dogs, he deliberately impairs or destroys the success of the trip. The average outing of a business man is not sufficiently long to permit him to condition his dogs properly. He should begin at least a month previous to his outing to give the dog a run night and morning when the temperature is coolest, gradually increasing the length of the run as the dog can stand it. If the dog is much blown at first, permit him to run but a few moments at a time, letting him run for exercise and walk at heel alternately—in this manner he can run longer than if run directly to a standstill. Much the better way is to keep the dog in at least fairly good condition during the open season, then there will be comparatively little trouble in getting him in working condition. Dogs which are started at work without preliminary conditioning afford the flattest and poorest sport, even if in a good game country.

In connection with handling, it is proper to mention that an owner, who has his dog trained by a breaker, should consider that it requires a longer or shorter time for the dog to become acquainted with his peculiarities: his methods of handling; tone of voice; manner of blowing whistle; hand signals, etc., differing from those of the trainer.

CHAPTER XXII.

THE INTELLIGENCE OF THE DOG.

Sportsmen who have had an extensive experience with dogs and their performances afield believe, in the generality of cases, that the dog is a reasoning animal. This belief is commonly a slow growth, a process of induction, opposed by the beliefs and prejudices of early teachings and the natural *penchant* of mankind toward self-exaltation, all of which are formidable obstacles to any concessions with respect to mind existing in the lower animals; moreover, it is a universal belief that mind is the distinguishing attribute which elevates man above all other organisms. It is unquestionably true that man transcends all animals in intelligence, but the possession of reason is that of superiority, not of exclusiveness.

In many parts of this work, much stress has been laid on the theory that the dog is a rational animal—it may be well to adduce some proofs which will make the theory more susceptible of belief, or at least less improbable to those who hold that the dog is endowed with no higher cognition than that derived from instinct. Also it may serve to engage the attention of some sportsmen who have not given the subject much, if any, thought. The trainer who is attempting to conduct a dog's training, requiring intelligent acts, on a theory of instinct, is groping in the dark and opposing the evidence of his senses.

At the outset, it may be proper to explain that the author

appreciates the vast scope and complexity of the subject in its psychological phases—the short chapter which is here devoted to the theme is insufficient to contain a concise statement of the elementary principles. It may afford some imperfect data, however, to those who wish to pursue the investigation further. If a spirit of observation and investigation could be once aroused, it would certainly result in removing the dog from the grade of purely instinctive organisms, to which he has arbitrarily been relegated by man, to his natural place in the domain of reasoning animals. Let the intelligent sportsman once begin to study the dog's acts and habits closely with a view to analyzing their purposes and to classify the associated mental phenomena, and he will become involved in a thousand perplexities and inconsistencies if he attributes the capability of the dog to acquire knowledge and retain it, to instinct.

That the subject may be treated fairly, we will briefly consider the commonly accepted reasons on which the belief that the dog's acts are instinctive are founded, to wit: Man is a reasoning animal, therefore there are no other reasoning animals—palpably a very illogical premise. All the inferior mental and physical attributes of the lower animals are carefully noted by man, but those which are analogous to his own are studiously ignored.

It might be anticipated that an extremely complex metaphysical process of reasoning would be required to prove that the dog is rational. Such is unnecessary. The most common phenomena are all that afford data for mental science, whether in respect to man or the lower animals; when dealing with abstractions of abstractions, the matter becomes wholly speculative, and then no two philosophers agree in their inferences. In respect to man, by observing his perception of means to ends, of cause and effect, we deduce that he is a reasoning animal, and although no man has seen more than a small portion of mankind, *a priori* we can infer that all men are reasoning animals.

To proceed understandingly, it is necessary to have at least a general definition of what is meant by the term *instinct*, it commonly being used loosely with a variable meaning, always with too much comprehensiveness, and therefore without a just precision. As to what constitutes the intrinsic properties of instinct, the greatest philosophers are wholly unable to define; it is in the realms of the unknowable; however, while they cannot define it, they can approximately define its limits and enumerate some of its extrinsic properties.

We will now clear some of the rubbish of popular belief from the purposes of instinct. It has been arbitrarily assumed that many acts of the dog are instinctively performed for the service of man, the fact that he could be trained to work being considered as conclusive evidence that he was specially created to so work. In his work aforementioned, Darwin says: "Again, as in the case of corporeal structure, and conformably to my theory, the instinct of each species is good for itself, but has never, as far as we can judge, been produced for the exclusive good of others."

Hence it is apparent that instinct is distinct and separate from experience, and in a measure independent of intelligence. Its purposes are for the good of the individual, or the preservation of the species. Instinctive acts do not improve by experience. The bird builds its last nest like all preceding ones; bees constantly build their honeycomb in the same shape, etc. On the other hand, all intelligent animals improve their methods by experience; the dog improves by experience, therefore the dog is an intelligent animal.

We will now consider briefly some of the elementary principles of mind. In its primary relations, mind has important physiological dependencies, or it is a dependency itself which greatly modifies or extends its powers under certain circumstances, which is simply the material phase of mind—this is in no wise concerned with the question whether mind is material or otherwise.

Prof. Bain, in his *Mental Science*, says, "The brain is the principal, although not the sole organ of mind; and its leading functions are mental. The proofs of this position are these:

"(1.) The physical pain of excessive mental excitement is localized in the head. In extreme muscular fatigue, pain is felt in the muscles; irritation of the lungs is referred to the chest, indigestion to the stomach; and when mental exercise brings acute irritation, the local seat is the head.

"(2.) Injury or disease of the brain affects the mental powers. A blow on the head destroys consciousness; physical alterations of the nervous substance (as seen after death) are connected with loss of speech, loss of memory, insanity, or some other mental deprivation or derangement.

"(3.) The products of nervous waste are more abundant after mental excitement. These products, eliminated mainly by the kidneys, are the alkaline phosphates, combined in the triple phosphates of ammonia and magnesia. Phosphorus is a characteristic ingredient of the nervous substance.

"(4.) There is a general connection between size of brain and mental energy. *In the animal series*, intelligence increases with the development of the brain. The human brain greatly exceeds the animal brain; and the most advanced races of men have the largest brains. Men distinguished for mental force have, as a general rule, brains of an unusual size. The average weight of the brain is 48 ounces. The brain of Cuvier weighed 64 ounces. Idiots commonly have small brains.

"(5.) By specific experiments on the brain and nerves, it is shown that they are indispensable to the mental functions."

The learned author then proceeds in a scientific exposition of the dimensions, shape and matter of the brain, and of the nerves and their action, and the power of sensation dependent on them; for instance, the sensations of sounds, tastes, sights, smells are known through the nerves of the ear, tongue, eye and nose respectively. It may not be correct to say *through*, but such is sufficiently accurate for the purpose. On these functional powers of the senses depend all the capability of acquiring knowledge, either in man or the lower animals. The dog has a brain containing white and gray matter, a nervous system and capabilities of sensation, since all will admit that he can hear, see, smell, taste and feel. He must have a perception of these else there would be no sensation, for it is plain that if the dog was not conscious of hearing, seeing, etc., he would have neither sensation nor perception. The dog has capability to become mentally excited, mentally deranged from diseases of the nerves or brain; and feels fatigue, pains in the body, etc. A blow on the head suspends consciousness, and may destroy his memory or intelligence. The shape of the head is indicative of intelligence, and dogs vary greatly in intelligence. Having a brain, a delicate nervous organization, and as many organs of sense as the highest order of animal life, it is fair to assume that, inasmuch as mind is dependent on these organs, their presence is indicative of mind; for it is not reasonable to assume that all these organs are concomitant to mind in one species, and not related to it in another. This is further sustained by analogous feelings exhibited—the dog has many emotions peculiar to mind, namely, anger, affection, resentment, gratitude, jealousy, pleasure, anxiety, surprise, wonder, sympathy, distress, mortification, etc.; and volition, cunning, love of home, anticipation, memory, etc., which are not related or necessary to instinct. Having the physiological organs of mind and exhibiting the phenomena of mind in his acts, why should any conclusion be derived therefrom in relation to instinct?

Physiologically, the analogy in the nervous organization and the organs of sense is not the only one. It could be shown, that in the organic animal world there is a close and related gradation of animal forms from man as the highest, down through the intermediate gradations to the lowest. Taking the highest type of man as the starting point, there are several regular descending gradations to the lowest type of man which have each distinguishing peculiarities of physical structure, noticeably in that of the brain, and distinct gradations of intellect, dependent on the peculiar brain formation and proportions of its matter which are present in each gradation; from the lowest forms of man to certain forms of the lower animals, the gradation descends with uniformity. This insensible gradation of forms is still more apparent in the skeletons; many animals varying greatly in their mature forms have skeletons showing close analogies. The similarity is even greater in the embryos. Widely different species, such as birds, snakes, mammals, have embryos which are so wonderfully alike that, up to a certain period of development, they are indistinguishable one from the other, although each species may present wholly dissimilar mature forms; all of which shows the analogy of animal organisms.

In the human species, the formation, weight and matter of the brain vary from that of the highest type, the Caucasian, through intermediate races to the lowest in certain savage tribes, thence in a descending scale of formations in the lower animals. It is reasonable to infer that the mental phenomena of the highest form of brain would be present in a lesser and lesser degree in all the brains that had analogous formations, but were successively inferior to it. That there are such differences in the mental powers of men, the different races afford proof. In tribes which have a brain formation approaching that of the lower animals, as, for instance, the aboriginal Australian tribes, the clay eaters of the Orinoco, etc., which lead an animal existence, the intelligence is very low, and incapable of extending to other than the simplest forms of abstraction. The reasoning faculties, unlike instinct, are notable for their variability and want of uniformity in individuals of the same family, tribe, or race; these mental differences are observable in the lower animals. By considering the close gradation in physical forms, in brain and nervous organizations, and the mental phenomena of different kinds of animals which conform to their brain development, there is proof of a gradation of minds as well as of physical forms.

While it is herein contended that a dog has mind, it will be explained that, as compared to that of man, it is in many respects very imperfect; some faculties appear to be wholly absent; on the other hand, some of its physiological functions appear to be superior, such as the sense of smell and hearing; and in other animals, the sense of sight. The most important absent faculty, *i. e.*, a failure to understand language, will be hereinafter dwelt upon.

Reason, one of the attributes of mind, is extremely difficult to define in a metaphysical sense. Every man is conscious of his own mind but wholly unconscious of that of others, hence *a priori* principles must be assumed. Only by certain phenomena can we judge of the existence of mind in others; and no one can analyze his own. Webster defines reason as follows:

"The faculty or capacity of the human mind by which it

is distinguished from the lower animals; the higher as distinguished from the lower cognitive faculties, as sense, imagination and memory, and in contrast to the feelings and desires, including conception, judgment, reasoning, and the intuitional faculty; the intuitional faculty, or the faculty of first truths, as distinguished from the understanding, which is called the discursive or ratiocinative faculty." This definition attempts so much in a small space that it accomplishes nothing. It is plain that the first clause is meaningless. The lower animals have not the slightest distinguishing relation to reason, for, if they were all destroyed, reason would exist continuously in man without reference to them. The rest of the definition is bad, since no one faculty is distinct to the exclusion of others, nor is there a uniform agreement amongst philosophers on the divisions of the intellect. The most comprehensive definition is "the consciousness of likeness and unlikeness," which also requires memory.

Referring again to the mind's sources of knowledge, *i. e.*, the senses, the feelings caused by them are called sensations. The consciousness of a sensation and its cause is called a perception. This has been concisely illustrated as follows: "If I simply smell a rose, I have a sensation; if I refer that smell to the external object which occasions it, I have a perception." Now, the dog has the power of sensation since he has the full number of organs of sense, and has the faculty of perception since he can discriminate and refer sensations to their cause conformably with the special functions of each sense—no one will dispute that to hit a dog with a whip, or to let him smell or see a piece of meat, or to call him by name, will cause both a sensation and a perception; but to grant this carries with it a concession of knowledge in the dog, and according to Prof. Bain, "All perception or knowledge implies mind." With respect to knowleage, Herbert Spencer, in the *Principles of Psychology*, concisely refers to it as follows: "Knowledge implies something known and something which knows." With respect to reasoning, he states it to be "the indirect establishment of a relation between two things." Now, it is worthy of remark that there are widely different grades of reasoning, some being very simple, others extremely complex. The ability to recall a mental picture of an object which was previously known by perception is called a representation. Beyond a few representations and their likenesses and unlikenesses some minds cannot go; others can grasp vast groups of abstractions, and abstractions of abstractions, with ease.

Undoubtedly one cause which largely contributed to the mental degradation of the dog from his true position in the estimation of mankind is the fact that he can have no knowledge unless his cognitions have been derived from direct experience, although some of the lower races of mankind have not much higher faculties. To illustrate, a man who has a knowledge of language, can gain a mediate knowledge of a certain object or idea by a description of it; but a succession of mental objects and attributes cannot be brought into a dog's mind by language except in the simplest forms of representation. The order *Find* causes the dog to hunt diligently for a dead bird, there then being undoubtedly a comprehension of the meaning of the word, learned from many experiences; but by having direct experience, the dog has a respectable scope of intelligence and perception of cause and effect. To be more particular, it may be illustrated by supposing an instance: By describing a gun and its uses to man, through the medium of language, a very good comprehension of it can be given—the dog cannot have such mediate knowledge; only by direct observation in practice can he learn its uses. The fact that the dog could not acquire knowledge by any mediate means (and therefore its absence being distinctly unlike the faculty of man) was very commonly observed; the fact that he could acquire knowledge by individual experience was observed by but a few. It was an easy deduction that, if he could not have a full cognition like mankind, he could not have any at all. After having acquired knowledge by direct experience he has quite an admirable reasoning ability. Having individual experiences every day, and a multitude of very complex experiences in pursuit of game, he gathers a vast amount of abstract knowledge from his direct experiences which he applies with an accuracy which denotes an understanding of means to ends. In referring to these intelligent acts, those who deny other than instinctive acts to the dog are unable to frame a language that is consistent with their belief; they are forced to use terms relating to reason. They properly speak of a dog's judgment in conducting his work; his quickness in learning; his knowledge of how to apply his training, etc.

To perceive a present cause and effect would not be very advantageous if no record could be kept of it in the mind. The dog has a memory and retains an intelligent cognition of his experiences. Innumerable instances of memory could be cited, but it is a fact so commonly known that it needs no proof. One or two, however, will be advanced. The fact that a trained dog shows the greatest delight when he sees his owner put on his hunting coat, take a gun in hand, or make other preparations significant of a hunt, shows an understanding and a memory. When a start is made he may lead the way to the fields, whereas, ordinarily, he might lead the way to the main road. Such act has the full implication of knowledge, the "something known and the something which knows." The memory of experiences of former states of consciousness and a comprehension of their purposes constitutes abstract knowledge. The application of this knowledge, with a perception of means to ends, can only be referred to a rational organization. By no possibility could he show abstract knowledge derived from experience if his faculties were limited to the senseless instinctive acts. Certain tones on the whistle, commands, signals, expressions of countenance of the owner, changes of route, etc., are understood, and are succeeded and responded to by certain rational acts. This branch, although treated briefly herein, is of great scope in physiology, and includes memory, association of ideas, cause and effect, etc. The saddling or harnessing of a horse, any unusual preparation, or energy of action, the preparation for meals, the purposes of methods in hunting and the multitude of details of domestic life, are remembered and understood if the dog has had opportunities to note their purposes—if novel, they excite his curiosity. Any unusual occurrence, even if trifling, will entirely change the current of the dog's thoughts and actions; acts which are many times repeated become habitual—he has favorite places to sleep in daytime, others at night, others again for sunning himself, favorite ways of working his grounds, circumventing the birds, etc. He quickly discerns such acts as are pleasurable to him, and such objects as are worthy of pursuit. Such as are pleasurable he will perform voluntarily; others he will refuse to perform, or perform because they are less painful than refusal with punishment.

If, when hunting in the field with another dog, the latter false points a few times, he will refuse to back his points thereafter, showing conclusively that he observed the points were purposeless, and the refusal to back showed a high degree of perception and reflection. In the case of the dog false pointing, and the other one refusing to back, the latter had a perception of subject and object attributes which required a process of ratiocination. It was a combined act caused by will, memory, perception of cause and effect, agreement and difference, and a knowledge of its valueless results. Instances are related where certain dogs would not remain with a shooter who missed frequently. All dogs will lose interest in their work if a bird is not shot occasionally or if no birds are found. Dogs which have been properly raised where there was poultry will not kill them; ones which have never seen poultry will hunt and kill them eagerly—the former have the necessary knowledge, the latter have not. Dogs are universally susceptible to flattery and approbation, which is also a very common property of high intelligence.

A sensible dog, when hunted a few times on certain grounds, learns the haunts of the birds, and, when hunting, will go from one haunt to another, thus showing knowledge and a memory of no mean capacity. If a trained dog is chained while his master goes afield, he becomes excited, barks violently and endeavors to break away to follow; if he fails, he utters howls of grief and disappointment. Mr. S. T. Hammond, an acknowledged authority on dogs and their training, in his admirable work entitled *Training vs. Breaking*, says: "Some dogs are possessed of remarkable reasoning faculties and appear intuitively to understand just what you wish, while others are slow to learn and require more time to develop their latent powers." In the American edition of Stonehenge, entitled "The Dogs of Great Britain and America," is the following paragraph, viz.: "This last (false pointing) was from a want of mental capacity, for it is by their reasoning powers that these dogs find out when they have made a mistake, and without a good knowledge box the pointer and setter are, for this reason, quite useless."

Nor are the acts mechanical during the primary lessons. The simple fact that the dog can comprehend the trainer's purposes proves the possession of pre-existing mental capabilities. The simple act of carrying an object to the trainer, in compliance with an order, is not a mechanical and meaningless act on the part of the dog, as is commonly taught and believed. The act is in full accord with the sum total of the dog's correlated experience. The greater number of the rational acts of life are devoted to seeking that which is pleasurable and avoiding that which is painful. In forcing a dog to retrieve, the trainer unconsciously considers his own complete knowledge as a standard, overlooking the fact that the dog cannot know the full application, since he has not had a full experience. When a dog will retrieve an object through the intermediate effects of the spike collar or other means, such acts are intelligently applied in accordance with his associated experience. He has learned by an association of ideas derived from special experiences that by performing certain acts in a certain manner he avoids pain, and that if he does not perform such acts he suffers pain. The mere presentation of the usual retrievable object to his sight after the necessary experience will cause him to grasp it forthwith without either command or punishment; in this act is shown all that constitutes the primary attributes of mind, a consciousness of agreement and difference, and a memory. Learning to retrieve from the application of force requires the exercise of complex mental processes in the dog. He must learn to grasp the object to avoid punishment; a new element is introduced when the order *Fetch* is associated with it. The association of ideas, although apparently simple to the trainer, are complex, nevertheless, for there is a discriminating complex mental process distinguishable in the intelligent performance of the act—the dog, after a brief series of experiences, associates a certain act with the sight of a certain object, and the performance or non-performance of it with or without pain respectively; next, he associates the act with a certain sound, called a command, with the same concomitants of pain or its absence; next, he learns to perform the act in a certain manner, and comprehends the relations of the different elements; thus he must consider the object to be retrieved, the act of retrieving, the manner of performing it, the command to perform it, the painful consequences of non-performance, the freedom from pain consequent on performance and the relations of the different parts. After a longer or shorter time contingent on the intelligence and willingness of the dog, skill of the tutor, etc., the intermediate element of punishment is unnecessary, and he associates the performance of the act with the necessary command; thus the act which in its inception was associated with punishment, and the command which was also associated with punishment, are then associated together independently of punishment. His acts thus intelligently concur with the extent of his experience, and as it enlarges, his comprehension expands with it.

These acts, although performed intelligently, are commonly attributed to an association of ideas, meaning thereby that they are not arrived at by any process of reason; but this common belief is erroneously opposed to their true meaning. An association of ideas may relate to a perception of cause and effect quite as much as to two material objects. An association of ideas presupposes the existence of ideas, and therefore mind. The fact that the dog can comprehend these relations as they apply to the simple act of retrieving, and, when subsequently afforded opportunities, comprehends its purposes and applies it intelligently in actual work, cannot be ascribed to an association of ideas which are independent of all ideas; nor can it be ascribed to the force of habit called mechanical. Acts which are so frequently and habitually performed as to be done without thought were not always habitual. All acts require thought and study in their primal stages; only by long continued repetition do they become habitual.

When the gun is fired and the dog is ordered to Find, there is then an exhibition of pure mind. There is no bird in sight. Hunting then for a dead bird, he shows a high degree of understanding, and deduction of effects from causes.

Some of the common acts which are supposed to be purely instinctive, such as pointing and following by scent, are, in a great measure, due to intelligence. The setter and pointer, when they first start a rabbit, follow by sight. Only by several failures do they learn to use their noses, and then they learn intelligently by degrees. In pointing birds the first attempts are very crude, and only become perfected by many opportunities. Undoubtedly they chase instinctively, but knowledge of methods only comes from experience. Hounds require great experience to solve the intricacies of the fox's cunning, and the most irregular capabilities are shown conformably to the irregular grades of intelligence. In pursuit, hounds do not depend entirely on the nose; if puzzled they will make wide detours to hit off the trail, thus trusting to their brains. Some setters and pointers will go entirely around the edge of a field to hit off the trail of any birds that have entered or left it; if puzzled on a trail, they make a wide circular cast to find the true trail; thus the dog does not wholly depend on the functional powers of nose to guide him in pursuit of his prey. The necessity for experience to perform good field work is known to all. The difference in the capabilities of two dogs of equal natural powers, the one having full experience, the other having none, is so great that every sportsman has observed the disparity. But it has been satisfactorily shown that instinct requires no experience; in fact, is independent of it. And it has been shown that the dog has the phenomena of mind, but must have his abstract knowledge from perception of objective phenomena. It could be shown that dogs have an understanding of each other's barks and actions to a certain degree, but such would not add to the force of what has already been adduced. The subject has been treated in its most elementary form as related to popular observation. While the belief of a mind in the lower animals may appear novel to some readers, it is respectably ancient. To gain a comprehensive grasp of the subject, it is necessary to read many voluminous works of natural history and metaphysics, besides being a close observer of nature.

The importance of the subject as it relates to the education of the dog is apparent. The most comprehensive object experience is necessary for him to acquire knowledge ; the commands are associated with objects in such a manner that, when re-presented in the dog's memory, he has a clear knowledge of their meaning ; it shows the absurdity of conducting a training on a theory of instinct ; it shows that the dog, being intelligent, should be treated kindly to develop his best effort ; and it shows the fallacy of hastily judging without proper investigation. The phenomena enumerated by no means include all that is peculiar to the dog ; they are simply cited for illustration, and not as being exhaustive.

CHAPTER XXIII.

FIELD ETIQUETTE.

There is no recreation which has more wholesome, pleasurable, health-giving properties than those which appertain to the dog and gun, or has, in its reminiscent phases, more pleasant memories when the surroundings were pleasant and companions agreeable; on the other hand there is none more repulsive if marred by the presence of a selfish, aggressive or noisy companion. Many accessory details contribute to the pleasure of the sport—the superb performances of an intelligent dog; the skill and knowledge necessary with respect to a gun; the beautiful in nature; the exhilaration from pure air and freedom—all have their full share in making a sum total of pleasure which redounds to the health and happiness of the sportsman.

Nevertheless, to derive the highest enjoyment from the sport when hunting in company, certain elementary principles of *meum et tuum* must be rigidly observed, otherwise the sport is stripped of its elegance and highest enjoyment. In no place are conventionalities more necessary than where the selfishness of all is directly appealed to by a common pursuit.

From an experience with all sorts and degrees of sportsmen, and a close observance of the individual peculiar excellences of each, the author has confidence in his ability to frame a code of etiquette wherein will be aggregated all the perfections which constitute the refinements of ideal sportsmen. To him who diligently observes them will come all the graces of a Chesterfield. They will also greatly add to the tyro's opportunities of learning how to deport himself properly in the company of other sportsmen. He will learn to avoid certain offensive violations of field etiquette to which beginners—some very experienced ones—are prone; acts which derogate from otherwise charming companionableness. Without a knowledge of the unwritten laws and amenities of sportsmanship, the beginner, whether experienced or inexperienced, will infallibly transgress them, either by extreme forwardness or backwardness, or both; for a painful and uncomfortable excess of modesty, or affectation of it, is quite as annoying, and at times as dilatory as its opposite. Sport which would be most pleasurable in every feature under polite circumstances may be marred or spoiled by the uncontrollable selfishness of one companion. If a set of rules were delicately presented to such to read, with certain marked passages in them which happily applied to his case, it might be conducive to his improvement if he were not so self-complacent as to preclude all improving innovations.

There are very few surroundings in civilized society which will develop a man's real nature so thoroughly and accurately as shooting in company, or an outing in camp. Under ordinary conditions, a man has two or three natures, one he shows to the world, one he does not, and one which he thinks he has. Too often the man whose nature is sunny when he is surrounded with comforts displays the most astonishing and unexpected selfishness, fretfulness or aggressiveness when circumstances afield combine to his discomfort of mind or body. For this reason the experienced sportsman is very careful in his choice of company. The man who is careless with his gun; who thinks that a hunt is synonymous with a carousal; who thinks it is a shooting competition; who thinks it is solely for his own use and behoof; who thinks that the pleasure of the sport is measured alone by the size of the bag, is a good man to encourage to go hunting with someone else.

In everyday society, there are certain little related circumstances which it may be proper to mention. There is no harm in "talking dog," provided that a man chooses and knows his proper time, place, and company; then it undoubtedly is edifying, æsthetically elevating and positively improving; but it is inexpressibly wearisome to have it perpetually obtruded into every conversation in every company, in season and out of season. If, by any chance, the company drifts away into the conversation from the dog topic, the enthusiast is unhappy and bides his time uneasily to again divert the conversation to his favorite theme, not always with the happiest tact in doing so or the approbation of the company when it is done.

The principles, particularly the *first principles*, embodied in these rules will be self-evident to those who read. The author has seen them practiced with great nicety of precision and grace of manner in all kinds of bird shooting, they being adjusted to the delicate comprehensiveness which should co-exist with first principles. No man can be at a loss as to the correct caper in etiquette who has a copy of these rules, whether in respect to his deportment as a guest, a companion or a tutor; all this from a sportsman's point of view.

Having thus explained at some length the necessities and benefits of them, and knowing the advantages to sportsmanship that will accrue from their general observance, they are herewith given:

As an essential principle, one which forms a broad groundwork for many other admirable qualities, you should begin and conduct your career on the assumption that you know everything appertaining to the dog and gun, a sportsman's encyclopedia; and let your actions and discourse be consistent therewith. Hold tenaciously to your opinions. There are many sportsmen whose cuticle and epidermis are so thick, tough and flinty, having such copious layers upon layers and folds upon folds, that no rules bearing on the subject can be made of sufficient acuteness to be knowable to their consciousness. So entirely are they in the murky clouds of their own selfishness that they do not discern the loss of respect or the contempt, the character of hoggishness which they justly suffer in the estimation of hunting companions, and as for perceiving their own low grade of sportsmanship themselves, it is not to be hoped for, for it is very difficult to correct nature by art.

When you are the guest of a friend, give your dog the freedom of his parlor. Tell him how much you love your dog, and let your manner be slightly austere ; this will be sufficient reason for turning his home into a kennel.

After completing your visit and therefore having enjoyed the hospitalities and shooting afforded by your host, tell your friends and acquaintances that his dogs are worthless ; that your own dogs completely and uniformly defeated them; that you beat your host shooting day in and day out, and that he is an overrated sportsman in every respect. Your host may have refrained from shooting, or may have given you all the shooting because you were a guest ; nevertheless, imply that the whole visit was a hot competition from start to finish. Your host, being solicitous for your comfort and pleasure, never dreamed of such ; but amiably construe his forbearance and courtesy to inability. You might, as an exhibition of tact and observational powers, criticise adversely every failing you could perceive in his dogs. You might even do this for the edification of your host personally. It would be a very gentlemanly return for his hospitality and care.

When you visit a friend whom you know is always plentifully provided with cartridges, make it a special point to forget yours, and as a guest you are sure to be supplied. Talk genially in respect to replacing them at some indeterminate time in futurity. By using them, you will demonstrate your confidence in your friend's loading, and if you make several successful shots you can delicately ascribe them to the superiority of his cartridges. Several sportsmen who understand this art, reinforced with skill in the art of borrowing, make some very beneficial gains in financial economy by their wiles and nerve every season. It is a trait worthy of note.

If your friend has a bevy scattered nicely, thus affording several nice shots, forthwith abandon your own range and go to him, get into the thick of the swim, and help him to kill all that you can. Often friends need help, and it is surely friendly to then give it. If you have a bevy similarly scattered yourself, keep the matter to yourself. You do not need any help, and besides, you are the best judge of the situation.

If you have been fortunate in marking birds which your friend, who is in company with you, did not see, send him a few yards away to hunt in the place where they are not. When you flush and kill them, tell him that they ran from the place where you marked them, and that you are grieved that he did not get the shots. It is so subtle that your friend will not detect it, hence you can play the trick repeatedly.

If your friend's dog points a bevy, mention an incident respecting your own dog, namely, that he smelt them a short time before and was taking a cast to them, be the same long or short, when your friend's dog stupidly pointed them. Let this incident occur in unbroken succession with every point, and be sure to mention it. What your dog did in your mind in the abstract should certainly be more meritorious than what your friend's dog did in reality, the fancy more than the fact.

Be officious and obstinate in arranging the route and its details. Make your companion's route subservient to yours. Suggest to him how he will work his dog. When he sends his dog to retrieve suffer yours to go also ; two dogs do so much better than one. Your friend may wish you under the dominion of the somber personage who presides over the destinies of the adverse orthodox hereafter, but you will have the sublime pleasure of your own will.

Watch patiently and ceaselessly for an opportunity to kill a bird which your companion misses. When you succeed in "wiping his eye," give full and hilarious play to your pent up feelings of exhilaration. Tell him you wiped his eye. Tell your friends and his friends of it. Within the following weeks refer to the fact that you wiped his eye. In every conversation introduce some topic that will craftily lead up to the opportunity of repeating that you wiped his eye. Thus you will exalt yourself as is your due, give full play to your excusable vanity simultaneously with an amiable exposition of your friend's unskillfulness. The time-honored custom of "wiping his eye" is obsolescent, but there is a worthy class which cherishes it as the sweetest morsel of field sports, and such should be duly revered for their numbers.

Assume an excessive affectation of modesty when the dog is pointing and your friend invites you to step forward and shoot. He will appreciate it, particularly if the dog has been pointing a long while, or the birds are running. If you do go forward, step closely and gingerly, and act as if you expected to flush a flock of rattlesnakes. It is very interesting to watch the extreme caution observed by some in flushing birds when no caution is necessary or desirable.

The delay, however, has some advantages—it will give the birds an opportunity to run still further, thereby affording excellent practice to the dog, particularly if the day is hot; providing that, from being disturbed, the birds do not rise out of range. Remember that the companion who, from a misconception of correct field etiquette, confounds obstructive delays with the purest ray serene of politeness is an educator; he educates his friends into shyness of his field society.

Carry your loaded gun lightly and gracefully resting in the elbow, the barrels in a parallel line with the surface of the ground. Keep them pointed at your companion. If your gun is cocked, as is frequently the style of some very good sportsmen who are authorities on this point, it will add materially to the potency of the act. If your companion silently shifts his position to the opposite side, immediately shift your gun likewise. If he suggests that the gun causes him disquietude, or is offensively threatening, beg his pardon, at the same time assume a mildly injured and strained air, assure him that you are noted for handling a gun with unceasing care and watchfulness, nevertheless change the position of the gun to oblige him—in two minutes have it back in its usual place, bearing on your friend with the same unceasing care and watchfulness. In walking through cover carry your gun on your shoulder, and let the muzzle point squarely in your friend's face when he is walking behind you.

When hunting with an experienced sportsman, if you happen to see his dog pointing, be sure to call his attention to the fact. If he appears indifferent repeat it two or three times; eventually he may understand you. This is particularly apropos if you are out with a professional trainer. The chances are a thousand to one that he saw the point before you did, probably saw the first signs the dog made of the recognition of the scent, but you will save yourself from any suspicion of dullness. The proper form to observe is to exclaim : *There he is!* HE'S GOT EM ! If the birds are at all wild or the dog timid, it is well to repeat this three or four times in louder tones.

Every time you miss a bird, stop and explain in elaborate detail just how excusably you did it. It will show that the miss, although a miss, was a commendable miss, and was made under such peculiar disadvantages of bad cartridges, ones either with the shot left out or which dropped out ; or no wads between powder and shot ; or bad powder ; hang fire ; aberration in the gun, it having too long, too straight or too crooked a stock, or is not balanced properly ; or the dog did not work just right ; or the birds flushed in an unusual manner ; or your friend stood in the wrong place— on the whole, the miss being so nicely executed, under adverse circumstances, that it unquestionably is superior to a clean kill. The sportsman cannot go wrong on any or all of these reasons, as they are sanctioned by common usage in some very good circles. Your friend, however, will merely consider that you made a plain, unornamented miss ; yet he will be delighted to listen to the descriptions and excuses after every miss. The manly reason of want of skill or error would concisely settle the matter, and your friend would then indorse your reason. Some very good sportsmen avoid the trouble of excuses or reasons by rolling out a voluminous, sonorous, full-fledged oath. It usually appears to be in the nature of a soliloquy and probably is due to an excess of self-consciousness.

If you are hunting from horseback, and your friend's dog gets in front of you, ride over him if he happens to stop ; or reach over and give him a vigorous poke in the ribs with the muzzle of your loaded gun.

Carry your gun loaded when on horseback or in a wagon.

It will conduce to your friend's peace of mind. If he requests you to unload, take offence. You are perfectly competent to handle a loaded gun, even if the horses should run away, the wagon upset, or break down, etc.

Blow your whistle and give loud orders continually. Keep the dog going to every likely place but the place he is in. Have five or six places that you desire him to work in at the same time. Claim, with great show of firmness, all the birds you can. If your friend's dog points when you are a quarter of a mile away, call loudly to your friend asking him to wait. It will be a great pleasure to wait, and make the pleasure divided a pleasure doubled.

When you walk up to your friend's dog which is on a point or back, never under any circumstances fail to have your gun, with your fingers on the triggers, pointed downward toward the dog, and as you walk around him, keep the gun bearing on him. In the few known instances in which the gun discharged prematurely, the dog was killed outright, hence there is no doubt of the effectiveness of the method.

If your friend has one day only in which to hunt, by all means try to make it entertaining. Narrate some long-winded yarns of what you have done on some previous occasion. Become intensely absorbed in the narration, stop your friend so that he can listen better, and let the dogs go on. Your friend can have no greater delight than in devoting three-quarters of his time to listening to some gross, highly-colored, apocryphal stories of self-glorification.

If the dog is on a point or back, be sure to walk straight over him as you go forward to flush the birds. There is unlimited space between a pointing dog and the horizon, but there might be some time lost if you deviate a finger breadth from a right line. The writer has seen this done with great nicety many times, much to the credit of the performer's determination to kill. It is particularly beneficial to puppies or timid dogs.

Point your gun at a companion at times. It is a delicate, friendly familiarity, and the distress, anxiety or fear produced will be intensely amusing and refreshing. Your friend may be killed, yet the possibility should not be considered. A friend who will not submit to some danger and distress for the diversion of a friend is not worth having. If fatal, it is only one more added to the list of "didn't mean to," or "didn't know it was loaded." Many true sportsmen justly consider the trick as being one of the most loutish and ruffianly that is possible, be the standing otherwise of the perpetrator what it may. The joker may know that the gun is not loaded, but the jokee cannot possibly know it, and the long lists of homicides from similar acts do not tend to allay his fears. No man can be considered a true friend who will wantonly terrify a friend, or jeopardize his life for amusement.

Always shoot on your friend's side of a bevy. It is an unnecessary refinement to shoot on your own side, although the practice is much in vogue amongst skillful sportsmen. If you are a poor shot but a good and consistent claimer of birds, it will add materially to your success.

Always make what should be a jointly pleasant hunt a keen competition or race. Banter your friend for a wager that you can beat him shooting; that your dog can beat his dog, and that your gun will shoot better than his—tell him so repeatedly. He will love you dearly for many qualities which hogs have not.

Make the fields resonant with your loquacity. Nothing is pleasanter or more conducive to success than an eternally prattling companion, particularly in cold, rainy or windy weather, when the birds are extremely wild. If you observe that your talk flushes the birds, you then have a subject of discourse for half an hour in assuring your companion that you know your talk did it, and you regret it so much.

Take the first shot invariably, and all of them if you can. You will be loved for acquisitive qualities common to certain domestic animals aforementioned. When you wish to go hunting, borrow your friend's gun and dog if you can. Ask permission to go hunting with your friend; for you can safely assume that one of two propositions is true, namely: If your friend desired your company, he would invite you; if you desire to go, you ask permission or cheerfully invite yourself—now, if you are wrong, you are the next thing to being right, which is a very good average—and a friend is no advantage if you cannot use him.

Always inspect your friend's gun. Open it and peer through the barrels, then slam it together. Cock it, pull the triggers, and snap it. Open it and slam it again. To do this correctly according to honored usage, it must be repeated six times at least, assuming a becoming look of idiocy during the performance; thus you will show that you know all about guns.

CHAPTER XXIV.

QUAILS, SNIPE, RUFFED GROUSE AND WOODCOCK.

A description of the peculiarities of these birds will be confined to such limits as relate to the training and handling of the dog.

The game birds commonly called quails in the North and partridges in the South are far superior to all others for training purposes. Their greater numbers, general distribution, habits and habitat render them unequaled, although certain sections from various causes may possess disadvantages. In many sections of New England and the Middle States, where the country is hilly and broken, swamps and thickets numerous, and the birds frequently disturbed by shooters, quail shooting is pursued under many difficulties. From two to eight or ten bevies are about all that can be found in a day of diligent seeking, the latter number being a very unusual one. In the Western States the shooting is less difficult, and the birds far more numerous, although the country is so vast and diversified that the character of the shooting varies greatly in different sections.

Quail shooting in the South is the shooting par excellence, the climate, topography and food supply all favoring the existence and multiplication of the birds. When the close season begins at the North enforced by statute law, and the still more stringent laws of Nature, manifested in the severe winters, quail shooting in the South is then in its prime. Usually the open season is limited to two or three months in the North, and many sections are periodically forced to protect their birds for two or three years at a time, in consequence of the enormous destruction caused by occasional severe winters. In the South, the season legally opens about September 1, and closes about March or April 1, thus affording six or seven months of an open season. The best months, however, are November, December, January, February and March.

A knowledge of their habits is of prime importance to the best success. Quails are early risers, and he who wishes to get the best shooting or the most opportunities for his dogs in a given time will be none too early if he is afield by the break of day. In the hot days of September, October, and early November, it is necessary, in training, to be abroad early in the morning, or in the cool part of the evening. During the winter months the trainers can find sufficient birds for their purpose in any part of the day. From twelve to thirty bevies are about the number that can be found in a day in the best sections, and from twenty to one hundred birds reward the efforts of the shooter. The birds are usually plentiful enough every season, but when a season is exceptionally favorable for breeding, they abound in great numbers. Quail shooting in the South may be said to be strictly upland shooting, differing in this respect from the like shooting in the East, where the birds go to dense, wet swamps at the first flight, and where it is necessary to pursue and diligently seek for them, if the success of the bag is duly observed.

In the South, the immense plantations, with their large sedge fields, plum thickets, cornfields, woods, large fallow fields covered with weeds, afford haunts for the birds, and the pea-patches and fields, sorghum fields, corn and wheat fields, Japanese clover, etc., furnish an abundant food supply during the fall, winter and spring. The habits of the birds are variable according to the means of supplying their necessities. Early in the season the wheat stubbles, the edges of corn or cotton fields, the vicinity of plum thickets, or along the edges of woods, or in the woods, are promising places to hunt, and occasionally they will be found in the most unexpected places. Early in the morning, the peculiar whistling cry of "bob-white! bob white!" can be heard in many directions far and near on a Southern plantation, and the peculiar note is a guide many times to the whereabouts of the birds. Later the sorghum patches are favorite resorts, the birds being very fond of the seeds. In the last of November and in December and January, the open sedge fields, along the plum thickets and the edge of woods, in fact anywhere except the bare fields, are good hunting places if the weather continues open and mild. When the cold days set in, there is an immediate change of habits. In January and February the birds usually abandon the open fields, if the weather is inclement, for the woods, such as have a good growth of sedge being preferred, although in the extreme South there is not much variation in their habits, the temperature rarely being so low as the freezing point. The Southern bird is quite as strong and rapid in flight as his Northern congener.

In the South, the dog can have an education that will fit him for work in any section, in open and cover, bevies and scattered birds, and he can be taught to work wide or close. The varying habits and increased cunning of the birds, as cold weather approaches, require that the dog should be intelligent and observing to acquire a knowledge of their habits. A manner of work which might be eminently successful on a mild, quiet day might be wholly inefficient in cold, rainy, or windy weather. Changes from settled to unsettled weather in the late fall and winter months always make the birds wilder and warier.

Usually, in the South, the trainer or sportsman hunts from

horseback, or has a wagon to follow convenient roads through the plantations, thus having a conveyance for a relay of dogs. With a good horse, a trainer can train ten or twelve dogs during the summer and fall, and about eight or ten in the winter. This number entails a great deal of hard work, however; one or two dogs, if backward, may greatly increase the difficulty. Hunting from horseback is the superior method. The cartridges, game bag and lunch can be tied to the saddle. The hunter rides while his dog is ranging for covies. From the elevated position he can see the movements of the dog a long distance away. If he points in sedge grass and is concealed, it is for the same reason much easier to find him. When the dog points, the hunter rides to within forty or fifty yards, throws the bridle rein over the horse's head to the ground, or a lariat is fastened to his neck and thrown on the ground, then he flushes and shoots. The scattered birds are then followed and good work obtained, if they do not fly to dense cover. After finishing work on the scattered birds the hunter mounts and resumes the hunt for bevies.

Good hunting horses are not plentiful; very few have the necessary requirements, namely, gentleness, endurance, intelligence, a good saddle gait and steadiness to the gun. A first class horse will also remain in the place where he is left in a field till the hunter returns; this by simply dismounting and leaving him to his freedom. A fast walk and a good fox trot are the best gaits that a hunting horse can have for this kind of work; and it is no demerit to him if he can jump a wide ditch or high fence. The introduction of wire fences in the South obstructs free riding in some sections, yet the plantations are so large that the fencing is of no special consequence.

A peculiarity of quails, *i. e.*, holding their scent at times when they light after being flushed, is a source of bewilderment to the novice. This peculiarity is not as frequently observable as is asserted by some writers. After marking a bevy accurately after flushing it, the trainer may be unable to find a single bird. The dog will take his casts to and fro, wholly unconscious of the proximity of birds. If, under these circumstances, the hunter will walk away to a proper distance and keep quiet until the birds begin to call, he can then return and secure point after point.

Quails are so plentiful, their haunts so permanent, the grounds so favorable for watching the work of a dog and for walking or riding; the birds are so game and cunning, yet withal so nicely adapted to the intelligent capabilities of the dog, that it is not surprising that they are the game birds, *facile princeps*, in the estimation of the professional trainer.

Ruffed grouse, while requiring a high grade of skill in both hunter and shooter, are very poor for training purposes; the conditions of dense cover, extreme wariness of the birds at all times, and their limited number and habitat, really make the training a special one, *i. e.*, the dog has to be taught to range close to the shooter, and to road with greater caution and deliberation; the dogs are extremely rare which can hunt ruffed grouse at a fast pace; such dogs necessarily have superior intelligence.

The woodcock is not worthy of consideration in dog training. The superiority of the shooting in the North is chiefly due to its being summer shooting, to the scarcity of the birds, and to the imagination of the shooter. In the last of December and early January, woodcock congregate in vast numbers in the woods of Louisiana, and other sections near the Southern coast, frequenting such places as have an undergrowth of clumps of briers, brush and patches of switch cane, or in woods which are comparatively open if the feeding grounds in that section are good. The most difficult grounds in that section are far easier to shoot on than the most favorable grounds in the North. At such times as the shooting is at its best, from forty to eighty birds can be killed by a single gun in a day. In the author's experience, and he noted the same results with others, the sport became very uninteresting after the novelty wore off, and quail shooting had the preference. The birds being migratory, the shooting is consequently very uncertain. The dog must be trained to work very close to the gun and the more intelligence he has, the better. Some shooters put a small bell on the dog when hunting woodcock and ruffed grouse, the gentle tinkle constantly giving warning of the whereabouts of the dog.

For training purposes, snipe are very unsatisfactory, owing to their erratic habits and migratory nature. On a windy or cloudy day, or a cold day succeeding warm ones, they are extremely wild, and in most instances rise out of shot, rising skyward with great swiftness, and flying out of sight. If the dog manages to secure a point during the prevalence of such weather, the bird usually flushes at extremely long range or out of range. On warm, quiet days, or days when there is a gentle, mild breeze, the birds will lie very close, particularly if they have good feeding grounds and are fat. Their flight then is slow and lazy, their bills hang pendulously, and the flight usually is short, sometimes but a few yards. When shooting, the better way when the bird is marked is to walk it up, keeping the dog at heel. Snipe generally rise and fly a longer or shorter distance against the wind, hence a skillful hunter makes it a rule to walk down wind on them; but on warm days, or when the birds are fat, it is immaterial how they are approached, so far as the wind is concerned. On favorite feeding grounds if they are of fair size, they may be successfully worked again and again if the weather is favorable and birds plentiful, the flushed birds taking a short flight and dropping back of the shooter; others come in to feed. They are the most uncertain of game birds in their habits, even in settled weather. Grounds which contained large numbers one day may have but one or two birds the next, or none at all. At times they are the easiest of birds for the dog to point, or the sportsman to kill; at other times they are incomparably difficult. They change their feeding grounds frequently without any appreciable cause, sometimes favoring the meadows, at others the wet uplands, plowed fields, or margins of small ponds.

The snipe shooting of the North is a very insignificant affair when compared to that of Louisiana and Texas. It is near their Southern migratory limit and they congregate in vast numbers, and the large prairies and fields afford ample feeding grounds for them. After the heavy fall rains, oftentimes in favorable seasons they are so plentiful that shooting ceases to be a pleasure. Forty or fifty snipe in a day to one gun is a common affair, and one hundred are not uncommon. There are authenticated instances where three or four hundred have been killed by one shooter in one day, he having two guns, which he shot alternately when one became overheated. This kind of slaughter required two or three assistants, one to carry the cartridges and spare gun, others to retrieve the birds. When the birds are so plentiful, a dog is wholly useless except as a retriever. The shooter simply walks along and will have more shooting then than he can attend to, if he happens to be favored with a good day. The fall shooting lasts several weeks.

In the winter, there is more or less shooting that is there considered very poor, but would pass for excellent at any season in the North. But it should be remembered that the winters in that section are very mild and open, the temperature rarely dropping to the freezing point. During March and April, the shooting is again good, although inferior to that of the fall. Often the hunter will find snipe in the cotton and sedge fields, while he is hunting for quails. They are frequently a nuisance to the quail hunter. Dogs, in many instances, become very fond of hunting them, and by constant hunting learn all their favorite winter feeding grounds. When hunting quails, the dog will suddenly remember one of these grounds if in the vicinity, and will take a straight line to it, perhaps half a mile away. If he finds one and points, there is then a long ride or walk for a bird so common that it is not valued highly, and the shooting of it is much inferior to quail shooting.

In working a dog on snipe, he must be corrected if he shows a disposition to press his birds too closely, for such acts, if habitual, are destructive to the sport. When snipe are scarce, the dog can range wide and fast as in quail shooting. An intelligent dog soon learns to work on snipe with greater caution and slowness than on quails, and if hunted on them week after week as can be done in Louisiana or Texas in proper season, the slowness becomes habitual to the injury of the dog's work on quails. The heavy grounds also contribute to the slowness. Considering all the uncertainties in the habits and nature of the bird and the unpleasant work of walking in muddy marshes or heavy upland, it is not a desirable bird to educate dogs on. The author has shot them week after week and always considered them far inferior to quails. It is quite fascinating for a few days when the birds are plentiful, but it soon becomes flat after the novelty wears off, and quails will have a superiority by contrast.

Prairie chicken hunting requires very little skill in man or dog early in the season, although there is no hunting which requires more endurance. The habitat of this bird is in the prairie country of the center of the United States from and including Dakota, Minnesota and Wisconsin on the North to Louisiana and Texas on the South; they are also plentiful to a certain limit northward in British America. They are rapidly becoming exterminated. Such a short time ago as 1882 and 1883, the shooting was uniformly good. It was then no unusual affair to kill from fifty to one hundred birds in a day. In the same sections where the author shot hundreds of them at that time, they now are a rarity. There is an enormous decrease every year excepting in a few favored localities; but the restless search for new grounds will eventually sweep all alike. The advent of the breech-loader and better dogs has sealed their fate.

In locating for a chicken hunt, it is much better to select a small town for headquarters. The large towns are always overrun with visiting sportsmen besides having a full quota of local shooters, a certain percentage of whom gather in a generous share of the birds before the legal season opens. This is so common, except in the vicinity of the large cities, or large towns which have game protective associations, that it is wholly useless to visit one of them with a view to hunting purposes. Unfortunately some of the associations are not always consistent in their practice as individuals with their promulgations as clubs.

Nothing is more destructive to the enjoyment of shooting than crowding. The chicken country, each season, is completely scoured by hunters, and every succeeding season witnesses an enormous accession to their numbers. During the few days prior to the opening day, the baggage cars on every one of the numerous lines through the chicken country are crowded with dogs, tents, guns and general shooting paraphernalia and camping outfits. On the opening day and several days thereafter, and in a lesser degree several days before, the country is swept. The sportsman who goes later in the season to enjoy the shooting and cooler weather will find but little to repay him for his trouble. Broken bevies, wild birds and the most irregular and unsatisfactory sport in consequence, is then the rule.

During the hot weather the chickens are comparatively easy for the dog to point, and the hunter to shoot. Their flights are slow and short; but when the nights begin to get cool and the fall winds set in, they become wilder and wilder, and in the last of August or early September, begin to pack, *i. e.*, two or three covies will unite in one flock, and as the weather gradually becomes more unpleasant and unsettled, the small flocks unite into larger ones. An old cock or two may be found here and there, which will not live with the main flock. Thus all the birds of a certain section are, after a time, in one or two large packs; consequently the shooting then is very uncertain since the pack must be found before any shooting can be done. If the weather is cold or unsettled, the pack when found will fly straightway out of sight. If the hunter should be so fortunate as to find it on a warm, quiet day, or if a gentle, warm breeze is blowing, the birds will lie like stones and their flights are shorter. If the pack lights in long grass and scatters after the first flight, the sportsman may have shooting that will reward many fruitless efforts. The birds will rise, one, two or three at a time, and it requires a steady nerve and cool judgment to take skillful advantage of the opportunities, and not get "rattled." Generally, when the fall weather sets in, the birds become so wild and unapproachable that there is very little sport in hunting them. If one bird flushes all go with it.

On windy days, the cornfields and sloughs covered with long grass are favorite haunts in September. A section in which corn is largely grown is a very poor one for chicken shooting. The birds fly to the cornfields and are then safe, save an occasional few that may be shot. On the whole, these birds afford the dullest, tamest sport, and about all that can be said in their favor is that they furnish some summer shooting. However, it requires a good man, dog and gun to show successful results after the chickens become strong and wild, but their excessive wildness and scarcity render the sport extremely unsatisfactory. Still there are shooters who find it excellent, and, after all, the sport that the shooter takes the most pleasure in is the best for him.

Two horses, which are not afraid of the report of a gun, and a strong double spring wagon, are the best for chicken hunting. A good, experienced driver, one who understands chicken hunting, is indispensable to good sport, and no other should be accepted. His knowledge of the country, habits and haunts of the birds, and skill in marking them down, are invaluable. When the dog points, if in a rolling or hilly country, the driver can take a commanding position on some elevation before the birds are flushed, and from his position in the wagon can mark accurately where they light. If the shooter is inexperienced, he will mark the birds inaccurately. After taking his eyes off the spot he can see fifty places just like the one he marked the birds by, there being a great similarity in the characteristic features of the prairie. Besides noting the exact place as carefully as may be, the shooter should mark it in a straight line with a straw or wheat stack, house, grove, or other prominent object somewhere between the chickens and the horizon. He can always then approach them directly. Sometimes they light nearer than they appear to, at other times farther, the absence of all objects for comparison rendering the distance difficult to estimate. When marking their flight the eye should not be taken off them for an instant, and only when they are seen to light, is there any certainty of estimating where they will be found.

Some prairie hay should be laid evenly on the bottom of the wagon for the comfort of the dogs when riding to and from the hunting grounds, or when they are resting. The weather in August is invariably oppressively hot, and therefore it is very distressing for dogs to work for more than an hour or two at a time. Plenty of water is indispensable. A bountiful supply should be provided before starting, particularly if the water is good. The quality of the water is not uniformly good, some wells having an alkali or lime impregnation. Many homes in the country get their water from a pit dug in low ground which contains surface water, while some depend on stagnant slough water; hence if the shooter neglects to supply himself before starting, it may occasion much inconvenience during the day. Dogs require an abundance of water, and must have it to work well. In the country, there is often great difficulty in caring properly for dogs. The housing for all domestic animals, and for the family, is frequently of the most primitive and inefficient character. When the frosty nights come, it is both cruel and ungrateful to make a dog shift for his sleeping quarters. It is pitiful to see his stiffness and painful movements in the morning after sleeping beside some haystack or even less comfortable place. If there is no barn in which he can be put, his crate can be placed on a bed of hay about two feet deep, and the whole covered with hay on the sides and top about six or eight feet deep, leaving an aperture just large enough for the dog to crawl in and out. Hay is always abundant and cheap. If there is no crate, some boards can be easily nailed together to make a substitute. If the hotel does not afford a sufficiency of scraps, a couple of old prairie chickens or ones badly shot may be boiled for each dog. Usually it is better to buy the dog-food and have it cooked, as there is every probability that a Minnesota, Iowa, Nebraska, or Dakota small country hotel will not have any scraps left—oftentimes the table itself is an inferior gathering of scraps, and dogs or cats dependent on leavings are trusting to a forlorn hope.

Chicken hunting is the hardest of all hunting on a dog, hence he is entitled to every care. The broad prairie offers no obstruction to the highest speed and widest range, the weather is warm, the birds scarce, consequently there is very little to relieve the constant exertion. A wide ranging dog is indispensable to good sport, and he must be hardened by exercise several weeks prior to the opening of the season.

An experience on chickens is not of much value as a preparatory experience for quail hunting. It brings the dog under control, but it frequently happens that a dog broken on chickens has to be rebroken for quail shooting. Theoretically the dog begins on quails with the same degree of perfection that he ended on chickens. Practically, it has very little beneficial effect, and in some instances is a disadvantage. The hard work on chickens, the difference in climate, etc., unfit a dog for several weeks for quail shooting in the South.

CHAPTER XXV.

THE TRAINING OF SPANIELS.

As compared with the setter and pointer, the spaniel has a limited sphere of usefulness, and his manner of hunting to the gun has not so many complex details as the working of setters and pointers.

The admirers of spaniels argue that the pointers' and setters' comparatively great range makes them less desirable for cover shooting as compared with the spaniel; but such is only partially true,—they are naturally much greater rangers, but they can be educated to work their ground as closely as the spaniel and, for the matter of that, to flush birds without pointing, or can be trained to flush them to order. On the other hand, the spaniel cannot take the setter's place as a finding dog. His usefulness is limited to such sections as have an abundance of game or such dense cover as precludes the use of setters,—cover which is very rare. His small size and short legs enable him to take the thickest cover with ease. In beating out narrow strips of cover, as in long narrow runs, in woodcock or ruffed grouse shooting, where one gun on each side, or a gun on one side, can command the width of the run, the cocker is useful. In the large areas of cover, as in ruffed grouse shooting, where the shooter must himself enter, the spaniel is then inferior to the setter. As he is out of sight and does not point his birds, many shots will be lost.

In the ruffed grouse and woodcock sections, setters are

used with admirable success, even in the thickest cover. Many shooters prefer to hunt a dog, in such cover, with a bell attached to the collar, thus by its warning tinkle always giving notice of the whereabouts of the dog; and as the dogs are trained to work close in, when the bell is silent the hunter knows the dog is pointing; he then goes to the dog and flushes, or approaches as near as he can and orders the dog to flush. Setters or pointers which are hunted much in this manner become wonderfully cunning in aiding the gun, and hold their point, or flush the bird to order with rare judgment, but, to maintain a uniform grade of excellence, they must be always handled correctly, always encouraged for good work, and reprimanded for inattention or willful errors. This, by the way, to show that the setter is a powerful rival in the spaniel's own special work, while the spaniel, in the setter's sphere as a finding dog, is a weak competitor.

The method of working spaniels is radically different from that employed in working setters or pointers. Spaniels do not point,—they road their birds to a flush. Their range should never exceed the distance at which the gun can kill, for it is self-evident that if a bird is flushed out of shot, the opportunity to kill is lost. From their narrow range, they beat out the ground very closely and few birds in their beat escape them, particularly when the shooter has a well trained team of them. It will thus be seen that as compared with training the setter and pointer through all the refinements of ranging far and near, pointing and backing, etc., the training of spaniels is a simple affair.

It is no small matter, however, to establish just the right beat,—to and fro within range of the gun, neither going out too far nor working too close. They are checked and restrained to this range until it becomes habitual, and they will work without any supervision. In roading, they should not press their birds too fast, otherwise they get too far from the shooter and flush out of shot. A bell is useful, when hunting in thick cover.

Spaniels which give tongue find favor with many, but noise in bird hunting is entirely out of place. When birds are wild the slightest noise will often alarm them, and an opportunity, which might have been the result of the work of hours, is lost.

The spaniel should be taught to retrieve; the system given hereinbefore applies equally as well to the spaniel as to pointers and setters.

Nothing is so utterly helpless and at the mercy of his trainer as a pointer, setter, or spaniel, when under the control of a spike collar, therefore the trainer should at all times be merciful. As with pointers and setters, trust more to frequent opportunity and slow progress than to violence and an intention to accomplish all in a few lessons.

Chasing rabbits should not be allowed. The same method, used with setters and pointers, will correct this fault. You should not forget that a dog can be broken from hunting certain kinds of game, and that by mismanagement in breaking him from hunting one kind, he may be broken from hunting all kinds.

The checkcord can be used in their training with even greater advantage than in training setters and pointers; their pace is comparatively slow and their range is limited, hence they are always within easy reach. All the commands taught to setters can be profitably taught to spaniels —the method is the same.

There are but few sections in the United States which are favorable to the use of spaniels, and where there is such cover, there is also so much contiguous open country that the hunter needs a setter or pointer for a finding dog. However, cocker and field spaniels are coming into favor. The distinction between the two in this country is more in the weight and size than in race, type, or characteristics, although there is a positive distinction with respect to the two latter. Some breeders have been striving to establish a type, having an extremely long body and short legs, but wherein such a type is an advantage in a working dog, the author has never been able to understand. Either the cocker or field spaniel is small enough to go through any kind of cover that game birds are found in, and if the extreme length of body and shortness of leg are to reduce their speed, the breeder has very little knowledge of how a dog's efforts can be controlled and guided by the trainer.

They are bright, affectionate and neat dogs, very companionable and susceptible of a high degree of training, they being very intelligent. Black spaniels have the greatest uniformity in type amongst cockers; other colored cockers vary in type to an astonishing degree.

The Clumber is about the weight of a small or medium sized setter, and works mute.

CHAPTER XXVI.

GUARD DOGS.

The guard dog does not undergo a regular, formal course of training as do the setter and pointer when educated for field work—his education is accomplished more by making a companion of him continually, thus affording unlimited opportunities for him to exercise his judgment and intelligence.

St. Bernards, mastiffs and Great Danes find great favor as house and guard dogs. It is a mistake, however, to suppose that any dog is a good guard dog simply because he is mastiff, Great Dane or St. Bernard. Lazy, stupid or physically inferior dogs are quite as common in these breeds as in others. In no dog is greater intelligence necessary than in one used as a watch dog, and in none is a good temper more desirable. A vicious temper is no indication of courage; often one possessing such a temper is a pitiful coward in time of danger. A vicious dog is wholly unfit for a companion for children; however, the St. Bernard and mastiff are commonly the personification of amiability and attachment, the Great Dane generally so. The mild temper and cool judgment which a guard dog must preserve even if he suffers provocation is wherein the breeds aforementioned excel. As for desperate courage and destructiveness, they are surpassed by some other breeds; nevertheless, a mild, amiable dog is sufficiently fierce if his temper is once thoroughly aroused as it is certain to be if the master he loves is assaulted, or any attempt made to injure children he associates with as guard and playmate. It is the nature of all dogs, even the most cowardly, when violence is threatened to the master or the household, to take the defence upon themselves.

To give a correct education, it should begin from early puppyhood, the dog having his liberty, and instructed more by association, with proper checking and encouraging as occasion requires, than by any system of formal training. He, by association, learns the everyday routine of the household, the habits of its members, and learns who are strangers, and even learns to discriminate between those which are suspicious in appearance and those which are not, probably being aided in this by observing the air with which different classes of callers are received. He also, from his own powers of observation, learns what are usual incidents and what are unusual, thus showing powers of discrimination.

The guard dog should, however, be taught to obey the common orders, such as "Come here," or "Come in," "Drop," or "Lie down," the methods for accomplishing this being the same as laid down for the training of setters and pointers in like branches.

Nothing is more destructive to a large dog's amiability and usefulness than to keep him chained, and nothing is so unwise or so quick to superinduce viciousness as to tease and worry him when so restrained. It also affects the dog physically if persisted in, large dogs not enduring the confinement without injury. If chained during puppyhood, they are sure to get more or less cow-hocked, out at the elbows, rickety, or twisted out of shape, and are pre-disposed to acquire a scowling or anxious expression of face which detracts from their companionable qualities. Only by thus treating the dog as a companion can he be made an intelligent guard dog, and but little should be expected of him until he has the experience and judgment of maturity, as no dog is capable of filling an office of so much responsibility before maturity.

CHAPTER XXVII

THE TRAINING OF FOXHOUNDS.

A very essential thing to the value and working capabilities of foxhounds is purity of blood. Any owner who resides where foxes, or other game on which hounds are used, are plentiful, will have good field dogs if they are properly bred. Hounds do not require the careful training that is given to pointers and setters. Given the hounds properly bred, if they are only taken to game and let alone, they will generally make good dogs, yet the manner of doing this well requires some skillful management which will be hereinafter described.

Too much care therefore cannot be taken in selecting and breeding foxhounds, for if there is any breed of dog that requires natural qualities in their highest perfection, it is the breed of foxhounds, particularly those which are used to run red foxes in the Middle States. It does not make so much difference about the pure breeding of dogs which are used to hunt deer, bears, wild cats or grey foxes, or for dogs that are used in the East to drive the fox by the stand of a shooter, and hence not strictly for the chase.

Hounds for catching red foxes should be selected from the best possible blood that can be obtained. A criterion of excellence should be breeding a uniform good lot, not a large litter with one good one in it, but a litter of, at least, good ones and the majority high class ones. To breed in this way, you must select stock which you know has high class natural qualities in physical structure and powers afield. This requires a pure ancestry as a prime factor; in fact, the breeding of foxhounds requires all the care and skill that is exercised in maintaining and improving other breeds.

As to the qualities to be desired, the hounds should be bred and trained so that they work almost as fast as the high class English setter of to-day. Their noses should be good enough to strike and trail up a fox, in favorable weather for hunting, which has passed along from twelve to twenty-four hours before; they should trail steadily, keep close together, and pick out the trail accurately and quickly—not scatter all over the country and go like wild dogs; but if the track is too cold to nose out, they should be intelligent enough to know it, but should stick to it until they get the course of the fox and go on circling from it for a mile or more if they cannot strike it in a less distance, and they should be dogs which would persist in trailing and working this way all day if necessary—not stop and give up in an hour or two if the fox is not jumped.

I like a dog with a clear, loud voice, one that gives tongue very freely while trailing and running, but not one that gives tongue when he runs over the track, and has lost the scent.

In chasing the red fox, when he is jumped, the pack should be very fast runners, stick close together and close to the trail; but on a loss of it, they should make wide casts for it and not turn too straight back; and if you have a dog that is too slow, one that does not pack well, one that runs over badly, or one that will quit a hotly contested race, he should be killed, not given to some friend who will probably breed from him or her. For red foxes they should be able to run and trail from twelve to twenty hours, and that singly if necessary. On favorable days, a first class pack nearly

AMERICAN FOXHOUND.

always catches a red fox in from two and one-half to four hours, but to do this they must make no mistakes and have favorable weather. One bad run-over, or loss, almost always gives the fox enough time to get far enough away to bring the pack to the trail, and if he is a good runner he will never allow them to get a close run on him again until he is so fatigued that he cannot possibly keep in front of them. To run a good old red fox to death that has got the advantage of a young pack in any way, you need dogs that will stick, all alone if necessary, from twelve to twenty hours; and it very often is necessary. To make a success of hunting red foxes, there should never be under eight good dogs that run and stay close together, and I think it much better to have twenty or more good ones. One poor dog in a chase does much more harm than good.

We are, in this section, as careful of the lives of our red foxes as we are of saving our pocketbook. I hope the Eastern hunters will adopt the plan of having more and better dogs, and quit shooting foxes.

We will now consider the subject of training. A foxhound puppy should not be allowed to run any until he is about eight months old, and if they are not well grown, healthy puppies at that age, they should be kept up and well fed until healthy and strong. When they are first taken out and started on a chase, they should accompany old, steady, broken hounds which you expect to train them with regularly, and they should first be run on rabbits about every other day. One hour at a time is sufficient, gradually working them longer if they are enduring the work well, until you get them so they can stand six or eight hours' good hard running after rabbits, remembering that they are always to be in company with the broken foxhounds that they are to be broken with.

While they are taking their first experiences with rabbits,

they should be taught to come to the blast of the horn or a call, and should be allowed to follow you on horseback around the country, occasionally, to teach them how to follow and not get lost. When they are about one year old and are well advanced in chasing rabbits, they should be taken out with the broken dogs next on grey foxes, or wild cats, if any are available. They never should be allowed to run a red fox until they are about eighteen months old, or are fully developed and strong enough to run from eight to twelve hours in a fast, closely-contested chase with fast hounds, and never should be taken out again, after a chase, until they are well rested. When started on grey fox or cat, as mentioned before, they should be accompanied by thoroughly broken, good, steady, working old dogs; not very fast dogs, but ones that will stick close to the trail and never quit following or trailing for twelve or fifteen hours, unless they capture their quarry or are stopped. The reason that I prefer dogs which are not so fast, to train puppies with, is because I want broken dogs which they can keep up with, and therefore can do some of the work themselves,—if the old dogs are too fast, the puppies will soon run down from their great efforts to keep up, or will be thrown out and learn to quit. They rarely ever forget their first experience after fox, and if they learn bad habits at first, they frequently retain them through life. When first taken out with broken dogs as already explained, they should be allowed to have their own way to a great extent. An assistant is necessary in training puppies. He can ride on with the broken dogs, occasionally blowing the horn for the puppies while you remain with them and cheer them off of anything they may be after. After the old dogs have struck a trail, the hunter should follow and encourage them a *little*, but do very little following; the other remains back and cheers the puppies in with the old dogs. They will soon learn to love the trail of a fox and will stay with the old dogs without much trouble. They should never be whipped much, and this especially should be avoided by the owner or trainer; they should be permitted to have their own way as much as possible.

Experience after the kind of game you hunt will gradually break them, and if they are whipped too much or broken too quickly, they will not make fast hunters and good strike dogs.

The best all-round dogs, which I have ever owned, were dogs which were hard to break, and, in fact, were not thoroughly broken till they were about three years old. My long experience with high class English setters and fox-hounds has taught me that it requires plenty of time and patience, and that a dog should be allowed to have his own way as much as possible, to make a first class dog out of him and develop his natural capabilities to the utmost. Of course, a puppy can be trained easier and quicker by starting his training while he is very young, but the great trouble is that the greater number trained after such a manner are worthless brutes.

Many hunters believe in running puppies and old dogs after a drag a great deal, but I do not believe in allowing a pack of hounds to run drags much, for I have seen good packs completely ruined by such practice; so badly ruined that they could not catch a good running red fox. They always learn to run-over very badly, and form many bad habits from this manner of hunting. If drags are run any with young puppies, it should be in company with old dogs which stick close to the track, and ones which cannot out-run them. The drag should always be manipulated by some one who is afoot, and should never be dragged in a road or pathway. The man should drag it about in circles as near after the course a fox runs as possible, through thickets, and never in a straight course.

In breaking and hunting, when a dog strikes a fox trail, give him plenty of time and wait until he has decided which way the fox has gone. Do not commence hurrying the hound and he will almost always learn to take the right end of the track, and, in trailing, I think the hunter should give the dogs plenty of time on any track that they can nose out, should always remain behind his dogs, try to keep them as close together as possible, and instead of continually harking them on, it would be better to call them back together and let them nose out the track accurately, if possible to do so. A hunter that always thinks he knows exactly where the quarry can be jumped, and is continually hunting his dogs on from trail to trail, never has a first class pack of trail dogs. It is true that very often, after this manner, he jumps his game very quickly, but to put him in a country where game is very scarce, he will more frequently spoil a good day's sport; moreover, after harking his dogs off a cold trail a few times, they soon get discouraged, and will not work at all. Any well bred pack of hounds that is broken and handled properly should, in favorable weather, work and trail a track all day, that is from ten to twenty hours old, and to get them to do that you must stay behind them, give them lots of time, try to keep them very close together, and let them nose it out. The great secret, I think, in catching red foxes is to have good stayers, ones that will run very close together. If there is a dog in your pack which is too fast or too slow and cannot be made to trail or run close with them, it would be best to kill him. One bad "run-over" dog will often ruin a large pack, and with a few such losses of time occasioned by this fault, they rarely ever catch any red foxes. While the pack should run well together and very fast, they should not "run-over" and make bad losses of time.

It is now apparent that, to endure the fatiguing exertion

and to train puppies properly to run long, hard races, they should be strong and have the necessary age before starting them after red foxes, and should be run with well broken dogs, so that they will learn no bad habits. I do not think any pack should ever quit running until it catches or trees whatever it is after; however, to have a pack of this kind you must have good blood in it. Kill any dog that will quit before he is stopped or catches his game, for he will turn some good young dog to stop with him.

A hunter should always endeavor to keep within hearing of his pack, and never go home and leave them running. If they learn once that you are a quitter they will be quitters also.

For good killing dogs for bears and deer, they should be trained and handled precisely the same as in hunting foxes, excepting that they should go a little slower and should not be good stayers in a chase; they should always stop running a deer, if he is not wounded, within one hour; for if you do not kill the deer in that time, he is so far away from the dogs that it is difficult to get a shot; the greater number of times they run off some ten or twenty miles. If game is plentiful, it is much more sport to get the dogs back in the drive and jump another deer. J. M. AVENT.

HICKORY VALLEY, TENN.

Mr. Avent's attainments as a trainer and field trial handler are well known, his success at field trials and prominence in dog matters for many years being a feature in the chronicles of field sports and within the personal knowledge of the larger part of sportsmen; yet except in the South it is not generally known that he is an enthusiastic and accomplished fox, deer and bear hunter, an owner of hounds for many years and a recognized authority on them; therefore, this chapter, coming from a recognized expert, should be accredited with the full measure of worth to which it is properly entitled. B. W.

CHAPTER XXVIII.

MISCELLANEOUS.

With respect to guns, it can be set down as the soundest of rules that it is always better to buy one manufactured by a reputable maker. The thousands of cheap guns distributed throughout the country, every country hardware store or general store having a stock with every imaginable kind of a trade name, or names closely resembling those of celebrated makers, evidently with the intention to defraud the purchaser, are not worth the trouble of accepting as a gift. They are made of poor material, badly fitted and balanced, and soon become shaky and unsafe, if not so at the beginning. These remarks, however, are intended to give the tyro some general suggestions with reference to the powder charges, gauges, etc., for different kinds of shooting. The subject with respect to gauges, weights, makes, etc., is in theory a most voluminous and diversified one, there being no end to opinions and controversies. In practice, there are certain data which afford ample information on all points. Usually the most important cause of failure to kill is that the gun is not held aright.

For general shooting, that is quails, chickens, ducks, snipes and woodcocks, the twelve gauge has the nearest approach to the properties of an all round gun, namely, weight, effectiveness and economy. To the sportsman who indulges his fancy in a gun, with a limitation relating to ways and means, the twelve gauge is the gun par excellence for general shooting. As to the weight, he must be governed by his physical capabilities, the weight of powder and shot loads he desires to use, the kinds of game that he will shoot most, etc. A half pound extra weight on a gun makes a perceptible difference in the greater fatigue of carrying or handling it all day. The favorite weights run from seven to eight pounds. A few shooters prefer guns of nine pounds or more, but they are extremely few; however, the extra weight is necessary if unusually heavy loads are used. It is an absurdity to claim that a light twelve gauge with light loads will kill as far as a heavy twelve gauge with heavy loads, if each gun is bored to give the best results with the respective loads. For upland shooting, a twelve gauge, thirty inch barrels, seven and one-half pounds in weight, bored to shoot from three to three and one-half drams of powder, and one ounce, or one and one-eighth ounce of shot, is ample. For chicken and duck shooting, a full or modified choke is not out of place. Many opportunities for long shots constantly occur, and, it being chiefly open shooting, if the birds rise too close, the shooter can wait till they get a proper distance away before killing. In chicken and duck shooting, a great deal of experience is necessary to acquire the ability to estimate distances properly, the tendency being to under-estimate them.

The sportsman whose shooting is confined to quails, snipes and woodcocks should use a sixteen gauge. It is also effective in the early part of the season on chickens. But, whether he uses a twelve or sixteen gauge for quails, snipes and woodcocks, a choked gun should most emphatically be condemned. A true cylinder is the gun. Quail shooting is usually close shooting. Usually the extreme range is less than thirty-five yards; the occasional shots at forty, fifty or sixty yards being no sort of consequence as compared to the bulk of the shooting. The average limit is from fifteen to twenty-five or thirty yards. If a full choked gun is shot at a target at twenty yards, the absurdity of shooting such a close mass of shot at a quail will be evident. A large percentage of birds are so mutilated by the use of choked guns that they are worthless, and occasional ones wholly destroyed. The author had the full choke mania some years ago, and for no other reason except that others used them, he purchased one. The whole character of his shooting changed. Shots that previously were easy became extremely difficult. Birds were blown to atoms, or partially blown away or minced, or cleanly missed at good ranges, yet the gun with all its atrocities of full choke and heavy powder charges was cherished, simply because it was the fashion. It was not a question of the shooting adapted to game, but a question of close pattern. By constant use, many faults were to a certain degree corrected, but there were always lurking the same fundamental principles of unfitness. The elements of the shooting were forced to fit the special features of the gun instead of having the gun adapted to the special features of the shooting. After persisting in the delusion about five years, the gun was bored out to a modified choke. This was a great gain, and improved the shooting qualities wonderfully.

A twelve gauge gun which will nicely distribute its load of one and one-quarter ounces of No. 8 shot, and place two hundred and fifty pellets in a thirty inch circle at forty yards, is amply sufficient for upland shooting.

The sixteen gauge should be about six pounds in weight, twenty-eight inch barrels. From two and one-quarter to two and three-quarter drams of powder, and three-quarter to seven-eighths ounce of shot is a load. It is very difficult to get a reputable manufacturer to make a cylinder bore. The popular estimate of a gun's merits is the closeness of its pattern at forty yards, and a maker dislikes to send out a gun that makes a pattern which might be considered inferior. The economy in the cost of shooting, ease of manipulation and comfort in carrying a sixteen gauge is much in its favor, and its capabilities are adequate to the requirements of quail shooting. If the shooter can afford it, it is much better to own special guns, a sixteen, ten and twelve gauge. The ten gauge should weigh from nine to ten pounds, and is superior for ducks and geese. It is commonly used with from four to six drams of powder, and an ounce and one-quarter of shot. The smaller bores will shoot small sizes of shot with nearly as much force as the ten bore, but the killing circle is less. The large sizes of shot can be used better in the ten bore. As for the smaller bores being equal in shooting capabilities to the large bores, it is an absurdity. Weight of powder, lead, bore and metal is palpably an advantage, else there would not be any more force in a cannon than a twenty bore.

The length and drop of stock must be determined by the sportsman himself. Every one has some peculiarities of physical structure which must be considered in selecting a gun which will fit properly, and the fitness can only be determined by actual trial either with an adjustable gun which large dealers usually keeps for a purpose, or by selecting one out of a large number. In shooting, it is a matter of prime importance to have a gun which is so shaped that it can be thrown into position easily and accurately.

Usually the large manufacturers or their agents give a discount of twenty-five or thirty per cent. from the list price, which would make a gun, listed at fifty dollars, cost thirty-five or thirty-seven dollars and fifty cents. This is as low as a purchaser should go in prices if he wishes to get a serviceable, reliable gun. The cheaper grades of American guns are far superior to those of foreign make of like grade in respect to price; but in the high grades, from three hundred dollars up, the foreign made gun is the best.

From fifty dollars to one hundred and fifty to two hundred dollars, the quality of the gun rapidly improves, but not in a regular ratio; for instance, there is a vast difference between the material, workmanship and finish of a fifty dollar gun and a one hundred dollar gun, but there may be only finer grades of the same material in a one hundred and a one hundred and fifty dollar gun, and the latter may have a better finish. Beyond the latter price, the value is chiefly in fine engraving, rare wood in the stock, and costly finish and hand labor. As serviceable and handsome a gun as a sportsman needs can now be bought of American make from several prominent manufacturers, for one hundred and fifty dollars or even less. They are quite as nicely balanced as the English high grade guns, and there is not the extreme difference that is commonly ascribed to them. A very small part is fact and a very large part is imagination. If a number of the higher grades of American guns and a like number of foreign guns were placed in a dark room so that the eye would not assist, it is doubtful whether any man is expert enough to determine the difference in them if restricted to determining by the balance alone. The American made guns in the higher grades are constructed of fine material, are finely fitted, artistically finished, nicely proportioned, and shoot equal to the best. If two guns, of eqnal weights and measurements, balance alike at or near the hinge, there cannot be a great difference in the handling of them even if one bears the name of an English maker, the other an American. While a nicely balanced gun is necessary, the exquisite, poetical, ethereal, dreamy balance is unnecessary for good shooting, particularly if it is necessary to pay two or three hundred dollars extra to secure it. The extra price is sure to react on the imagination of the purchaser in such a manner that he can perceive a delicacy of balance which is superior to all others.

In purchasing a gun, due regard should be paid to the weight of powder and shot charges which are to be used in it. Different charges require a special boring to perform at their best. Besides, every gun has its individual peculiarities and will shoot one certain load better than any other and such as a matter of course, is the best load for it. Some guns will shoot all sizes of small shot well, others only one or two. The best load can only be determined by repeated trials. Two ordinary felt wads or one thick one over the powder and a card board wad over the shot is all the wadding necessary for ordinary shooting. In early shooting, many good field shots use but one felt wad over the powder, and it appears, from the successful results, to be amply sufficient.

For chickens, No. 8 shot are fine enough early in the season. In September and October 7's and 6's can be used to advantage. For snipes and woodcocks, 9's and 10's are good. For quails, 8's and 9's, the former size being used after the birds get strong and heavily feathered. In cold weather, when strong and well fed, quails will often fly a long distance before falling, when hard hit with 9's or 10's, and occasionally with 8's, hence the former do not give the uniformity in clean killing that the 8's do.

There are several important items of information concerning the carriage of dogs which are very advantageous to know before starting on a long railroad trip with dogs in charge. Always give the preference to a road that runs through trains, even if the rates are higher. Changes of cars are very inconvenient and sometimes occasion unnecessary delay. Nearly all roads refuse to assume any responsiblity for dogs, or their handling or baggage. They are carried simply as a matter of courtesy. If there is a change of cars there is always enough to engage the station baggageman's attention, and any request for assistance must be accompanied with a fifty cent piece or a dollar. There is no time to adjust differences. The delay of a minute may be the cause of a missed train.

Long journeys by rail are very disturbing to the dog's system, particularly if he is nervous and fretful. During the stops for meals, the owner or man in charge can take him out for a short run, thereby giving opportunity for the necessary act of defecation. Many dogs will retain urine and fæces an injuriously long time, if confined in a crate, thus suffering a great deal, arriving in bad condition and requiring several days to recover. Sometimes a bad diarrhœa is caused by neglecting to take the dog out of his crate as mentioned. It is better to feed sparingly a day or so before starting, and during the journey. Give a few scraps of meat and all the water he needs. He will suffer less from the effects of the journey and recover quicker than if fed liberally. No sportsman should think of traveling with a dog without putting him in a crate for protection and to guard against escape; besides, the dog is much more comfortable and easy to handle. It may save the hunter a great deal of annoyance also, for some railroads will not carry dogs which are not crated. When a baggage car is crowded with heavy baggage, a dog on chain is in constant danger of injury or loss of life from falling trunks, or others being thrown or rolled into place, and loss or escape under these circumstances is not infrequent. Moreover, he is constantly in the way of the baggageman, and is frequently a sufferer in consequence; for the baggageman does not always use the gentlest means; in fact he is generally so hurried that it is impossible for him to do so. A gratuity at the start is a very discreet act, if any favors or attentions are desired. There is not a day on any of the great lines but what there are special personal claims on his attention, and naturally they grow wearisome. Unless he is rewarded, there is no reason why he should consider one personal claim any more than hosts of others. As a class, if treated courteously and considerately, they are obliging. That they should not always be pleased at the sight of dogs is the outcome of good causes. Their experience with dog owners is not always of the pleasantest kind. They meet the individual dog owner who is perpetually wanting something, even at the busiest moments; then there is the imperious gentleman who thinks the presence of his dogs paramount to all other business of the road, and demands what he should request; there is the gent who is gentle, but persists in telling the antecedents of his dog to a maddening length; and there is the numerous element who try to evade the payment of tariff or gratuity. Nearly all roads have an established tariff on dogs, which in most instances goes to the baggageman as a perquisite. Some roads will not take dogs unless the owner or his agent signs a form releasing the road from all liability for death, injury or escape. It is very unpleasant to know that in many instances the experience of railroad officials with a certain class of sportsmen made this protective course necessary; thus all have to suffer for the acts of a few. When five or six dogs are taken along, the tariff is very oppressive. One or two are allowed to go free by most roads; when the sportsman has more than that number, it is better to write to the general baggage agent and make special arrangements if possible before starting. If the journey is long, it is particularly desirable to get full information. Some roads have a rule which allows the hunter, who is a passenger, only carriage for two dogs—over that number they will not carry. It is obvious that if a hunter had a ticket over such line and had more than two dogs with him, he would find himself very unpleasantly circumstanced. Also some roads very properly refuse to carry dogs which are not in crates. All these matters are very simple, apparently, but they assume a great importance five minutes before train time in a strange city.

A good, cheap crate is herewith described. It is light, strong and durable. The dimensions are as follows: Height, 26 inches; width, 25 inches; length, 30 inches. The frame should be of ash, 1½ x 1½ inches. Pine slats, 2 x ⅜ inches. The bottom strip should be 6 inches wide to keep the dog's feet or tail from slipping out, and also to retain the bedding. The bottom should be of ¾ inch pine boards. Brace diagonally across the top to give the necessary stiffness. Light wrought nails or screws are the best for fastening. A door in the end, with a hasp, staple and hinges, is necessary. A small box, opening on the top, and made a part of the crate, is convenient for carrying food, chain, etc. A light crate is easier to handle, is more pleasing to the eye and is a direct saving of money when dogs are sent by express, double first class rates being the expressage on dogs. Painting protects the crate from becoming water logged by heavy rains, and also is desirable on the score of neatness. A case, made of oilcloth or other waterproof material, can be made to nicely fit the top and sides. This will be of frequent use in traveling as when driving from place to place on stormy days, or in changing cars where there is a wait of several hours and the weather is rainy or cold. If, on arriving at a strange place where there is no shelter for dogs, the crate, thus protected, is impervious to rain or wind, and is a very good kennel for the time being. With respect to protection from idlers whose curiosity is so obtrusive as to be irritating impertinence, and is a source of constant annoyance, a crate having slats is inferior to one having a solid top and sides, with narrow slots closely grated, although the latter is not so comfortable

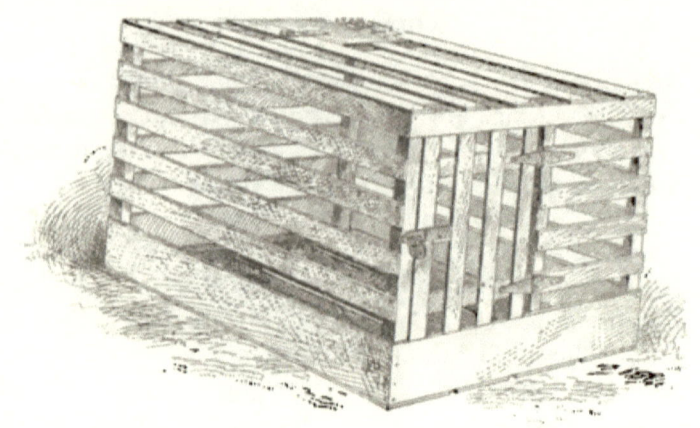
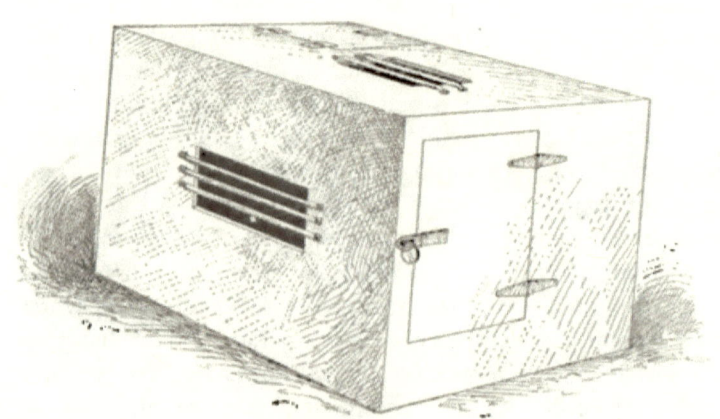

DOG CRATES.

in hot weather. Some sportsmen use crates with a false bottom under which are placed spiral springs, which add greatly to the dog's comfort.

There are some faults occasionally exhibited by the dog which do not properly come under the head of training, but which need correcting when they appear, namely, killing chickens and sheep. If the dog kills chickens, make an effort to catch him in the act. Put a spike collar on him and tie the rope around your waist, this merely to hold him. Both hands are then free. Take the chicken in one hand and the whip in the other, hit him lightly over the head with the chicken, and at the same time give a severe cut with the whip. Whip and scold alternately. Graduate the punishment according to the needs of the dog, which is determined by his disposition, number of offences, etc. The principle is identical with that of breaking a dog from chasing rabbits, etc., namely, he blinks them.

For chasing sheep, the dog must be soundly thrashed if caught in the act. Then put a line on him and lead him toward the sheep; if he shows the slightest disposition to chase, repeat the whipping; continue the treatment till he will shrink at sight of them. While giving the whipping, repeat at intervals the exclamation *Hi!* or such exclamation as is preferred, to make the dog desist. He will soon learn to heed it. If a dog acquires a habit of sheep-killing through hunting with sheep-killing curs, he becomes cunning and usually selects the night hours for his depredations. When his master is present he may not notice them. Bad management of the owner is responsible for such viciousness. If the dog cannot be caught in the act, there is no certain way of breaking him of it. Hutchinson, I think, recommends tying one end of a stiff stick to the dog's collar the other end to the horns of a strong ram, the severe jerking and consequent terror caused by the efforts of the ram to butt the dog being considered effectively curative. As a matter of opinion the author would consider it to be of doubtful efficacy. The dog is too intelligent to be deterred by such treatment, or the more absurd one of tying a piece of sheepskin to his mouth so that the taste and annoyance of the wool will create a dislike to catching sheep.

KENNEL SECRETS.

HOW TO BREED, EXHIBIT AND MANAGE DOGS.

FROM "KENNEL SECRETS."

By "ASHMONT."

PRICE, - - - - - $3.00.

ADDRESS

J. L. THAYER PUB. CO., - 248 Boylston St., Boston, Mass.

Extracts from Press Comments. *(Continued.)*

"Of its intrinsic worth to breeders, fanciers, exhibitors, and all interested in dogdom, it would be impossible to speak too highly."

American Field.

"The most beautiful book yet published on matters pertaining exclusively to the dog is 'Ashmont's' new work entitled 'Kennel Secrets.'"

The Sportsmen's Review.

"To say that it is a superb work is to put it mild. The text is of inestimable value to every dog man in the land. The illustrations, 170 in number, are the finest executed half-tones ever published."

Pacific Field Sports.

"The consensus of opinion is, that it is the best and most elaborate book of the kind ever turned out by a publishing house. At $3.00, the sale of the first volume should be enormous."

Turf, Field and Farm.

"It is truly a grand production, and by far the most valuable addition to canine literature that has been made. * * * The value of the illustrations, showing as they do specimens nearest perfection, and in so many different positions, is well-nigh incalculable, for fanciers can now create near ideals of the dogs they must breed to advance the work of improvement."

New York Herald.

"Ashmont has given to the dog fancier a most valuable little book on the diseases of the dog, and few indeed are the kennels where it is not to be found, or where it is not immediately consulted on the first symptoms of anything being wrong, but his earlier efforts are entirely eclipsed by 'Kennel Secrets,' a work of 344 pages, devoted to the care, management, and breeding of the dog. The scope of this book is great; none but an experienced 'dog man' would have dared to have attempted it. But, although Dr. Perry aimed high when he undertook 'Kennel Secrets,' no one can deny that he has hit the bullseye. * * * It has proved an enormous success, and the verdict of the fancier seems to be that nothing so good has appeared since 'Stonehenge' produced his famous work on the dog."

Boston Herald.

"The 'secret' is out — that is, 'Kennel Secrets,' and it is worth the waiting. Already we have made favorable mention of the work, judged from the advance sheets and proofs of the illustrations. The complete volume more than fulfils the promise of these harbingers. If the mind is educated through the eye, then the pictures in this book are a whole college course in dog lore. Most of them are absolutely perfect, and show only the best type of the breed illustrated. That is, the pictures of the dogs, and perhaps the statement might be extended to include the gentlemen here represented; for they are surely worthy types of dog lovers. The price of the book is $3.00, and it contains nearly 350 pages of attractively printed wisdom on the breeding, management, and exhibition of dogs. Every dog man will wish to own a copy."

Dog Fancier.

Extracts from Testimonials. *(Continued.)*

"Your great work has been my constant companion for many evenings, and it is needless to add that the company has been most agreeable and profitable. In face of the many praises from competent critics, anything from me would be superfluous, but I cannot refrain from pronouncing it a wonder and the kennel book of this or any other age."

Mr. Charles E. Bunn.

"Am extremely well pleased with the typographical appearance, and its splendid engravings, but more especially with the reading matter, which is certainly the best ever given the Dog Fanciers of this or any other country."

Mr. A. E. Pitts.

"'Kennel Secrets' is an evidently scientific and practical work, showing advanced thought and great labor on the part of our esteemed 'Ashmont.' It can be trusted, and I commend it as a guide in the care and treatment of our much loved friend — the dog."

Dr. A. G. Aldrich.

"I am delighted with the binding and elegant engravings, but what is of a more priceless value to us doggy men is the good solid food for study it contains — written in a clear concise style that needs only to be read to be appreciated. It is certainly a boon to a lover of the dog, whether he owns only one or a large kennel. Should this book be read as extensively as it deserves, there will certainly be less mistakes from ignorance in the breeding and care of dogs in the next decade than there has been in the last."

Mr. W. B. McCloud.

"I do not hesitate to say that it is the most complete and comprehensive work on the subject that has ever been brought to my notice. Every line in it testifies, not only to the author's scientific attainments, but also to a thorough knowledge of dogs and their treatment, which could only be obtained by many years of close observation and practical experience."

Mr. James Mortimer.

"'Kennel Secrets' alone tells how to breed and exhibit dogs successfully.
'Kennel Secrets' alone tells how to properly feed and raise puppies.
'Kennel Secrets' alone tells how to wash and condition show dogs.
'Kennel Secrets' alone tells the best hair growing treatment for Yorkshires.
'Kennel Secrets' alone introduces the fancier to the secrets of the kennel.
'Kennel Secrets' alone portrays the grandest dogs of two kennel worlds.

"Manifestly, then, 'Kennel Secrets' stands alone, and he who disregards its teachings will count many losses and but few blue ribbons."

Mr. Charles H. Mason.

"After a thorough examination and perusal, I do not hesitate to pronounce it the most remarkable book that has ever been published relative to the Dog. Not only remarkable for its beautiful and perfect illustrations, which excel anything of the kind that has ever been published, and for its general handsome appearance, but also for the masterly manner in which the subject has been handled by its distinguished author, who has gone into this work with a thoroughness of detail that is immeasurably valuable to all breeders and others interested in dogs."

W. L. Washington ("Kildare").

CONTENTS.

PART I.—MANAGEMENT.

CHAPTER I.

THE NATURAL DIET.

The dog of to-day. — Diet best suited to him. — Familiar faults in feeding. — Quantity of meat required daily. — Influences which modify it. — Force of individual peculiarities. — Dangers of **excess of meat.** — Relations between effects of animal and vegetable **foods.** — The right proportions **of** the ingredients of **a** mixed diet. — **Allowances** that should be made **for** existing circumstances. — Distinct **lines** on which to formulate diet-tables 3

CHAPTER II.

VARIETIES OF ANIMAL FOODS.

Proportions of meat required by puppies. — Penalties for over-feeding. — Special value of raw meat. — Prejudices against it duly considered. — Relation between an animal's disposition and his food. — Meat and the scenting powers. — Important facts about common foods. — When horse-flesh is wholesome. — Milk in its various forms. — Eggs as a food and medicine. — Their action in health and disease. — Fish, how it should be cooked and served 19

CHAPTER III.

VEGETABLE FOODS.

Capabilities of dogs' digestive powers. — Special effects of vegetables on the blood. — The various starchy foods. — Wheat and its products. — Much about bread remnants. — Prejudices against corn meal. — The foundations for the same. — Right method of use. — Oatmeal, and its peculiar effects. — Rice, and its admirable qualities. — Nutritive value of barley and rye. — How starches should be cooked. — The proportions of them allowable 35

CHAPTER IV.

DIETARY FOR PUPPIES.

The right period for weaning. — Essential preparatory steps. — Various foods to be used. — Proper quantities of each. — Number of feedings demanded. — Of what each should consist, up to the eighth month. — The great secrets of puppy-raising. — Means of preventing deformities. — Many absurd notions combated. — Ruinous results of overfeeding. — Treatment of common affections by dietetic means . . 49

CHAPTER V.

GENERAL DIETARY.

The foods, quantities, and combinations for toys. — Of what each meal should consist. — Special directions for feeding the overweighty. — Rules against over-feeding. — Many valuable hints for novices. — How mature dogs should be fed. — The number of meals they should have. — Methods of preparing meat. — Quantities required under various conditions of life. — Foods that should be associated with it. — Requisite proportions of each. — Treatment of dainty feeders. — In total loss of appetite 65

CHAPTER VI.

KENNELLING.

The most primitive kennels. — Their glaring defects. — A suitable kennel. — The best situation for it. — Complete directions for builders. — Its various furnishings. — Absolute requisites to health. — To secure freedom from vermin. — Method of fumigation by sulphur. — Important considerations in large kennels. — Precautions to be observed in stable quarters. — An efficient deodorizer 81

CHAPTER VII.

EXERCISE.

Physiology of exercise. — Baneful results of too close confinement. — Yards for puppies. — Prime requisites. — Infinite importance of cleanliness. — Yards for mature dogs. — Economy and efficiency duly considered. — Devices for exercising in cities. — How to estimate the amount of work imperative for puppies. — For the mature. — Special requirements for dogs in the stud 93

CHAPTER VIII.

THE DRINKING WATER.

Dangers in foul water. — Some important physiological facts. — Prevalent theories that are unsound. — Symptoms caused by denial of sufficient water. — Excess rarely, if ever, to be feared. — One of the first essentials in all kennels. — Difficulties in maintaining healthfulness where there are many inmates. — Water for puppies. — Its peculiar beneficial action on digestion 109

CHAPTER IX.

WASHING AND GROOMING.

When frequent washing is imperative. — Injurious effects of cheap soaps. — The required articles of toilet. — General rules for washing. — Egg shampoos. — Necessary treatment after bathing. — Remedies where the coat is harsh. — Influences which greatly injure fine hair. — Absolute essentials to its health. — When it falls out. — The common causes. — Safe and efficient hair restorers 116

CHAPTER X.

TROUBLESOME INSECTS.

Nature and habits of fleas. — Agents that are obnoxious to them. — The most potent preventive. — Powerful flea-destroyers. — Insect powders. — Tinctures of the same. — Cheap and potent solution of carbolic acid. — Real facts as to flea-soaps in general. — To afford relief from flies. — Sure remedies for lice. — For the removal of wood-ticks. — Treatment of kennels when infested 129

PART II. — EXHIBITING.

CHAPTER I.

PREPARATORY WORK.

The real danger of infection at shows. — Infinitely less than generally supposed. — Much of interest about distemper and mange. — Amount of work required. — Expedients where opportunities are limited. — Erroneous notions that are productive of much harm. — How sporting dogs are often injured. — Medicines commonly used for conditioning. — Serious results which follow their use 143

CHAPTER II.

THE FEEDING.

Special requirements of common varieties. — The most nutritive and digestible foods. — Number of meals required daily. — The methods of preparation. — Forced or spoon feeding. — The feeding of toys in general. — An absurd notion dispelled. — The foods they should have. — How the same should be cooked. — At which meals they should be given. — The quantities and proportions of each. — Remedies to be found in the feeding-pan. — Dietetic treatment of the overweighty . 155

CHAPTER III.

CONDITIONING THE COAT.

When the work of improvement should commence. — Character and amount of grooming required. — Expedient to be resorted to in extreme cases. — Special precautions to be observed in all instances. — Where novices are liable to be at fault. — The last wash before the show. — Formula for the best kennel soap. — Washing with eggs. — How to wash a Yorkshire terrier. — Each step in the process fully described 166

CHAPTER IV.

TO AND FROM THE SHOW.

A suitable crate. — Injunctions as to feeding while on the cars. — A mistake that has often proved fatal. — Choosing a caretaker. — Rules which he should observe. — A provision against mange and eczema. — The return journey. — Precautions against the transmission of contagion. — Disinfection after home is reached. — Dietetic restrictions that are advisable. — The only medicinal treatment generally required. 177

CHAPTER V.

ON THE BENCH.

The feeding. — When the appetite is impaired. — A common custom to be avoided. — The first essential to the maintenance of good condition. — Before the judges. — Ring etiquette. — Grave mistake of many exhibitors. — **Golden rule for all to follow.** — Hints for show management. — Delusions about disinfectants. — **Unwarrantable** inflictions upon dogs and visitors. — Measures of relief advised . . . 185

PART III. — BREEDING.

CHAPTER I.

SELECTION OF SIRE.

Methods of the average breeder. — Glaring faults uncovered. — Why failures are so common. — **The prime essentials to success.** — Lines on which sires should be chosen. — **Breeding sporting dogs.** — Advantages of in-breeding. — Its pernicious effects. — **Influence of the** previous sire. — Unsound theories combated. — **Where misalliance** occurs. — Importance of pedigree. — Interesting **experiments in hybridizing.** — Valuable lessons therefrom 197

CHAPTER II.

IN SEASON.

Too early mating and maturity. — Effects on the mother. — On the offspring. — Is mating at the first season justified? — The method of "shaping." — Maturing periods. — Signs presented during the "rutting season." — When to mate is possible. — Successful service. — Absolute essentials in both subjects of a union. — One common **cause of great mortality among puppies.** — Breeding at every season. — Obesity and sterility. — When a cure is possible. — **The** treatment required. — The right condition for breeding 214

CHAPTER III.

BEFORE WHELPING.

Exercise during gestation. — Its infinite importance. — **Essential precautions.** — Signs of pregnancy. — Some pronounced absurdities. — Diet of the bitch in pup. — Highly instructive experiments. — The real effects of raw meats. — Bone-making materials. — The one that promises best. — The whelping **quarters.** — Important measures against worms. — Bed and **bedding.** — Popular fallacies regarding them. — **Abuse of cathartics and laxative foods** 229

xii   *CONTENTS.*

CHAPTER IV.

TREATMENT OF THE MOTHER.

PAGE

First signs of whelping. — Companionship advocated. — Puerperal mania. — Hints for attendants. — Danger to puppies from crushing. — Measures of prevention. — Temperature of the whelping quarters.— Phenomena of labor. — After treatment of the mother. — Of the puppies. — The puppy-eating habit. — The various influences which cause it. — The remedy required in most cases. — Diet after whelping. — Of what each meal should consist. — Constant liberty for the nursing mother 243

CHAPTER V.

CARE OF THE NEW-BORN.

The favorable season for whelping. — Degrees of heat required by puppies. — Fatal faults emphasized. — When the milk secretion is scanty. — Milk fever. — Foster mothers. — Considerations in making selections. — Nourishing artificially. — By various animals. — Weeding out litters. — When suffocated by the mother. — Impediments to nursing. — Remedies for sore breasts. — Poisoning by the mother's milk. — How it may be detected. — Treatment of the mother. — Of the puppies 260

CHAPTER VI.

EARLIEST PUPPYHOOD.

Infinite importance of warmth. — A cause of many failures in breeding. — Ill effects resulting from sleeping-boxes. — Measures for the removal of vermin. — Treatment of colic. — Hygiene of the puppy quarters. — Poisons generated in milk. — Grooming and washing. — Prevention of deformities. — Golden rules for fanciers. — Worthless puppies. — The destroyer to be used. — Cautions against over-stocking. — Notions about teething. — Operation of docking. — The removal of dew claws 281

CHAPTER VII.

TRAINING.

Earliest education of puppies. — House-breaking. — Introduction to new homes. — Qualities essential in the educator. — Right methods of restraint and correction. — Perversity and self-will. — Power of kindness. — Some very annoying habits. — The use of the whip. — Happy effect of association. — Training of watchers. — A dangerous method. — The right way. — Retrieving and its advantages 304

CHAPTER VIII.

INTESTINAL PARASITES.

The course of infection. — The most potent means of prevention. — Symptoms of worms. — Peculiar action of the pests. — How they cause death. — Post-mortem appearances. — Treatment of nursing puppies. — After the weaning. — Dangers in anthelmintics. — Much of interest about santonin. — The first mixture to be used. — A stronger preparation. — Definite rules for estimating doses. — Relief in desperate cases 314

CHAPTER IX.

POTENT WORM-DESTROYERS.

Directions for treatment of toys. — Areca nut. — Its peculiar action. — Safety lines. — Rule for adjusting doses. — Best methods of administration. — Remedy for tape-worm. — General treatment for worms. — A shot-gun mixture. — Its preparation. — Influence of diet on worms. — Preventive measures. — Liability of infection in kennels. — Precautions which should be applied 331

The postage on "Kennel Secrets" is 34 cents. The express rates are the same, provided charges are PREPAID. The purchaser would do well to inclose this sum with his order, otherwise the book will be sent "collect." In which instance the express charge is quite sure to be greater than that stated.

www.ingramcontent.com/pod-product-compliance
Lightning Source LLC
Chambersburg PA
CBHW032356230426
43672CB00007B/725